WHO INTERVENES?

Who Intervenes?
ETHNIC CONFLICT AND
INTERSTATE CRISIS

David Carment, Patrick James, and Zeynep Taydas

The Ohio State University Press
Columbus

Copyright © 2006 by The Ohio State University Press.
All rights reserved.

Library of Congress Cataloging-in-Publication Data
Carment, David, 1959–
Who intervenes? : ethnic conflict and interstate crisis / David Carment,
Patrick James, and Zeynep Taydas.
   p. cm.
Includes bibliographical references and index.
   ISBN 0–8142–1013–9 (cloth : alk. paper)—ISBN 0–8142–9010–8 (CD-
ROM)
   1. Ethnic conflict—Case studies. 2. Conflict management—Case studies.
3. International relations—Case studies. 4. World politics—Case studies. I.
James, Patrick, 1957– II. Taydas, Zeynep. III. Title.
   HM1121.C37 2006
   305.8'009'051—dc22
   2005018560

Cover design by Dan O'Dair
Type set in Sabon
Printed by Thomson-Shore, Inc.

9 8 7 6 5 4 3 2 1

For my father David William Carment (1928–2004)

For the future–Patrick James Wayne and Sarah Smith Brenda

For Kahraman, Aynur, and Mehmet Taydas

CONTENTS

LIST OF FIGURES

LIST OF MAPS

ACKNOWLEDGMENTS

We owe a great deal to those who have read this book in its previous drafts and offered help. Ahmet Sözen provided insightful criticism and suggestions on our Cyprus chapter. We also are also indebted to Özgür Özdamar for making our figures and providing helpful suggestions; Janet Bradshaw for extensive help with word processing; and Azat Atadjanov, Balkan Devlen, and Leslie Liu for research assistance.

The inspiration for this volume springs from the International Crisis Behavior project's goal to develop a systematic and comprehensive study of international crisis. As a doctoral student, David Carment was privileged to have worked with Michael Brecher and the International Crisis Behaviour project team at McGill University. Carment's dissertation, upon which this book is partly based, was written with helpful feedback from Mark Brawley, Patrick James, Hudson Meadwell, and T.V. Paul. Subsequent comments and reviews of the theoretical and case study literature were provided by Bruce Bueno de Mesquita, Stuart Kaufman, Stephen Saideman, Shmuel Sandler, Hemda Ben-Yehuda, and Jonathan Wilkenfeld. David Carment would like to recognize the support of many of his research assistants at Carleton University, including Michael Penner and Troy Joseph. Financial assistance for this research was provided by the Social Sciences and Humanities Research Council of Canada, the Security and Defence Forum of Canada, and the Centre for Security and Defence Studies at Carleton University.

Each of us is blessed by having good friends and family who have helped in ways that go beyond the content of this book. David Carment would like to thank his family and friends who have made the journey interesting and fruitful. Patrick James is grateful for the support of his family, most notably, Carolyn, Ben, Bob, Carol, Jim, and, of course, Puppy. He has received encouragement from William James Booth, Daryll Clow, Jamie Hayden, and Ian Sirota during some challenging times. Zeynep Taydas feels the same way: This book would not have been possible without the encouragement and support of friends, family, and colleagues who have been at her side since the beginning of this journey. Zeynep is indebted to her family—Kahraman, Aynur, Mehmet, Nazan, Defne, and Emre Taydas, whose presence, support, and smiling faces over the years have been essential to realizing her dreams.

Zeynep also wishes to thank some wonderful people, Tansu Demirbilek, Yasemin Akbaba, Çigdem Kentmen, Özgür Özdamar, and Ramez Sünna, for being there every time help was needed.

Finally, we are grateful to our editor, Malcolm Litchfield, and everyone at The Ohio State University Press for their extraordinary work at every stage of development for this book.

CHAPTER ONE

Ethnic Conflict:
The Neglected Interstate Dimension

> The conflicts which are of global concern involve deep issues of ethnic
> and cultural identity, of recognition and of participation that are usually
> denied to ethnic minorities in addition to issues of security and other val-
> ues that are not negotiable. (Burton 1987: 5)

1. The International Politics of Ethnic Conflict

Seemingly banished to the sidelines of international politics by the Cold War,
ethnicity is back at center court. Two decades ago, Brecher and James (1986)
argued that many interstate crises have their origins in political, economic,
and social upheavals at the domestic level, while in other cases, these events
have fueled the fires of internal disruption.[1] Ethnicity is at the forefront of
such processes, regardless of the direction that is emphasized for cause and
effect. The politicization of ethnicity in general and ethnic parties in particular is regarded as a "major threat" to democratic stability (Chandra 2004: 1).
Although the crises of the late-twentieth century and new millennium no
longer are subsumed within overarching ideological competitions and rivalries—conflict settings that shaped perceptions for the almost half-century-
long Cold War—the assertions from Brecher and James (1986) remain no less
valid today.[2]

   While sources and manifestations of ethnic conflict are studied primarily
at the domestic level, the epigraph to this chapter points out that much of
today's ethnic strife is internationalized and naturally associated with foreign
or interstate events. In this context, interstate ethnic conflict entails a set of
deliberate strategic interactions and processes by which the behavior of one
state creates a crisis for one or more state actors who perceive a core threat
to values, finite time for response, and a heightened likelihood of military
hostilities (Brecher and Wilkenfeld 1997a; Carment and James 1997b;
Goertz and Diehl 1997; see also Weiner 1992).

Various questions need answers: Why do some ethnic conflicts lead to interstate crisis and even war while others do not? When interstate ethnic strife does erupt, why do some states pursue covert involvement while others adopt open and conciliatory approaches? In answering these questions, this book contributes to an understanding of the interstate dimension of ethnic conflict in three ways. First, the book develops a framework to account for the origins and patterns of interstate crises in relation to the combination of ethnicity and political institutions for a given state. Second, five case studies of ethnic intervention are used to assess the framework's performance in practice by testing propositions derived from it. Third, and finally, specific policy recommendations are derived from the case studies.

More advanced understanding of interstate ethnic conflict is important for several reasons. For example, Brecher and Wilkenfeld (1997a) find that ethnic conflicts with state-to-state interactions generally are more violent and involve more coercive crisis management techniques than do their nonethnic counterparts. They also discover that interstate ethnic conflicts tend to be more protracted and therefore more difficult to resolve within a single crisis. Given the high stakes involved, intense interventions can be difficult to sustain and control (Brecher and Wilkenfeld 1997a). This is because leaders and their constituencies may be deeply divided about issues related to support for an ethnic movement. In such instances, the relative autonomy of the leader, in combination with the distribution of political gains and losses at the domestic level, is fundamental to the credibility of, and commitment to, crisis escalation. More importantly, if internal constraints do impose significant limitations on what leaders can do in the foreign policy domain, it may be possible (and desirable) to address the interstate dimensions of ethnic conflict by tackling its sources at the domestic level.

To advance this argument, a framework is developed to link the causes of ethnic conflict at the domestic level to interstate conflict, crisis, and war. This process begins by building on the work of Heraclides (1990, 1991, 1997), Lake and Rothchild (1996, 1998), Saideman (1997, 1998a, b), Taras and Ganguly (1998), and the Minorities at Risk Project (Marshall 1997), among others, through an assessment of interactions between affective and instrumental interests that influence a state's choice about whether to intervene in ethnic strife. Affective motivation refers to the pursuit of self-esteem through ethnic group identification, while instrumental interests pertain to material desires such as land or employment (Chandra 2004: 8–9). A comprehensive vision of ethnic politics in general and intervention in particular must take account of both affective and material interests. The framework identifies how leaders pursuing an ethnically oriented goal might respond to, and even take advantage of, incentives within both the international system and domestic political structures. Carment (1994a, b; see also Davis and Moore 1997; Davis, Jaggers, and Moore 1997) establishes that interstate ethnic crises are driven primarily by a combination of opportunities represented by ethnic divisions in neighboring states and ethnic alliances and constraints that correspond to a state's institutional configuration and ethnic composition. In other words, ethnic crises are products of the classic combination of opportunity and willingness (Most and Starr 1980; Siverson and Starr 1990).

This argument couples purposiveness, rather than inevitability, with escalation. Interstate ethnic conflict is not a predetermined outcome. Nor do the roots of a conflict necessarily lie in centuries-old hatred (Kaufman 2001). By attaching a sense of purpose to political ambitions, the framework asserts that leaders choose strategies to maximize their security and that of their followers. Accordingly, ethnic leaders sometimes can be anticipated to generate crises as a means of holding on to, or increasing, their share of domestic political power (Saideman 1998a, b). This expectation is based on the fact that in many emerging states, political participation and opportunities are defined along narrow bands of ethnic sensibility. Coupled with deliberate suppression of nonethnic issues, the result is a narrowing of policy options, which leads to interethnic confrontation, crisis, and war.

Decision makers' strategies, according to the framework, are limited by two factors. First, strategic choice is constrained by ethnic arrangements inherent within a state. Structural factors of primary concern include the relative size of ethnic groups and divisions between and among them. Second, preferences for nonviolent strategies are a function of institutionalized forms of political order. Thus the state is much more than a unified actor that reacts to domestic strain by extending it into the international system. Instead, the state is a rational actor constrained by *both* internal and external forces. This point can be established in three ways.

First, the vast majority of ethnic leaders respond to incentives, threats, and coercion in rational and predictable ways (Fearon 1998). Collectively, ethnic conflict appears to be irrational because it leads to undesirable social outcomes over the short term, such as destruction of property and economic decline. However costly and irrational it might seem in human and material terms, conflict is a means of regulating behavior and maintaining social order. In short, a collectivity, much like a state, will pursue conflict, even violence, if it safeguards advantageous and long-term political and economic outcomes (Kriesberg 1997).

Second, and related to the first point, conflict itself can have positive attributes. For example, ethnic conflict plays a role in building group solidarity. It also creates mobilization opportunities through which free-riders can be identified and more readily sanctioned. Under such conditions, performance expectations are one way to ensure mobilization, cohesion, and stronger support (Kriesberg 1997; Marshall 1997; Fearon 1998). In this sense, conflict serves a functional and positive role for ethnic elites and their followers; leaders may generate strife as a means of increasing cohesion among the groups. Identification of a common enemy provides an opportunity for a group ridden with antagonisms to overcome them (Coser 1956; Rummel 1963; Wilkenfeld 1973; Carment 1994a, b; Carment and James 1995, 1996, 1997a, b, 1998).

For example, from the perspective of an ethnically oriented leader, long-term gains from a dispute, such as territorial consolidation, enhancement of political power, and increased ethnic homogeneity, are enhanced dramatically if a conflict can be pursued within limits. On occasion, leaders may not even be interested in resolving a violent dispute: Since representing an ethnic group can provide specific benefits like prestige and military power, leaders may be more interested in prolongation and even future escalation of a conflict. For elites who play on the fears of their constituency, the perceived and real benefits of escalation can be appreciable.

Third, and finally, the label "ethnic conflict" itself reveals very little about what underlies intergroup tensions (Lake and Rothchild 1998). A widely held belief still exists that ethnic conflicts are distinct from others. This outlook assumes, on the one hand, that all identity-based disputes possess similar underlying causes and, on the other hand, that identity is what makes these conflicts distinct. In essence, this perspective holds that ethnicity is a primordial sentiment reactivated in the modern context. Ethnic conflict arises out of the systematic denial by the modern state of minority aspirations, goals, and values. From this sense of exclusion and denial, ethnic struggle arises and becomes violent (Taras and Ganguly 2002). However, it also should be noted that ethnic identification can be manipulated. For example, Chandra's (2004: 102, 260) authoritative study of politics in India establishes that ethnic parties with a nonexclusionary basis, all other things being equal, enjoy greater success because of their ability to incorporate new sources of support without permanently marginalizing ongoing member groups that may temporarily lose leadership positions to those coming onboard later on.

Interstate ethnic conflicts are not new. More than two decades ago, Connor (1978) described the pervasiveness of multiethnic societies and predicted at the time a decline in the congruence between the nation and the state. More recent studies of state- and nation-building argue that creation of national societies is very much a process, just as it is in Eastern Europe, the former Soviet Union, and much of the rest of the world. It generally is assumed that ethnic conflicts now are more numerous and violent, even though the evidence, as will become apparent momentarily after three points are considered, does not support this conclusion.

First, much of what has been called a resurgence of ethnic strife in Central Asia and Southeastern Europe, for example, is in fact conflict between groups that have been in confrontation with one another for a long time. The most prominent example of that is the ethnic-based violence in the Balkans during periods of regime crisis and breakdown, such as the last phase of Ottoman control leading to the Balkan wars, the final throes of Hapsburg rule, and the collapse and dismemberment of the Yugoslav state in 1941. In general, nationalist wars and ethnic violence follow the collapse of empires. The examples that follow are especially notable; in each instance, the location and name of the empire(s) appears, respectively: South America in the nineteenth century (the Spanish Empire), Europe after World War I (Russia, Austria-Hungary, and Ottoman Turkey), and Asia and Africa after World War II (Belgium, Holland, France, Britain, and Portugal).

Second, an upward trend in ethnic conflict reached its peak in the mid-1990s, but it began in the 1960s and is associated most closely with decolonization. Indeed, since 1945, over sixty protracted conflicts involving more than one hundred ethnic groups came into being; expand the criteria to include interstate conflicts with ethnic dimensions, and the numbers increase to well over that many in progress for the same period (Brecher and Wilkenfeld 1997a).

Third, the end of the Cold War did not create many of the animosities or aspirations that triggered these conflicts. In quite a few conflicts, preexisting problems have played key roles in escalation (Stack 1997). To be sure, as long as superpower bipolarity shaped the character of the international political system during the Cold War, the tendency for peripheral conflicts to acquire an East-West dimension militated against overt involvement by the major powers. Within the context created by this struggle, international instruments developed to hold in check the aggressiveness of some states and prevent ethnic conflicts from spreading. Maintaining international stability became a systemwide concern.

Today, despite a change in the matrix of competing claims and entrenched interests, the internationalist ideal persists in the belief that sovereignty, territorial integrity, and independence of states within the established international system, and the principle of self-determination for peoples—both of great value—are compatible. The most recent evidence indicates that ethnic violence is in modest decline. According to analysts at the Integrated Network for Societal Conflict Research (INSCR), ethnic rebellion and nonviolent protest gradually increased between 1945 and 1980 (http://www.cidcm.umd.edu/inscr/mar/home.htm). Levels of rebellion reached their peak by the early 1990s and have declined after that time (Gurr, Marshall, and Khosla 2001).

While it may be true that ethnic conflicts reflect problems related to human rights, participation, justice, and distribution, the manifestation of these issues becomes ethnic only because that is the basis for exclusion or repression (Gurr, Harff, and Speca 1996). Indeed, many conflicts are only superficially ethnic and are stimulated by a combination of nonethnic factors (Ryan 1998). More generally, ethnic conflict refers to the form the conflict takes, not to its causes. To say that ethnic conflict arises because there are distinct ethnic groups is tautological. By themselves, ethnic differences are insufficient to guarantee either political mobilization or intergroup conflict. The important fact is that groups are organized and draw their strength and resilience from ethnic attachments and seek benefits for members on that basis (Gurr 1996). Such factors usually become salient because they are invoked by contemporary ethnic leaders to mobilize support (Gurr 1997; Lake and Rothchild 1998).

This inquiry unfolds in seven additional chapters. First, a framework specifying the precise causal relationships among the selected variables and their interaction effects is presented, along with propositions, in chapter 2. Second, case studies—the Indo-Sri Lankan crisis, Somali irredentism, Thai Malay separatism, the breakup of Yugoslavia and its immediate aftermath, and the Cyprus puzzle—are used in chapters 3 through 7 to evaluate the propositions. Third, and finally, based on the degree of support for the propositions from the case studies, the framework is refined and contributions to theory and policy are presented in chapter 8. The remaining sections of this chapter pertain to internationalization of ethnic conflict, vertical escalation, the institution of ethnic conflict, and a more detailed overview for the rest of the book.

2. The Move to Internationalize

Analysts recently have argued, in an effort to make sense of ethnic strife in the post–Cold War world, that these conflicts constitute a salient threat to international peace and security. In many more cases, little agreement exists on the extent of the threat or the likelihood that such conflicts could become uncontrollable beyond a state's borders. The combination of conceptual innovation and a desire to embrace unorthodox approaches has led some scholars to elevate ethnic conflicts to the domain of high politics—a realm previously occupied exclusively by ideological conflict, international crisis, and war.[3]

Viewed as high politics, the collective claims of the literature on the relationship between security and ethnic conflict are that ethnic strife leads to internationalization in three different ways: (1) ethnic diversity and weak institutions compound existing political and economic problems within states, which leads to intensified competition for resources and a weakening of the state; (2) ethnic conflict carries serious risks of contagion and diffusion through processes known as *horizontal* escalation; and (3) ethnic conflict leads to *vertical* escalation that culminates in interstate confrontation, crisis, and war (Lake and Rothchild 1998). All of these claims have some basis in reality. Each is examined in turn, and the third and final process is the focus of this book.

Ethnic conflicts weaken state structures and can lead to both state collapse and intervention; this point is self-evident. According to Ted Robert Gurr, founding director of the world-renowned Minorities at Risk (MAR) Project from the University of Maryland, over twenty new post–Cold War new states have experimented with democratic institution building. Much of the recent upsurge in communal conflict, Gurr argues, is under way in precisely these states and as a direct consequence of opportunities for institutional change, through which communal groups can pursue their objectives more openly (Gurr, Marshall, and Khosla 2001).

Since ethnic disputes are prone to disagreement about abstract values that serve as basic organizing principles for other political activity, the potential for spillover into the international domain is high (Marshall 1997). For example, in an exposition on international law and minorities, Ryan (1988, 1998) argues that self-determination is a key legitimizing principle for mobilization; structural incompatibilities between the ideology of nationalism and national minorities significantly influence whether a group will seek out external support in its struggle. Similarly, Azar and Burton (1986) argued that internationalization begins with denial of separate identities, the absence of security for minorities, and a dearth of effective participation for these minorities. For Smith (1986a), internationalization is associated largely with the growth of an ethnic intelligentsia and emergence of a repressive, "rational" state that is dominated by a specific nationalist group (see also Marshall 1997). Internationalization occurs when a state's treatment of its minorities fosters noncompliance with the prevailing norms of international relations (Väyrynen 1997; Goertz and Diehl 1997).

Posen (1993) applies the realist concept of the security dilemma to ethnic conflict. He argues that after the fall of imperial regimes, the race for power and the security dilemma helped ethnic conflicts to emerge. According to this logic, when ethnic groups feel insecure, due either to violence or assimilationist policies, they ask for outside help in order to obtain protection. At that point, ethnic groups believe there is no way that the state, on its own, will guarantee their survival. In other words, when ethnic groups start to experience fears collectively about assimilation and physical safety, violence is to be expected. It is therefore not a coincidence that heightened mutual distrust and fear coincide—creating a security dilemma—and requests for outside help naturally follow (Snyder 1993; Posen 1993; Kaufman 1996; Lake and Rothchild 1998; Taras and Ganguly 2002).[4]

Horizontal escalation is a process related to a weakening of state structures. It refers to a situation in which events in one state change directly the ethnic balance of power in a neighboring state (Lake and Rothchild 1998). Through this means, ethnic displacement, refugee flows, and spontaneous population transfers constitute a form of contagion (Lake and Rothchild 1998). Movement of displaced ethnic groups directly changes demography and thereby creates regional instability. For example, the violent outflow of Tutsis and moderate Hutus alike from Rwanda to Zaire and Burundi in 1994 and from Kosovars to Albania in 1999 had the potential to create a new class of militant ethnic leaders in these neighboring states.

Ethnic conflicts also expand horizontally when groups in one country prompt those in another to make more extreme demands. This takes the form of a demonstration effect. Groups in one state, witnessing ethnic mobilization by those in another, may as a result increase their own political activities. The latter recognize that internationalization of their demands can both simultaneously encourage internal mobilization and weaken the salience and effectiveness of the state by creating international forums for substate grievances. This legitimization process is facilitated by the existence of supranational and human rights organizations that provide a forum for subnational ethnic claims. Consider, for instance, the 25 June 1991 declarations of independence by Croatia and Slovenia, in turn, as a demonstration effect that emboldened both states to commit to full separation from the Yugoslav Federation.

Finally, horizontal escalation occurs through information flows and transnational media networks that condition the behavior of ethnic diasporas. Information flows directly influence the levels of protest, rebellion, and mobilization among ethnic brethren. Ethnic diasporas provide both material and nonmaterial support for politically mobilized ethnic groups. These affective links are crucial for an ethnic separatist movement to prosper and grow

(Davis, Jaggers, and Moore 1997). Diffusion has come under scrutiny within political science only in the last two decades (Most and Starr 1980; Most, Starr, and Siverson 1989; Starr 1990; Siverson and Starr 1990, 1991), and its application as a concept to the study of ethnic conflict is even more recent (Zartman 1992; Marshall 1997; Lake and Rothchild 1998). Contagion and diffusion often are used interchangeably, but contagion should be defined as a subset of diffusion because the latter is systemwide, whereas contagion is first and foremost a process that alters the behavior of states within that system (Marshall 1997). The MAR Project defines contagion as the spread of protest and rebellion throughout a region and measures it as a function of those actions for a particular ethnic group within a region. Information flows shape the level of communal protest and rebellion and the extent of ethnic mobilization.[5]

Horizontal transmission of ethnic conflict appears, in sum, to be tied inexorably to transnational identities and associated movements of people, resources, and ideas. Groups that believe they are threatened may seek out support from their ethnic brethren in two notable ways. The first is the linkage entailed by shared particularist identities between groups that straddle borders. The second is the impact that a global diaspora can have on development of ethnic leadership pools in nonneighboring states. While the former, according to Horowitz (1991) and others, may lead to mutual restraint between states, the latter is a more explicit and well-known foundation for development of ethnic protest and rebellion (Davis and Moore 1997).

While horizontal escalation can occur in the absence of directed state activity, vertical escalation refers to a set of deliberate strategic interactions and processes by which the behavior of one state creates a crisis for one or more state actors who perceive a core threat to values. Vertical escalation means internal ethnic conflict that leads to crisis, intervention, and possibly war with other states.[6]

When the word "escalation" is mentioned, the first thing that comes to mind is a potential armed assault on one state by another. Two points are worth noting about escalation. First, any effort to interfere with or disrupt the internal affairs of states can lead to escalation. Both covert and overt activities would be included in this definition. Intervention of this kind may include the calculated use of political, economic, and military instruments by one country to influence the domestic or foreign policies of another. The second point is that escalation will not be and, indeed, has not been confined solely to interactions between states through military means. It encompasses a broader range of state-to-state activities. The next section examines these activities in greater detail.

3. Vertical Escalation and the Neglected Interstate Dimension

Vertical escalation leading to interstate ethnic conflict is a dynamic process in which stages of escalation and deescalation can be identified (Brecher and Wilkenfeld 1997a; Kriesberg 1997).[7] These include (*a*) a latent stage in which differences between ethnic groups are made salient but without overt interstate conflict or crisis; (*b*) an onset phase whereby a "trigger" creates the conditions for interstate violence; (*c*) a peak point that leads to large-scale confrontation between states; (*d*) a deescalation phase; and finally (*e*) a termination phase that either resolves or transforms the conflict (Kriesberg 1997; Brecher and Wilkenfeld 1997a). Interstate ethnic conflicts can last months, years, and even decades. The most salient are "protracted" conflicts, fluctuating in intensity over the course of several decades and involving entire communities, with periodic outbreaks of violence. Prominent examples of protracted conflict include Arab-Israel, Kashmir, and Cyprus (Bercovitch, Diehl, and Goertz 1997).

Today's world features a great deal of variation in types of ethnic groups and conflicts associated with them. By one estimate, fifteen years ago over five thousand ethnic groups could be identified (United Nations Report on Ethnicity and Development 1987). This substantial number, however, signaled an impending global crisis in the waning days of the Cold War. The forms that ethnic conflicts take vary widely across time and space, and the sheer number of groups is not a cause for concern, at least in isolation. Only a handful of ethnic groups—fewer than 20 percent—have the capacity for political activity. An even smaller number of groups are engaged in violence. For example, in the 1980s, the MAR Project identified 233 such groups which, in 1990, made up 17.3 percent of the world's population; the comparable figures for 1995 are 268 groups and 17.7 percent. (See http://www.cidcm.umd.edu/inscr/mar/home.htm for full details.) Within this subset of groups, over a five-year span, approximately eighty were involved in significant protracted conflict and a small number engaged in interstate crisis or war (Wallensteen and Sollenberg 1996: 354; Ellingsen 1996).

Characteristics of interstate ethnic conflict are identified readily using the logic of opportunity and willingness, derived from the work of Siverson and Starr (1990; see also Most and Starr 1980 and Starr 1978) and applied by Davis, Jaggers, and Moore (1997) and Marshall (1997) in the context of ethnic conflict. According to Davis, Jaggers, and Moore (1997), many, but not all, interstate ethnic crises are dyadic and involve dispersed ethnic groups across borders. Geographic contiguity, therefore, is crucial to escalation of interstate ethnic strife (Most and Starr 1976, 1978, 1980; Vasquez 1992;

Zartman 1992). Within the context of interstate ethnic crises, borders establish the opportunities for, and parameters within which, most hostile and friendly interactions occur between states (Davis, Jaggers, and Moore 1997). In a similar vein, Zartman (1992), Marshall (1997), and Maoz (1997a) argue that ethnic conflict does not necessarily diffuse across the entire system, but rather is constrained by interactions among sets of states within a specific region (see also Fearon 1998).

Willingness is determined by the presence of ethnic affinities—a kind of nonstate alliance—that influence state behavior (Carment 1994a, b; Davis, Jaggers, and Moore 1997). Aside from instrumental reasons such as the desire to make gains at the expense of another state (Grieco 1990), ethnic affinities influence a state's willingness to support brethren (Zartman 1992). A potential intervening state always faces a trade-off between supporting minority ethnic brethren in a neighboring state and maintaining or developing a cooperative relationship with the government of that state. The willingness of an intervening state to expend resources on behalf of ethnic brethren is assumed to be a direct function of its relative interest in the issue (Carment, James, and Rowlands,1997). Elites not only view ethnic affinity as useful, but specific groups on whom they rely for support also perceive these international linkages as potentially helpful. For example, transnational affinities may enhance a state's interest in a conflict (if not for leaders directly, then at least through pressures from constituents) and, under certain conditions, can determine the intensity of preference for intervention (Carment, James, and Rowlands 1997). Different levels of willingness, defined by ethnic affinities, therefore distinguish the opportunities generated by respective interstate ethnic crises.

For the purposes of this study, irredentism and separatism provide the basis for comparative case studies. Such conflicts are specific classes of hostile, occasionally violent, military-security interactions that take place at the international level (Brecher 1993; Brecher and Wilkenfeld 1997b). Both geographic contiguity and ethnic affinities are present by necessity. Thus, after having reviewed the components of interstate ethnic conflict, a basic question of definition and an answer to it can be presented at this point in relation to crises in world politics: Is an *interstate conflict* also an *interstate ethnic crisis*?[8]

For the answer to be yes, two criteria must be met. One is that the case must correspond to an international crisis as defined by the International Crisis Behavior (ICB) Project, that is, a disruption in process and a challenge to the structure of the international system.[9] The case therefore also will fulfill requirements for a foreign policy crisis for at least one state, as follows:

a situation with three individually and collectively sufficient conditions, deriving from changes in a state's internal or external environment. All three perceptions are held by the highest-level decision makers of the actor concerned: a threat to basic values, awareness of finite time for response to the value threat and a high probability of involvement in military hostilities. (Brecher and Wilkenfeld 1997b: 3)

The other criterion is that the case must fulfill either or both of the conditions for an irredentist or separatist conflict. Each of these types of conflict is defined below.

Irredentism means a claim to the territory of an entity—usually an independent state—wherein an ethnic in-group is a numerical minority but forms a regional plurality (or even majority). The original term "terra irredenta" means territory to be redeemed. It presumes a redeeming state, as well as such territory, so irredenta are interstate ethnic conflicts by definition. Either an ethnic nation-state or a multiethnic plural state may seek redemption. The territory to be redeemed sometimes is regarded as part of a cultural homeland or historic state (or as an integral part of one state). The claim to territory is based on existing or cultivated transnational ethnic affinities and is conditioned by the presence of cleavage between the minority in-group and its state-center (see also Saideman 1998b for a similar interpretation).

Irredentist conflict entails an attempt to detach land and people from one state in order to merge them into another, as with Somalia's claim to the Ethiopian Ogaden, Serbia's claims to parts of Croatia and Bosnia, or Germany's claims (at different times) to the Sudetenland.[10] This summary follows Weiner's (1971: 668) classic exegesis of irredentism, which assumes the existence of a "shared" ethnic group crossing the international boundary between two states. Two subvariants exist: (*a*) an ethnic group transcends multiple borders but does not itself constitute a state (e.g., the Kurds in Turkey, Iran, Iraq, and Russia) and (*b*) irredentist claims are made only with respect to territory "cleansed" of the ethnic claimant (e.g., Armenian claims to eastern Anatolia). This study focuses on those irredenta that include both an ethnic group and territory to be redeemed (for examples, see Sullivan 1996: 115–17).

Irredentist conflicts are by definition interstate in scope and involve third-party support, as with Pakistani patronage of an Islamic Kashmir. Since the conflict involves two or more states in dispute over a specific territory and claims about an ethnic group, there is a high potential for crisis, violence, and war. Pursuit of aggressive tactics may result from an ethnic ideology (e.g., Panslavism), a sense of historic injustice (e.g., Danzig), or even a perceived threat to values that justify some kind of future society—perhaps one in which all of the relevant territory and people are reclaimed (e.g., Greece and Macedonia). A high threat to values is more likely to be perceived in such situations because irredentism pertains to another state's territory, a core value (Carment 1994a). Thus an irredentist conflict can produce an interstate ethnic crisis in three overlapping ways: (1) by triggering a foreign policy crisis for one or more states through an internal challenge supported by the redeeming state; (2) external threats made by one or both states; and (1) and (2) can trigger (3), that is, foreign policy crises for allies of the two states.

For example, throughout the 1950s, Great Britain had attempted to create a viable political structure in Oceana that would include Brunei, Sarawak, Sabah, Singapore, and Malaya. All of these states had majority Muslim Malay populations that shared a strong cultural and religious heritage. Plans for a Federation of Malaysia, however, conflicted with the territorial claims of the Philippines and especially the Muslim-Malay state of Indonesia. In February 1963, President Sukarno announced that Indonesia opposed a Malaysia Federation. Indonesia set about disrupting the ethnic and political cohesion of the fragile federation through a policy of "confrontation" that included covert military incursions in West Malaya. On 11 July the federation was formalized, which triggered a foreign policy crisis for Indonesia. In response, Indonesia requested that the federation be delayed until a UN-monitored election could be held to determine the interests of the people. On 14 September 1963, the results of the vote indicated that preferences lay with a Malaysia Federation. Indonesia responded by refusing to endorse the results. On 17 September the new state of Malaysia severed diplomatic ties with Indonesia and the Philippines, and both sought and obtained important international support. For example, the International Monetary Fund withdrew its offer of promised credit to Indonesia—a significant action with respect to a relatively poor developing state. The crisis faded with both sides claiming victory (Brecher and Wilkenfeld et al. 1988: 262).

Separatist interstate ethnic crises are less easily defined. These crises are generated from within a state but spill over into the international domain. Separatist interstate ethnic crisis refers to formal and informal aspects of political alienation in which one or more ethnic groups seek, through political means, reduced control by a central authority (this may not be formal or declared separation as in secession sensu stricto). The ensuing confrontation may involve politically mobilized, organized, ethnic insurgency movements and the use of force. As Heraclides (1990: 344) points out, the separatist threat includes (1) a degree of in-group legitimation that endorses the aims and means of the conflict; (2) a military capability; and (3) some tangible or political support from external states. Both the state-center and/or separatist group can be expected to seek out external support. This competition exacerbates internal disruption and leads to interstate conflict and possibly crisis. In some cases, the minority group may make a formal declaration of independence that certifies it as secessionist sensu stricto.[11]

When ethnic groups refuse to recognize existing political authorities, ensuing conflict can lead to an interstate ethnic crisis in four nonmutually exclusive instances: When ethnic groups refuse to recognize existing political authorities, they can (1) trigger a foreign policy crisis for the state in question (i.e., internal challenge leading to external involvement); (2) trigger foreign policy crises for the state's allies, which leads to an international crisis; (3) invite external involvement based on transnational ethnic affinities (including threats of involvement) of one or more state interlocutors that support the separatist group, which triggers an international crisis; or (4) invite external involvement by one or more states based on ethnic affinities that support the state-center, which triggers an international crisis.

For example, the international crisis over Bangladesh took place from 25 March to 17 December 1971. In mid-February 1971 the military rulers in West Pakistan decided to suppress the growing fervor of East Bengal nationalism (i.e., what later became Bangladesh). They posted military personnel in the east. On 1 March, President Yahya Khan postponed opening of the assembly in East Bengal. The Awami League protested that action and launched a noncooperative movement on 6 March. Approached by Bangladesh in March 1971, the UN declared the matter internal to Pakistan but could not disregard the effect of the war on ethnic minorities, referring respectively to Muslims in eastern India and Hindus in East Bengal. While fighting raged over the spring and summer, an estimated nine million refugees fled from East Bengal to Bengal in India. On 21 November, the Indian Army crossed into West Pakistan, already at war with East Bengal. Indian forces quickly overwhelmed the Pakistani troops in the seceding territory. The war ended on 17 December 1971 with Pakistan's surrender and the emergence of Bangladesh, a new sovereign state on the Indian subcontinent (Brecher and Wilkenfeld 1997b).

Not all domestic ethnic conflicts leading to interstate crisis, to be sure, have reached the level where either irredentism or separatism are readily identified. Some international crises exhibit the characteristics of both irredentism and separatism, which makes the task of identification more difficult. In the former instance, ethnic leaders may prefer low-intensity conflict with the stated goal of a separate state or reunification to follow if the struggle ultimately succeeds. In the latter context, irredentist impulses and separatist tendencies interact considerably (Heraclides 1997). For example, Horowitz (1981, 1991) argues that many irredenta have their origins in third-party support for separatist movements. From a third-party state's perspective, a short-term strategy of strengthening a separatist movement, which may lead to restoration of territories and peoples over the long term, generally is preferred to an outright and potentially costly irredentist struggle (Horowitz 1991). The net result is a hybrid of irredentist claims and separatist struggle interacting to create a unique type of interstate crisis. Support for a separatist movement may entail lower probable costs than irredentism (Horowitz 1981, 1991). Leaders of separatist movements and supporting states use ethnic connections to advance their interests. These leaders initially may espouse reunification. A crucial point is reached, however, when leaders of separatist groups no longer rely exclusively on external state support; separation then becomes viable and self-sustaining, with the irredentist goal as a secondary consideration.

4. Outline of the Book

Development and assessment of a framework in order to identify the origins, manifestations, and patterns of interstate ethnic crisis is the goal of the remainder of this book. Seven chapters follow this introductory one.

Chapter 2 develops a framework for the analysis of interstate ethnic crises. Key explanatory variables, such as ethnic composition and political constraint, are identified, and their interaction effects are assessed. Contingency factors, including ethnic affinities and ethnic cleavage, also are examined.

Chapters 3 through 7 convey case study research. Chapter 3 covers a secessionist case, the Indo-Sri Lanka Crisis of 1983–96, in which the Indian government sent a "peacekeeping" force into Sri Lanka to prevent the Tamil secessionist conflict from spilling over onto Indian soil. This case provides an opportunity to examine interactions between institutionally constrained, ethnically diverse states.

Chapter 4 examines Somalia's recurring irredentist crises. No fewer than seven international crises are related to Somalia's quest for a "Greater Somalia," the most notable being the Somalia-Ethiopia war of 1977–78. This chapter determines how changes in institutional constraints, in combination with ethnic affinities, can account for interstate ethnic conflict in a protracted setting. The case is notable because the most intense period of interstate conflict occurred when Ethiopia experienced very high ethnic cleavages while Somalia's military junta went through the process of consolidating power.

Chapter 5 examines the Thai Malay secessionist conflict in southern Thailand. Since the turn of the twentieth century, a minority Malay community continues to seek secession from Thailand. This case is selected not only because it exhibits all of the important elements of an interstate ethnic conflict with its intense interstate violence. The Thai Malay conflict also encompasses both irredentist and secessionist dimensions. While not unique, this combination of factors may provide insights for both refinement of the framework and principles of conflict management. The Thai Malay conflict also is unique among those included because it does not feature an interstate ethnic crisis, which makes the case potentially useful in producing insights about how such events can be averted.

Chapter 6 deals with the Yugoslav conflict, which also exhibits both irredentist and secessionist characteristics. This conflict is selected for two additional reasons. First, its complex nature, which includes multiple actors, issues, and crises, should prove useful for development of the framework. Second, from a policy perspective, the case presents an ongoing challenge to the international community. Greater understanding of this conflict would provide insight into the future of ethnic conflict management and resolution.

Chapter 7 examines the Cyprus conflict, one of the most complex ethnic problems in the world. This chapter explains how the domestic and institutional characteristics and the perspectives of Turkey and Greece, in combination with ethnic ties, can account for an intense and violent interstate ethnic conflict. This case is chosen for several reasons. First, it is a protracted ethnic conflict that spilled over into the international arena. Second, the case of Cyprus shows how difficult it is to solve deeply rooted conflicts between ethnic groups and how third-party activities can prove insufficient to solve the key issues. Third, it is an interesting example because two democracies have struggled with each other for so many years. Fourth and finally, the case shows not only irredentist but also secessionist characteristics. Investigating this case should reveal much about the characteristics, motivations, and actions of two ethnically dominant states.

Chapter 8 summarizes the contributions of the preceding chapters in order to assess how interstate ethnic crises might be more amenable to management and even prevention. In this final chapter, contributions to theory and policy are presented in light of the findings.

CHAPTER TWO

The Two-Level Game of Ethnic Conflict

The most stubborn facts are those of the spirit not those of the physical world and one of the most stubborn facts of the spirit remains nationalist feeling—at different scales. (Gottman 1951, quoted in Knight 1982: 520)

1. Toward a Framework for Analysis

Why do some ethnic conflicts lead to interstate war while others do not? Why do some third-party states pursue covert involvement in ethnic disputes while others adopt open approaches? Furthermore, why do some intermediaries seek to manage or resolve ethnic strife while others try to exploit conflict for their own purposes? The epigraph to this chapter suggests that ethnic identity, both for states directly involved in disputes and third parties, will play an immanent role in styles of conflict management and escalation.

To address the preceding queries, this chapter is organized in six additional sections. In the second section, the metaphor of a two-level game is introduced as an effective technique for analysis of ethnic relations between states. Third, domestic processes, international ambition, and rational choice are linked together to develop a new perspective on decision making. Section four focuses on ethnic composition and institutional constraint, variables that are combined to develop a framework of analysis for third-party intervention and interstate ethnic conflict. In the fifth section, conditions enabling ethnic conflict—namely, ethnic affinity and cleavage—are introduced. Sixth, propositions are derived from the framework. The seventh and final section explains the case selection and summarizes the accomplishments of this chapter.

2. The Two-Level Game of Ethnic Conflict

With a focus on the behavior of the potential intervener in an ethnic conflict, the framework is kept relatively simple: a state's choice of strategy is determined by a limited number of elements, which facilitate a diagrammatic and diagnostic exposition. Analysis of these elements can be divided into three stages. The first stage examines the roles of ethnic composition and institutional constraint in the formation of ethnic foreign policies. Interaction effects are then assessed in light of two enabling conditions that are deemed necessary for an ethnic conflict to reach the interstate level. These are transnational ethnic affinities and ethnic cleavage. In the third stage of the analysis, types of states that are more or less likely to use force in ethnic interactions are identified on the basis of the interaction effects and enabling conditions.

Structure and decision-making motivations combine to form an integrated framework. The emphasis is on linkages between and among structural conditions, normative constraints, and strategic opportunities that are conducive to escalation and intervention. Under certain conditions, motivations and interests arise as much from domestic considerations as from the structural conditions associated with them. For example, instrumental and strategic interests may relate to larger system-level and regional considerations, while affective motivations pertain to a particular set of issues within a conflict. The meaning of these motivations and interests may be context dependent and variable in salience.

Accordingly, an actor-oriented theory of interstate ethnic conflict encompasses two levels of interaction. These levels pertain, respectively, to willingness and opportunity (Most and Starr 1980; Siverson and Starr 1990; Cioffi-Revilla and Starr 1995) of a state with respect to adoption of an ethnic foreign policy.

One tier of interaction includes the processes of decision making, based on some preference ordering, which explains the specific route taken to select a certain policy option. Analysis focuses on substantive aspects of the choice of one option over others. A state's foreign policy is said to be ethnically based when ethnicity is the most salient component within its relations of cooperation or conflict as expressed in the statements and actions of its leaders.

Deciding whether ethnicity is the most salient aspect of an interstate conflict can be a challenge. States may act on a variety of impulses that include instrumental concerns with only a remote connection to ethnic conflict. For the purposes of this inquiry, a state external to a conflict that either expresses or implements support for a state-center or a minority group is said to have an ethnic foreign policy. Support may be expressed through various means, such as diplomatic recognition, the transfer of arms, facilitating the efforts of insurgents, financial aid, provision of sanctuary, and direct intervention

(Heraclides 1991). The state-center, in turn, is said to have an ethnic foreign policy if internal identity-based conflict influences and shapes relations with one or more states.

Interventionism, whether ethnic or otherwise, cannot be "read off" from political structure alone. Instead, politics influence the formation of a decision maker's preferences and resulting actions (Brecher, Steinberg, and Stein 1969; Meadwell 1992). Decision making involves risk and sources of uncertainty that are internal to the state; constraints and opportunities are created by, for instance, ethnic groups and political institutions. External factors also exert influence; a state's capabilities and alliances, for example, would be two obvious, realist-oriented considerations.

This kind of linkage politics perspective portrays elites as essentially non-self-sufficient individuals who respond to their environment and adapt, with varying degrees of success, to the influence of mass sentiments.[1] Elites will seek to optimize results in light of other actors' preferences and options. Accordingly, elites must be able to set priorities among alternative goals in light of both domestic and international constraints. At the national level, domestic ethnic groups pursue their goals in various ways, most notably by pressuring the government to adopt favorable polices. While minimizing the adverse consequences of foreign developments, governments seek at the international level to maximize their ability to satisfy domestic pressures (Putnam 1988). Sometimes, due to international and domestic constraints, which can work at cross-purposes, the choices made may be suboptimal and relatively unsuccessful, although decision making still is considered to be rational in at least a procedural way.[2] Interstate ethic conflict, when it does occur, is a product of instrumental considerations and affective linkages in combination. Less clear in accounting for this behavior are the precise linkages between and among normative and strategic determinants of elite decisions. An important component of decision making is the strategic interaction inherent in contact between masses and elites (Kaufman 1996).

Another aspect of the approach based on linkage politics is that certain structural features within and between states may be conducive to escalation. For example, elites facing high levels of institutional constraint may be more sensitive to the interests of groups whose support they seek and therefore choose overt and even forceful intervention for reasons different from their low-constraint counterparts. This occurs because under certain conditions, external conflict can serve an important functional role for elites that is specified by a causal link between domestic and interstate conflict. Internal turmoil can lead to international conflict, which in turn has a positive impact on overall support for the leader and internal cohesion.

Leaders of ethnically dominant and institutionally underdeveloped states face a different set of opportunities in pursuing foreign policy objectives than their more constrained and diverse counterparts.[3] Elites of these states can and sometimes will become adept at manipulating mass opinion in order to bring it in line with their foreign policy and nation-building objectives.

3. Domestic Pressures, International Ambition, and Rational Choice

Decisions to intervene are rational calculations even when based on ethnic attachment. Leaders must take into account the wide range of constraints impinging on their choices. Although events in the target country are the main concern for an intervener, the decision to intervene still is inferred to be the result of a thorough cost-benefit analysis. The internal dynamics of the intervener as related to perceived national interests, probability of success, and possible human and material cost are all important parts of the rational calculus (Regan 2000). While it is difficult to reconcile identity-oriented behaviors with a presumed chain of events, as will become apparent, instrumental and affective motivations can be combined to tell a more complete story about ethnic intervention.

Third-party support for an ethnic minority will reflect the degree of approval for such ideas within a leader's ethnic constituency. Exacerbating these societal tensions is competition among elites for public office, which makes their decisions even more responsive to the aspirations of the masses. A two-level game approach implies that the credibility of an intervention depends in part on the likelihood that it will be carried out, which increases with domestic support for such a commitment (whether the intervention is successful or not is another issue). Conversely, the more powerful the domestic groups that anticipate a resulting disadvantage, the less credible and sustainable will be any presumed policy of involvement.

For example, while everyone within an ethnic group may long for a historically derived state based on shared identity and history, only a few elite members can and will act on it. As positional players at the domestic level, elites try to optimize political choices that are favorable relative to any potential counterelite. In making choices, decision makers must consider the dispersion of preferences and interests of the constituent elements that make up the domestic affairs of the state (Bueno de Mesquita, Siverson, and Woller 1992; Bueno de Mesquita et al. 2003). Ambitious leaders can be expected to draw on nationalist identities, political symbols, and ideologies to manipulate mass sentiment. According to Putnam (1988: 434), "the unusual complexity of this two-level game is that moves that are rational for a player at one board—may be impolitic for that same player at the other board. Nevertheless there are powerful incentives for consistency between the two games." Thus, in this context, rationality refers to finding the most efficient means under a given set of circumstances to accomplish a specified set of objectives.

Decision makers must be able to comprehend the nature of objectives and the characteristics of the environment in which goals arise (Maoz 1990, 1997a; Brecher 1993). From this perspective, preferences and strategic choice are a function of the decision maker's role as a leader within a specific institutional framework and ethnic group. Based on procedural rationality as described above, this approach shares some basic similarities with prominent foreign policy research in terms of the assumed linkage between structure and foreign policy orientation (Snyder, Bruck, and Sapin 1962; Maoz 1997b; Mintz and Geva 1997; Reed 2002).

Diagnosis of a foreign policy problem, as revealed by a classic examination of bureaucratic behavior, will reflect threats or promises to the organization or entity that decision makers represent as well as to the state as a whole. In other words, "where you stand depends on where you sit" (Allison 1971). Less bureaucratic in orientation is Stein and Tanter's (1980) analytic model, which postulates that decision making emerges from a careful assessment of risks, along with costs and benefits, of alternative options: Decision makers are expected to choose the option with the greatest expected utility, measured in terms of the value of each possible outcome of an action weighted by the perceived probability that it will occur.[4]

Taken together, the preceding models highlight the fact that in the formation of foreign policy, linkages between group structure and individual preferences ultimately determine choices. The maximization of expected utility is the end result of a process, not its sole characteristic. Expected utility maximization emphasizes relativism—plausibility of each choice is assessed relative to others (Maoz 1990).

Interventionist states, however, are more than unified actors that react to domestic strain by projecting it into the external system. Instead, the state is regarded as a rational actor constrained by both internal and external forces (Rummel 1963; Tanter 1966; Wilkenfeld 1968, 1972). Past research on conflict linkage indicates that domestic politics plays an important role in the promotion of international conflict and cooperation. Studies over the last decade show that foreign policy can be explained, at least in part, by domestic factors (Ostrom and Job 1986; James 1988; Putnam 1988; Mastanduno,

Lake, and Ikenberry 1989; James and Oneal 1991; Morgan and Campbell 1991; Bueno de Mesquita and Lalman 1992; Carment and James 1995; Maoz 1997a). It is no surprise that domestic considerations affect the rational state's pursuit of foreign objectives (James 1993).

In a compelling investigation of regime change and its relationship to foreign policy performance, Bueno de Mesquita, Siverson, and Woller (1992) find that leaders are well advised to consider the dispersion of preferences and interests among constituents because a misadventure in foreign policy can lead to reduction or even loss of power. While existing studies establish that foreign policy decisions are influenced by domestic constraints, the role of ethnicity remains largely unexplored. One of the most important questions facing a decision maker then might be this one: If I make a foreign policy decision considered favorable to my ethnic group, what are the long- and short-term ramifications of this decision for my own political standing vis-à-vis my ethnic group, the other ethnic groups within society, and relations with other states? In other words, whether explicit or implicit, a foreign policy that includes demonstrations of support for ethnic brethren can both identify and legitimate a leader's actions. It also sets boundaries for foreign policy choices in terms of salient constraints.

4. Ethnic Conflict from a Two-Level Perspective: Affective Motivation and Institutional Constraint

Credibility of support for ethnic brethren, from the two-level game point of view, depends in part on the likelihood that it will be carried out. The likelihood increases with the degree of domestic support for making such a commitment. In deciding to commit support, a leader or head of state must coordinate actions at two bargaining "tables," which correspond to domestic and international politics. By monitoring strategies and tactics in each arena, it becomes possible to understand puzzling developments. More specifically, initiatives in one domain may reflect constraints or opportunities present in the other. This kind of decision-making process is known as a two-level or "nested" game because both domestic and international constraints and opportunities must be taken into account (Putnam 1988; Tsebelis 1990).

Several traits distinguish the two-level game as an outlook on international bargaining and, for the purposes of this study, as a metaphor for understanding and clarifying third-party strategies toward intervention.[5] Interpretation of these strategies emphasizes (1) complex patterns of interdependence that create opportunities, not just constraints, for statecraft; (2) the head of state as the central strategic actor; and (3) simultaneous and interactive calculation of opportunities and constraints at both the domestic and international levels. The most distinctive phenomenon within the two-level game is synergy, where international actions are employed to alter outcomes otherwise expected in the domestic arena (Putnam 1988).

Several assumptions drive two-level explanations of international politics. The first is that decision makers must consider the dispersion of preferences among constituent interests (Bueno de Mesquita, Siverson, and Woller 1992). Citizens can separate a foreign policy that they consider a legitimate reflection of their values from one that does not. Thus, the second assumption is consistent with the first: a foreign policy cannot be considered viable if it contradicts the preferences of a decision maker's constituency. The third assumption is that national leaders must retain some minimal degree of support among their constituency to stay in power. The COG (Chief of Government [Putnam 1988], head of state, etc.) otherwise loses power, except for the head of an authoritarian government, who can resist political pressures of opposition up to a certain point.

Two-level game analysis will build on the confluence of ethnic structures, normative determinants, and strategic choice. In particular, how do political constraints and opportunities interact with ethnic composition in influencing decisions about whether to intervene in an ethnic conflict? Since elites play politics at two different levels—domestic and international—the payoff structures of both must be considered (Putnam 1988: 434). It will be assumed that a state is represented by a single leader (with independent policy preferences) in search of a foreign policy that is attractive to his or her constituents. Depending on interaction effects between variables, some leaders will prefer confrontational policies because of anticipated domestic payoffs, while in other instances the configuration of domestic variables will inhibit such tactics and shift the elite toward more covert or possibly even peaceful measures.[6]

These conclusions follow from certain principles—what Putnam (1988) calls "win-sets"—about available choices. A win-set at stage one is defined as all the successful foreign policy strategies that would "win," that is, be considered successful by the masses. The first part of this analysis concerns stage one wins-sets. The size of a stage one win-set is governed by several factors, and for obvious reasons the interaction effects have important implications for determining the strategy pursued (Evans 1993). Simply put, stage one win-sets influence a state's calculation of the cost-benefit ratio in pursuing involvement in an ethnic conflict.

Figure 2.1 shows how win-sets are anticipated to vary on the basis of interaction effects, which create four ideal types of state. (The examples listed within the figure are explained in subsequent chapters.) This does not mean that all states can fit in these categories exactly—in practice, a continuum is expected to exist along the dimensions corresponding to institutional constraint and ethnic composition. The win-set is minimal for high-constraint, ethnically diverse states (Type II_b) and maximal for low-constraint, ethnically dominant states (Type I_a). All other things being equal, these opposite ends of the typology are driven by two distinct logics: system- and constituency-driven for low- and high-constraint situations, respectively.

Preferences for involvement in an ethnic conflict are reflected in the win-set's size. Since states of Type I_a from the figure can choose from a broad range of options that would be satisfactory to the masses, *belligerence* is preferred. Here a leader may adopt a "hawklike" stance while incurring the lowest domestic political costs. Differences between Types I_b and II_a are difficult to predict; each is expected to fit between extremes. Type I_b states are inhibited because of diversity and engage in *passive lobbying,* while II_a states are constrained by institutions and exhibit *sporadic interventionism.* Both are labeled as moderate, although outbidding can increase II_a's propensity toward intervention. In these instances leaders succumb to being agents of particular groups' ethnic foreign policy interests, if that support is crucial. Options contract as interaction effects between ethnic composition and institutional constraints exert full force. Thus a Type II_b state, under normal conditions, is least likely to find an outcome that is acceptable to its constituents. Overt support to ethnic brethren across national borders, all other things being equal, will not be an attractive option, so *realpolitik policies* will prevail. The situation of each ideal type of state vis-à-vis intervention will be considered in turn.

4.1 Type I_a: Low Institutional Constraint and a Dominant Ethnic Group

Interaction effects will be considered first for low institutional constraints in dominant and diverse settings, Type I_a and I_b, respectively. Analysis begins with these arrangements because of relative simplicity in the relationship between elite and masses. Where constraints are low, first stage win-sets are large. In more formal terms, if W is the size of the winning coalition and S refers to the size of a "selectorate" of those eligible to be in W, then W is much smaller than S in Type I_a political systems. At a substantive level this would correspond to a rigged electoral system such as that of any Eastern

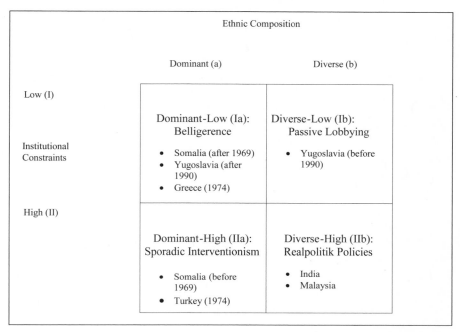

Figure 2.1. A Typology of Potential Intervening States: Ethnic Composition and Institutional Constraints

Bloc state during the Cold War (Bueno de Mesquita et al. 2003: 54). The only formal constraint on elites in these cases is the bureaucracy or military. If the elite comes to power through force (e.g., Somalia in the 1970s), it will depend on a narrow band of support from specific groups, such as the military and bureaucracy, which are comparatively free of domestic pressures. The relationship between the military and the elite therefore is an important, but not enervating, constraint. Indeed, compared with high-constraint elites, these leaders are more able to manipulate the size of their stage one win-set. When present, checks on executive authority tend to be "on paper only" because in low-constraint settings, affect is important in influencing political interactions between decision makers and the overall population.

For example, in Type I_a cases, a dominant ethnic group controls an ethnically homogenous military that will mobilize the population through manipulation of group symbols in order to pursue foreign policy goals. Consensual procedures in the formation of foreign policy decisions, if present, are likely to be "rubber stamp" operations. Power will be concentrated heavily, and the elite is assumed to be relatively immune to domestic pressures. Foreign and domestic policies are designed to appeal to the dominant ethnic group, but not in a way that would threaten the power base of elites.

In one sense, it is an oversimplification to categorize intervention as either elite or mass led; obviously, an ethnically based foreign policy cannot continue long without both leadership and mass support (Kaufman 1996). Nevertheless, in some cases, elite action, independent of the masses, is decisive in shaping outcomes. When the elite is relatively immune from domestic pressures, as with Type I_a cases, there will be a greater tolerance for gaps between elite and mass preferences, and the interests of the masses are subordinated to those of elites.

Without democratic pressures, elites obtain an extra resource with which to mobilize support, namely, affect, a low-cost political device. Type I_a means that, in essence, the elite leads and the population follows. Elites in a low-constraint situation are not expected to pursue an ethnic foreign policy if it constitutes a threat to their power. When constraints are low and an ethnic group is dominant, the elite is unlikely to face significant criticism at home for pursuing external involvement that leads to confrontation. Elite foreign policy is influenced primarily by the identity of its constituency. Pursuit of an ethnically oriented foreign policy therefore becomes an optimal strategy in a relatively wide range of situations. Thus the win-sets at stage one are large and the maximum that possibly can be obtained.

Type I_a elites will pursue involvement if it means achieving specific goals in the international arena. The payoffs in this case are situated at the international rather than domestic level. Such a policy will be heavily imbued with ideology, but it need not be inherently aggressive. If elites are assumed to act rationally, their choices will allow for a range of factors and constraints that include their capabilities, power discrepancy, alliance structures, and so forth. Thus Type I_a is associated with belligerence in figure 2.1.

Absent internal constraints, an elite can find its international position strengthened. Minimal uncertainty about domestic politics could translate into higher resolve in the international arena. In this instance, the ability to control domestic outcomes can be achieved through a "forced" convergence of interests between a national leader and the state being represented. Lower levels of domestic uncertainty have important implications for interactions with other states (Evans 1993).

Elites in unconstrained situations are in a better bargaining position than those whose power is dispersed. The former are less prone to involuntary defection because they can control domestic political outcomes. However, given that unconstrained elites do not have to worry about the ramifications of an ethnic foreign policy for the masses, they might be more tempted to "voluntarily" defect because of the low political costs of doing so. In other words, unconstrained elites in dominant settings can be expected to behave as rational maximizing egoists as represented in the game of prisoner's dilemma (Axelrod 1984, 1977). Rent-seeking imperialism is expected among dictatorships rather than democracies (Olson 1993).

Under such conditions, observed differences in state strategies and goals reflect what could be achieved within the constraints set by the external political situation. Anarchy and the self-help system will create the appearance that these states have a uniform set of basic goals and interests. Decisions to intervene would seem to reflect distinctive "hard-shelled," unitary rational actor characteristics. A rational elite would take into account a limited number of international factors, including absolute and relative capabilities, alliance structure, and so forth. From a realist perspective, foreign policy then would be understood as a function of external constraints in terms of the distribution of military and economic power, the level of uncertainty in the regional and local system, the cost of bargaining, and similar concerns. States of this kind are most akin to self-sufficient units operating in an international environment that provides a reasonably predictable and stable set of constraints within which to pursue intervention.

4.2 Type I_b: Low Institutional Constraint and Diverse Ethnic Groups

In diverse, low-constraint settings, or Type I_b, issues important to the mass public of a specific ethnic group are unlikely to influence policy choices among elites because the magnitude of anticipated payoffs is low. Leaders of ethnically diverse, low-constraint states are unlikely to pander openly to the interests of any one ethnic group. If the military is of a different ethnic group from the majority population or if the elite represents more than one ethnic group (i.e., diverse), then it would be impolitic to pursue a confrontational ethnic foreign policy unless the opportunities to do so provide sufficient international *and* domestic benefits. The size of the stage one win-set will be smaller than that of Type I_a and outcomes initially will be suboptimal.

Lower incentives exist for pursuit of an ethnically oriented foreign policy because of potential ramifications for domestic politics. Countercoups motivated by ethnic allegiance would be the most prominent risk to the regime status quo or internal balance of power. Making ethnicity a salient aspect of foreign policy also is risky because it could incite potential internal enemies to seek support from neighboring states (e.g., Rwanda's covert support for rebels in the Congo in the 1990s). While expecting gain from opportunism in a foreign country, the costs can increase incrementally to an ultimately unacceptable level. This can provoke ethnic violence within the state itself and eventually weaken state institutions. If no such risks are present or can be managed, an ethnic foreign policy is more likely. Unlike those of Type I_a, these states are not immune to involuntary defection. Their ethnic diversity increases the chance that leaders of a group either cannot or will not cooperate on certain policies. At the international level, this makes these states more vulnerable to defection on agreements. Therefore, to maintain support, Type I_b elites need to monitor and control defection, which includes creation and exploitation of international rules and institutions that derive from a sense of shared vulnerability. Thus, Type I_b in figure 2.1 is labeled as the passive-lobbying variant. Elite behavior approximates the concept of the inhibited state that Jackson and Rosberg (1982, but see Saideman 1998a, 1998b for contrary evidence) use to describe the maintenance of African boundaries in the 1970s and 1980s.

For Type I_b states, inhibitions on behavior can be countered by "reverberation" inherent in putting foreign policy into place. Normally, rational choice approaches require that the structures of issues and payoffs be specified in advance (Putnam 1988: 454). In this case, however, reverberation refers to the way in which preferences are altered unintentionally by external pressures. The extent to which the state mobilizes social resources to mount a credible campaign to assist ethnic brethren is arguably as much a function of strong preferences about issues at stake as compared to capabilities. Transnational ethnic linkages can create extreme preferences that compensate for a deficiency in capabilities in weighing options related to intervention as in the case of Rwandan support for rebel groups in the Congo in 2004 (Carment and James 1995).

Consider, in that context, recurring Iraqi threats against the low-constraint, ethnically diverse state of Iran over disputed territories after the Islamic revolution of 1979. In this instance, Iraqi threats reverberated within Iran's domestic political scene and increased support for the new Khomeini regime. Furthermore, Iraqi threats did not generate substantial internal opposition. As a result, Iran's capacity for carrying out foreign policy objectives exceeded the level that normally would be expected for a multiethnic state. In other words, Iraqi pressures on Iran may have been counterproductive—"international pressure reverberates negatively if its source is generally viewed by domestic audiences as an adversary rather than an ally" (Putnam 1988: 456).

Normally, Type I_b elites express a moderate preference for involvement. The leaders of these states prefer not to galvanize significant domestic oppo-

sition and narrow the base of popular support; all other things being equal,
it is unlikely that they will engage in interventionist policies. The phenomenon of reverberation, however, demonstrates how these preferences can be
altered and expanded. Reverberation can increase an elite's domestic win-set
so that it derives greater utility from an interstate ethnic conflict than would
be normal otherwise.

4.3 Type II_a: High Institutional Constraint and a Dominant Ethnic Group

Accurate predictions about the choice of strategies and potential size of stage
one win-sets for elites in high-constraint situations can be made only after
more extensive interaction effects are considered. Leaders of these states are
constrained simultaneously by the ethnic affinities of their supporting coalition and formal institutional arrangements. Foreign policy decisions regarding separatism or irredentism are acute particularly in democratic societies in
which the degrees of internal constraint upon decision makers are expressed
in terms of party formation, electoral politics, and cabinet composition
(Bueno de Mesquita and Lalman 1992).

For high-constraint situations, the size of the state one win-set is relatively small. Preferences for belligerence are limited because to be considered successful, an ethnically oriented foreign policy must satisfy several additional
conditions in comparison to low-constraint states. These factors in turn will
influence potential interstate ethnic conflict. According to Morgan and
Campbell (1991: 191): "[C]onstraints should be greatest when competition
is highly institutionalized. Well-organized permanent parties that compete in
a systematic fashion provide a ready outlet for opposition to a leader and
constitute a focal point around which opposition can form." Elites, in sum,
will be "hamstrung" in pursuit of foreign policy goals by the competing interests of various groups—including ethnically based ones.

For Type II_a cases, where institutional constraints are high and elites represent a single and "like-minded" ethnic group (i.e., dominant), leaders go
along with the ethnically oriented sentiments of the population. If not, they
may end up being replaced by rivals. When the majority of the electorate
belongs to a single ethnic group, leaders are vulnerable to challengers who
claim that the interests of this crucial constituency have been betrayed.
Concerns about involuntary defection will be paramount. In this case, as
opposed to either Type I_a or I_b, the elite is expected to follow rather than lead
the masses. Therefore, Type II_a in figure 2.1 is expected to engage in *sporadic
interventionism*.

"'Like-minded,'" as used a moment ago, refers to those cases where even political opponents offer "all-purpose" support to an ethnic foreign policy. This support is crucial to expanding the stage one win-set; indeed, Type II_a elites may go along with an ethnic foreign policy even if it appears irrational in the international arena (i.e., there may be a threshold as to how much cost is borne, if it promises domestic payoffs to all elites [Putnam 1988]). A good example of that situation is Turkish intervention in Cyprus. In 1964, the Turkish government thought about intervening in the island after a cost-benefit assessment, but intervention did not occur because of strong opposition from the international arena, particularly the "Johnson Letter." U.S. President Lyndon Johnson, speaking as a superpower leader, changed the calculus of costs and benefits for Turkey with his firmly worded letter that opposed intervention. However, in 1974, despite the ongoing Cold War and strong domestic opposition, the Turkish government decided to intervene in Cyprus. Domestic considerations, determined both by affective and instrumental ties, seemed to outweigh the constraints imposed by the international arena through Cold War rivalry, which had not been the case a decade earlier.

Elites will seek to enhance their position in the stage one game by increasing political resources through side payments (such as increases in power and influence) or by minimizing potential losses (like electoral defeat). For example, a head of government may seek popularity anticipated from pursuit of a politically rewarding foreign policy. Indeed, viewing the elite as an individual without preferences opens the possibility that constituents and political opponents may be more eager for an aggressive ethnic foreign policy.

Management of the discrepancy between their constituents' and political opponents' expectations and the outcome is the main problem facing the elites of these states. Leaders must be aware of the choice of tactics by opponents, which can be influenced heavily by ideology, a sense of historical injustice, perceived grievance, or a threat to values that justify a future society. Elites are more likely to be successful if they channel such interests toward their objectives.

Another way of describing the behavior of a Type II_a state is to observe that elites can be expected to persist with involvement when benefits are situated primarily in the domestic arena, while costs may come at the international level. Empirical instances of Type II_a in its present form are unusual, largely because states with some kind of institutional constraint rarely are dominated by a single ethnic group that supports policies across the board. (Japan and Germany would seem to be notable exceptions.) Implications for newly democratizing states dominated by a single and relatively like-minded ethnic group, such as those in the Balkans, are clear. Past cases of ethnic conflict, including confrontations between Greece and Turkey over Cyprus, would suggest that high-constraint states are not immune to the pursuit of aggressive policies (Russett 1993; Maoz 1997a).

4.4 Type II$_b$: High Institutional Constraint and Diverse Ethnic Groups

When the constituency is composed of members of several different ethnic groups (i.e., diverse) and institutional constraints are high, a leader will face new incentives and constraints and therefore exhibit different policy preferences. In Type II$_b$ cases, a foreign policy based on ethnicity remains unlikely as long as elites can withstand the pressures of ethnic outbidding. The size of the stage one win-set will be the minimum of the four types examined, and the disposition toward an ethnically oriented foreign policy will be the lowest of all. This is particularly true if force is anticipated to be used against members of a group sharing an ethnic affinity with at least some constituents. Use of ethnicity for political gain is a risky strategy because supporters easily can become divided. Elites therefore can be expected to promote self-policing policies that downplay ethnicity as a source of foreign policy. Due to all these characteristics, Type II$_b$ in figure 2.1 is labeled as *realpolitik*.

Institutional constraints will reduce even further the opportunities for pursuit of a risky foreign policy (Morgan and Campbell 1991). COGs in these cases, all other things equal, will be the most "dovelike" of the four types. Success in the role of a dove opens up possibilities for alternative strategies (Maoz 1997a). Depending on the degree of dovishness, the COG still could become involved in covert operations when no public and mutually acceptable action is feasible (Zartman 1992: 38). Furthermore, a more dovelike, neoliberal type of state that supports international norms and nonintervention in spite of the presence of ethnic affinities might be rather close to its neighbors on some scale of cooperation (Carment, James, and Rowlands 1997). Solidarity between states, as dictated by domestic sensitivity and mutual inhibition, diminishes incentives for third-party intervention even further. Under these conditions, a Type II$_b$ state can be expected to adopt a relatively mild position on the autonomy and political goals of ethnic brethren (Maoz 1997a). Efforts to mediate become more likely and positive experiences in the role of a dove could facilitate a more conciliatory approach (Russett 1990, 1993).

Specific instances of Type II$_a$ or II$_b$ ethnic outbidding arise when a leader faces a population composed of only part of a single ethnic group. Political competition may become intense through multiparty ethnic factionalism. A kind of extreme hypernationalism is likely to emerge from leaders who become interested in "outflanking" other political parties. In this case, an ethnic foreign policy is "heterogeneous" to the extent that there is greater factional conflict on this issue (Kaufman 1996; Saideman 1997). For example, Downs (1957) shows that political parties in two-party systems tend to imitate each other and become ideologically immobile. Both parties strive to appeal to as many different viewpoints as possible, and the result frequently is that moderate views prevail. Multiparty systems, by contrast, often accentuate ideological "product differentiation" (Downs 1957: 141). New parties that stress an aggressive, ethnically oriented foreign policy may emerge when there is a great deal of similarity between two moderate parties. All other things being equal, multiparty systems are more likely than two-party systems to give birth to involvement in ethnic strife. In the Type II$_b$ case, for example, the initial size of the stage one win-set is small because of institutional constraints, but elites often will seek to increase their options by initiating issue-based conflict through processes of interelite confrontation (Tsebelis 1990).

As noted by Tsebelis (1990), special interest ethnic parties are most prevalent where both internal and external imperatives of the ethnic group exist in relation to others. Cases such as Kenya, Sudan, Sri Lanka, Malaysia, Nigeria, and Yugoslavia, at varying points in time, come to mind. Nigeria, for example, had major party systems based on three ethnic cleavages during periods of democratic rule (Sklar 1980). Similarly, studies of Sri Lankan politics suggest that attempts at nonethnic multipartyism will eventually be displaced by ethnically based parties (Horowitz 1985; Chandra 2004: 291 n. 9). If two groups exist with only one party each, then distances between them should become minimal and conflict can be brokered. If, by contrast, each group is represented by more than one party, then outbidding can be expected to occur (Saideman 1997).

Multiethnic parties, defined as those that do not serve as champions of "one particular ethnic category or set of categories" (Chandra 2004: 3), occasionally are able to withstand outbidding processes. For example, during the 1960s, the Indian Congress Party maintained control because it (a) developed a minimally successful compromise on language issues; (b) overrepresented in state cabinets the group with the stronger flank party; (c) allowed a Sikh to lead the party between 1956 and 1964; and (d) had representation at both the state and national levels (Nayar 1966; Brass 1974, 1990).

When a democratically elected multiethnic party succumbs to parties on one or both sides, a shift occurs to a one-party state (e.g., Zambia, Kenya).

This, put simply, represents Type II_a outbidding. Unable to satisfy either side, the original multiethnic party will be left with a shrunken base, and single ethnic parties become the norm (Horowitz 1985).

Either way, to maintain support, leaders of an ethnic group may strive to be its best representative (Horowitz 1985). Such competition in Type II_a and II_b cases could lead to a more aggressive foreign policy than otherwise would be expected. The political party with the greatest interest in an ethnic foreign policy will have the most extreme position on that issue; if its rivals (including the governing party) can offer effective resistance, then an ethnic foreign policy is almost certain to be played down.

Options contract as interaction effects between ethnic composition and institutional constraints take hold, so a Type II_b state, under normal conditions, is least likely to produce an outcome that is agreeable to all constituents. High institutional constraints oblige leaders to retain at least a plurality of popular support in order to maintain political power. Leaders therefore will not pursue any policy that serves the interests of one group at a real expense to others, and ethnic adventurism becomes unlikely. This prudent approach can be called *realpolitik* because it reflects calculations about power at home and abroad and results in caution in the face of multiple constraints. Ethnic interventions can be expected to occur only when there are strong, even overwhelming preferences among the state's ethnic groups or where a general consensus exists that the state has important reasons for involvement abroad.

4.5 Summing Up the Typology

Outbidding can increase the win-sets for both Type II_a and II_b states, so the latter still have some limited potential for an ethnic foreign policy. The unconstrained Types I_a and I_b have a broader range of choices that would be considered satisfactory and therefore reveal high and moderate dispositions, respectively, for intervention. Accurate predictions concerning differences between Types I_b and II_a are difficult because both are expected to fit between the two extremes. Type I_b states are constrained by ethnic diversity, while Type II_a states are held back by institutions. Both are labeled as having moderate preferences toward intervention, although outbidding can increase the disposition of Type II_a.

The preceding metaphors provide insight into how foreign policy strategies are shaped through the interaction between ethnic composition and political constraints. The argument sketched out above establishes that, in specific instances, elites must attend to the domestic political ramifications of their foreign policy actions. The analysis also offers insight into which states are likely to engage in confrontational policies. The larger the win-set at stage one, the more probable it becomes that a confrontational ethnic foreign policy will be implemented.

5. Enabling Conditions: Ethnic Affinities and Cleavage

Enabling variables may impact upon the size of a stage one win-set. Such factors can increase the chances of a state initiating an ethnically oriented policy that leads to crisis. What, then, will affect the size of the stage one win-set? For an ethnic foreign policy to result in interstate conflict and crisis, the most important set of factors pertains to a state's own ethnic characteristics and those of other states. As noted in defining interstate dimensions of separatist and irredentist crises in chapter 1, two elements distinguish these kinds of conflicts from nonethnic crises: the presence of transnational ethnic affinities and ethnic cleavage. These characteristics create opportunities to be exploited and therefore increase the probability of involvement in irredentist and separatist conflict. For low-constraint states, international opportunities are more important than domestic ones. If there are domestic implications, affinities and cleavage heavily influence the strategies of highly constrained elites. After all, these elites must be sensitive to the interests of constituents—even those beyond the state's borders.

COGs may be pressured by political opponents or more directly by the masses to act on ethnic linkages (Davis, Jaggers, and Moore 1997). The resulting foreign policy can lead to intensified interstate strife when ethnic minorities search for credible support from ethnic allies in neighboring states (Zartman 1992: 37). When these allies cannot commit to a policy of nonintervention, then crisis and war may ensue.

Ethnic affinities relate directly to the problem of sovereignty, that is, the ability of states to implement authoritative claims. Efforts to control the flow of people, culture, and resources are significant in interstate ethnic conflicts. Quite often, authority is not defined solely in terms of territory; fragmentary sovereignty exists and will shape the size of a state's win-set (Saideman 1997).

Transnational ethnic affinities exist among most groups in the international system, especially those that have undergone the experience of diaspora. Russians living in the Ukraine and the Baltic, the Tamils of South India, and the Chinese of Southeast Asia, Kurds in Turkey, Iraq, and elsewhere are a few prominent examples (Taylor and Jodice 1983; Taylor and Hudson 1972; Neilsson 1985; Gurr 1992, 1997). Defining transnational affinity is difficult, however, because there is more than one way to establish ethnic identity (Rothschild 1981; Horowitz 1985; Smith 1993a, 1993b). Race, religion, tribal (kinship), and linguistic cleavages may not coincide, so affinity in one area (e.g., linguistic) may be at odds with another (e.g., kinship) (Chazan 1991). Moreover, elites can attempt to mobilize other transnational identities (pan-Arabism as opposed to Islam, for example) or cultural subsystems at the expense of transnational ethnic affinities. In sum, ethnic linkage with a group in another state does not guarantee mutual interest (Zartman 1992; Midlarsky 1997).

When a greater number of affinities exist (e.g., linguistic, race, religion) between members of an ethnic group in two or more states, the anticipated connection is stronger. When identities converge, it becomes more likely that an ethnic group will seek external support (Stack 1997). Both the state-center and an internal minority adversary will try to take advantage of such linkages. In some of these cases, elites may be carried along by mass ethnic fervor (Chazan 1991). Moreover, mutual interests are strongest for groups that experience high international ethnic affinities and perceive the "other" group as an enemy of the supporting state. The other or "out" group in this instance can be either the state-center or an ethnic minority (Zartman 1992; Saideman 1997).

States that experience intervention will feature a high level of ethnic minority consciousness due to regime repression, civil unrest, and loss of civil liberties. These states have highly divided political loyalties and are less likely to develop civic cultures conducive to the pursuit of policies that manage and reduce ethnic conflict. The degree of division is comparatively high for those minorities who seek to transform the political status quo through force and/or external assistance. Such ethnically based divisions are referred to as "cleavages" (Gurr 1992, 1996).

As noted in chapter 1, relationships involving ethnic affinity and cleavage can be understood best through the use of two overarching concepts: *opportunity* and *willingness* (Most and Starr 1989). An intervening state always faces a trade-off between supporting ethnic brethren in a neighboring state and maintaining or developing a cooperative relationship with that state. The willingness of a potential intervening state to expend resources on a minority brethren's cause is assumed to be a direct function of its relative interest in the issue (Carment, James, and Rowlands 1997). Elites not only view ethnic affinity as a possibly useful trait, but specific groups on whom elites rely for support also perceive these international ethnic linkages as potentially valuable. For example, transnational affinities may enhance a state's interest in a conflict—if not for leaders directly then through constituencies that pressure leaders to act.

Under certain conditions, these affinities can determine the intensity of preferences for intervention (Carment, James, and Rowlands 1997).

6. Propositions

This chapter offers a framework that builds on rational choice arguments
without positing isolated and self-sufficient decision makers. Instead, interdependence between elites and masses is assumed. Both the choices of elites
and masses, along with their interaction effects, are important from the outset. While seeking to minimize adverse consequences of foreign developments, leaders also must attempt to satisfy domestic needs. The causal mechanism linking domestic structure to conflict behavior for unconstrained and
diverse states focuses almost entirely on various ethnic segments that
encroach on an elite's hold on power. Thus the only constraints on such decisions are those that operate through a leader's perceptions of how the decision will affect their ability to remain in power (which remains important to
even the most entrenched dictators) and the state's security. However, in the
absence of institutions, ethnic groups will find it very difficult to mobilize,
short of the use of force, against leaders (Carment and James 1996). Since
military regimes have a comparative advantage in the use of force, ethnic
opposition will be relatively weak as compared to high-constraint states
unless external military support is forthcoming. To summarize:

> 1. Mechanisms are available to states that allow them to pur-
> sue ethnic foreign policies. For example, states can manipulate
> ethnic divisions within other states and reinforce transnational
> ethnic affinities through material and diplomatic support;
>
> 2. The leaders of a state will be penalized if they fail to protect
> their ethnic groups (i.e., domestic constraints) or if they pursue
> objectives beyond their means (i.e., international constraints);
>
> 3. For a multiethnic, institutionally constrained state, the pre-
> ferred strategy is one that focuses directly on the strategy the
> other player is using; in particular, it is best if this strategy
> leaves room for development of interstate cooperation. This
> conclusion is consistent with the "governing principles" identi-
> fied by Bueno de Mesquita in his exposition on the strategic
> approach toward international politics (2000): Leaders always

choose what they believe best for themselves after carefully evaluating all developments and factors. No foreign policy action can occur without taking into consideration domestic political consequences; in sum, relations between leaders and nations are driven by strategic considerations.

These points illustrate a three-stage process of interstate ethnic conflict. For example, at stage one, there are four ideal types of states, each with different preference structures for supporting ethnic brethren. At stage two, affinities and cleavage can create a security dilemma for third-party states. Elites face the decision of whether and how to commit to support for an ethnic minority. Choices may create problems for a leader's internal political situation. For states that face high domestic costs because of institutional constraints and ethnic diversity, the use of force is the least attractive choice in finding a solution to the dilemma. Domestic repercussions could exacerbate that state's security dilemma. Possible stage three processes include the onset of crisis, efforts at mediation, diplomatic activity, and use of force.

Whether a state will use force depends on the extent to which there is a discrepancy between elite and mass preferences. Sometimes elite action is decisive in causing conflicts to become violent (Kaufman 1996). Keeping in mind the size of the stage one win-set, the use of force in interstate ethnic conflict becomes most probable for interactions involving Type I_a (i.e., low-constraint, ethnically dominant) states and least probable for Type II_b (i.e., high-constraint, ethnically diverse) states, with Types I_b and II_a in between.

Since the behavior of these Type I_a states is inhibited primarily by international rather than domestic constraints, confrontations including them will depend on international benefits provided by involvement in ethnic conflict. The expectation of relatively low constraints in both environments can create policies of intransigence that lead, in turn, to use of force. The COGs of these states would be expected to pursue interests with an international payoff, such as reclaiming territory. Interstate ethnic crises involving Type I_a states could become the most violent of all with commensurate compensation.

All other things being equal, low-constraint elites in diverse settings do have to worry more than their counterparts in dominant settings about implications of an aggressive ethnic foreign policy for their ethnic groups. Indeed, relative to the extent of domestic ethnic conflict, only a few African interstate crises have escalated to open warfare. Collins (1973) suggests that the fear of ethnic disorder inhibited conflict between states in Africa, while Saideman (1997, 1998a) takes up this point in greater detail and provides evidence to the contrary. When conflict does arise, it is because these states experience greater instability or sensitivity to disorder (Jenkins and Kposowa 1992). For high-constraint states, the potential for interstate conflict will affect the choice of strategies and tactics. In a conflict between two constrained, multiethnic states, for example, the elite of each state should try to minimize the other side's win-set, that is, ensure that its counterpart does not formulate a policy of aggression. When ethnicity is politicized it becomes a double-edged sword. On the one hand, the larger the win-set, the more capable a state becomes in carrying out its foreign policy objectives, including those with an ethnic basis. On the other hand, under certain conditions, enlarging the win-set could weaken a leader's domestic position. For a constrained but dominant (i.e., Type II_a) state, enlarging the win-set through outbidding, for example, may lead to dangerous and potentially irreversible aggressive behavior that produces a political calamity at home. Regime type and ethnic composition are highly visible characteristics of states, as elites of other states will seek to exploit advantages these characteristics make available to them. For example, Hitler used the Sudetenland Germans as a pretext for taking over Czechoslovakia in 1938 and knew that the badly divided and ineffective democracy in France would work to his advantage, in the form of poor morale and fighting effectiveness of Germany's traditional adversary, if a war occurred.

Doubly constrained states are expected to be cautious in confrontations with those of the same kind. Under such conditions, if ethnicity does become a salient issue, both sides may try first to resolve their differences through negotiation. Elites also must consider the long-term, possibly unanticipated ramifications that hostile policies engender (Putnam 1988). Strategy selection and change therefore are determined by preference structures: For example, how does a very large domestic constraint influence preferences? The likelihood of substantial domestic political costs decreases the expected value of strategies that involve the use of force (Bueno de Mesquita and Lalman 1992). In interstate ethnic interactions an elite's best strategy is not independent of those used by others. Elites engage in "safety" strategies that minimize domestic costs (Maoz 1990, 1997a).

Strategy selection must be understood in a larger context that includes significant links between domestic ethnic politics and third-party intervention. The costs associated with politically constructed "strategic ideologies" are too high to make them reliable sources for interventionist strategies in ethnic conflicts. Whether mediation, tacit support for an ethnic challenge, or forceful intervention, a single strategy is unlikely when a COG depends on a domestic constituency. Leaders and their constituencies can have preferences that diverge over support for ethnic "brethren." Thus the first of five general propositions about interstate ethnic conflict and crisis is as follows:

P_1—Constrained states will pursue multiple strategies when intervening in ethnic conflict.

When international initiatives (including interventionist strategies) arise out of limited autonomy (i.e., where both executive aims and constituency desires are fundamental to the dynamics of a choice of strategy) for COGs, the tension between elite and domestic preferences will result in interventions of lower intensity. This pattern is expected because interventionist initiatives can awaken dormant domestic constituencies that undercut or even redirect a COG's initiative in an unfavorable direction. Thus a second proposition is derived:

P_2—Ethnically diverse states are less likely to initiate crises with violence.

Conversely, forceful intervention is most likely when costs and benefits are highly concentrated. Minimal political resistance from constituents (i.e., an authoritarian regime) or generic, all-purpose support from members of the same ethnic group (i.e., ethnic group dominance) produces this expectation. A third proposition therefore emerges:

P_3—Crises are likely to be more severe when unconstrained, ethnically dominant states are involved.

Interstate ethnic crises that are conditioned by high levels of cleavage and affinity present additional opportunities and constraints. Thus a fourth proposition arises:

P_4—High cleavage and affinities increase the probability of intense interstate ethnic conflict.

Fifth, and most encompassing of the propositions, is the one about relative likelihood of ethnic intervention:

P_5—Ethnic intervention is more likely, in descending order, for Type I_a (low-constraint, ethnic domination, i.e., belligerence), Type II_a (high-constraint, ethnic domination, i.e., sporadic interventionism), Type I_b (low-constraint, ethnic diversity, i.e., passive lobbying), and Type II_b (high constraint, ethnic diversity, i.e., *realpolitik*).

Various structural, normative, and strategic features of interstate ethnic conflict combine to reveal that as power is distributed among more than one ethnic group, interethnic cooperation becomes more likely. The phenomenon of nested games is used to explain high-constraint domestic political situations. When power is concentrated in the hands of a few leaders, as in the case of military regimes, the decision makers are less constrained in their domestic actions, and the nested game shifts to interelite strategic interaction within the international arena. Some elites, therefore, may be disposed toward finding relatively cooperative arrangements to resolve a dispute, while others may lead in the direction of more confrontational policies.

7. Summary and Case Selection

Determining which states are more likely to become involved in interstate ethnic strife so far has been a matter of a priori reasoning. This chapter has derived a framework based primarily on interaction effects for two variables, ethnic composition and institutional constraint. Each set of interactions will result in varying levels of decision making and implementation costs to elites. Conceptual analysis has focused on the *framework*, which begins with an explanation of elite preferences for involvement in ethnic strife, according to four ideal types or metaphors. This analysis includes the underlying logic and presumed linkages of the framework.

In short, this chapter has developed a framework of analysis for interstate ethnic crises. This framework, which pays close attention to the characteristics of the potential intervener, can provide useful insights regarding third-party intervention in ethnic conflict. It applies to any ethnic conflict that includes a potential intervener. The collective purpose of the five case studies in this volume is to illustrate the value of the framework in explaining how interstate ethnic crises do (or do not) come about. In other words, case studies will reveal whether the presumed linkages from the framework are valid interpretations of reality. We are mainly interested in theory *development* rather than *testing*. Thus the case studies are intended to show the value of our framework in explaining interstate ethnic crises and third-party activities.

The cases have been selected to include an example of each type from the typology, along with some regional diversity. We try to understand how interventions take place. In other words, by looking at the history in some detail, we try to determine whether the mechanisms suggested by our framework are consistent with events on the ground.[7]

In a classic exposition, King, Keohane, and Verba (1994:130) warn about dangers of selection on the dependent variable: "The cases of extreme selection bias—where there is by design no variation on the dependent variable—are easy to deal with: avoid them! We will not learn about causal effects from them." Researchers usually are curious, however, about some specific, important event, like a revolution, war, transition to democracy or breakdown of a democratic regime (Collier 1995; Geddes 1990; Collier and Mahoney 1996). Along these lines, Collier, Mahoney and Seawright (2004: 87) suggest that selection of these extreme cases is a well-established tradition in case-oriented research. In fact, under some circumstances, this kind of selection becomes useful because it allows the researcher to gain knowledge of a previously understudied or even generally unknown phenomenon that is of direct interest. In this study, the focus is on intervention in ethnic crises and it does include minimal variation, at least in terms of intervention that reaches the crisis level. While we are interested primarily in intervention as related to crisis, we also have included one case short of that level, that is, the Thai Malay.

The following chapters will examine the processes by which an ethnic conflict leads to intervention, interstate crisis, and sometimes even cooperation.

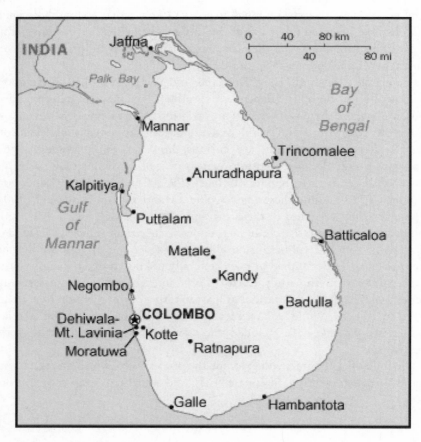

Sri Lanka, 2004. http://www.cia.gov/cia/publications/factbook/

CHAPTER THREE

Disintegration of Paradise:
The Indo–Sri Lankan Crisis

> Quotas racially applied in the work place or on campus do not work.
> They rip societies apart; so does linguistic separatism or historical revi-
> sionism in pursuit of ethnic self-esteem. Scholars or politicians who pro-
> mote such policies based on the romantic notion that ethnic groups
> should use state power to preserve their distinct identities should be sent
> to Sri Lanka to witness the fallacy of their theories (McGowan 1992).[1]

1. Introduction: The Disintegration of Paradise

The Indo-Sri Lanka crisis is characterized by a complex formation of issues,
perceptions of adversaries, and decision-making tasks that emanate from
internal as well as external sources. These sources indicate that deeply divided societies can influence decisions by outside actors to become involved in
an internal conflict (Zartman 1992). As will become apparent, India's
involvement in Sri Lanka's domestic protracted ethnic conflict had a double-
edged nature. On the one hand, India's direct involvement consisted of acts
of compellence, mediation, and physical intervention in an attempt to transform the highly centralized, unitary Sri Lankan state into a decentralized federation. On the other hand, indirect Indian involvement consisted of an
increase in the flow of materials and weapons from India to Sri Lanka in support of the Tamil insurgency, along with the training of Tamil separatists on
Indian soil.

Internal dimensions of the case reflect the impact of both the Tamil insurgency in the north and east of the island and the Sinhalese nationalist Janatha
Vimukthi Peramuna (JVP) insurgency in the south. Both conflicts can be
characterized as hostile internal acts to the extent that they represented challenges to the unity of the Sri Lankan state. This internal dimension continued
to play a significant role in influencing the relationship between the governments of India and Sri Lanka.[2]

This chapter, in an attempt to reveal patterns of Indian interest and involvement in Sri Lanka, examines the issues and events within the regional conflict. The primary focus is on the decision by India to send peacekeeping troops to Sri Lanka. In the second section of the chapter, the historical and political background of Sri Lanka's protracted ethnic conflict is scrutinized. The precrisis, crisis, and postcrisis periods are presented in the third and fourth sections. In the fifth section, implications of the conflict for the framework's propositions are assessed. The sixth and final section reviews the findings of this chapter.

2.   Assessing the Ethnic Factor: A Regional Perspective

2.1 The View from Sri Lanka—Dominance or Diversity?

Sri Lanka's population of over 18 million consists of six major ethnic groups. Census data indicates that about 75 percent of Sri Lanka's population is Sinhalese, that is, Buddhists who speak Sinhala. They originally came to the island from India and mostly live in the southern, western, and central parts of Sri Lanka. The second-largest group is formed by Sri Lankan Tamils, or Tamils of Sri Lankan citizenship, who comprise approximately 12.2 percent of the population or more than 2.23 million.[3] (The population data are drawn from 1995 UN population estimates.) Sri Lankan Tamils are predominantly Hindu and speak Tamil. Sri Lankan Tamils traditionally have occupied the northern and eastern parts of Sri Lanka and they are basically split in two groups: Jaffna Tamils, mainly descendants of tribes that arrived on the island more than fifteen thousand years ago, and Indian Tamils, brought to the island by British tea planters during the nineteenth and twentieth centuries. They comprise 5 percent of the population. The remaining 7 percent of the population is made up of Tamil-speaking Muslims, Moors, Burghers, descendants of European colonists, and Veddahs. Some Muslims speak Sinhala and others Tamil due to the location of their homes. Muslims, located mostly in the eastern province, are mixed in with Sinhalese and Tamils. Other Muslims live around Colombo and the west coast (Shastri 1997).

Another important piece of demographic information that should be mentioned regarding Sri Lanka's ethnic conflict concerns India. In the southern part of India is the province of Tamil Nadu, in which more than 80 million Tamils live. This is significant because ethnic affinities have played a crucial role in Sri Lanka's ethnic problem (Taras and Ganguly 2002). According to Taras and Ganguly (2002), the relationship between Sinhalese and Tamils is not only an example of peaceful coexistence but also traditional rivalry. Due to centralized colonial administration, for a long time the problematic issues between the two sides—political, religious, cultural, linguistic, or economic—were held in check by the British. However, when Sri Lanka became independent and the Sinhalese majority obtained political power, these issues came to the surface.

Political arrangements for ethnic groups and their degree of influence over the state and its decision makers are determined in part by historical experience (Horowitz 1985). Indian dominance in the political and social life of Sri Lanka played an important role in shaping the Sinhalese political order and Tamil reaction to it. India's relationship with Sri Lanka exhibits four significant characteristics.

One characteristic is the self-perception that the Sinhalese are a threatened people—they, not the Tamils of Sri Lanka, should be regarded as the minority. Surrounded by an overwhelming Hindu Tamil majority in the region—52 million including South India—the Sinhalese have, over time, developed a "reverse psychology" of superiority. Specifically, the Sinhalese claim lineage to the Aryans of northern India. In turn, this historical legacy is related to the idea that Sri Lanka is an island that had been conquered by the Buddha in order for the Buddhist religion to flourish (de Silva et al. 1988). Primacy of Buddhism on the island and commitment of political leadership to overcome threats to the Buddhist order are two historical perceptions deeply embedded in the collective subconscious of the Sinhalese people of Sri Lanka. Myths of Sinhalese cultural primacy have been bolstered by interpreters of ancient mythology that Buddhists have proprietary rights over the island.

Second, the Sinhalese have had a twenty-five-hundred-year history of political and religious affairs in which the sacred Sinhalese Buddhist texts describe the southern states of India as the main oppressors of the Sinhalese people (The Dipavamsa 1959). The identity of India as an external and threatening force is the most salient aspect of historical relations between India and Sri Lanka. This perception is reinforced by India's continuing status as the greatest power in South Asia.

Third, like India, the political system in Sri Lanka is elitist and personalized. The politics of Sri Lanka belong to a select few—members of either a "plantocracy" or English-educated political elite. In the early years of mass politics, transfer payment schemes and the state patronage system of the Sri Lankan government translated into the kind of participatory democracy that commonly is associated with welfare states. Decision making remained highly centralized and controlled by an elite group of Colombo-based politicians (Carment 1987, 1991). In other words, due to the fragile nature of democracy, ethnic tensions could be manipulated by Western-educated elites in Sri Lanka.

Fourth, and finally, the Sri Lankan political system continues to exhibit aspects of institutional incompleteness. An illustration is the transformation of the Sri Lankan constitution over the past twenty years. These changes reinforced the powers of the president and the unitary political system while, more recently, attempts have been made to devolve power to provincial councils. The failure of devolution to take hold after the death of President Ranasinghe Premadasa in May 1993 and the subsequent election of the Sri Lanka Freedom Party (SLFP) meant that regional politics remained subservient to that of Colombo. In sum, the unitary nature of the state has two implications: First, politics is direct—leaders are selected on the basis of their willingness to protect the group and appeal to voters on that basis. Second, a unitary state implies a lack of flexibility in finding solutions related to autonomy.

Congruence among Sri Lankan elites with respect to the historical understanding of Indo-Sri Lanka relations cannot be interpreted as an absence of conflict among Sri Lanka's decision makers. Differences among Sri Lanka's elites consistently have focused on how to deal with the Tamil separatist movement, Indian involvement in the conflict, and relations with the chauvinist *sangha* (the influential Buddhist clergy).

These historical and social elements combine to create a centralized system based on identity politics that proved to be ill-prepared for the political mobilization of Sri Lanka's minority Tamils. Despite inheriting a legal and constitutional system that emphasized individual rights and liberties, democracy quickly became equated with quotas, applied both in the government and higher education (McGowan 1992; de Silva 1993). Interethnic elite interests converged initially during the 1920s, but that goal then had a simple and unifying character: to end colonization. Subsequent elite interests became fragmented along ethnic lines, especially after 1956, when ethnic nationalists swept into power on promises to restore Sinhalese preeminence.

2.2 The Origins of Sri Lanka's Protracted Ethnic Conflict

Figure 3.1 shows a time line for the protracted ethnic conflict, which can be traced to political mobilization of the Tamil minority in the early 1940s. At independence in 1948 the main issue regarding ethnic politics became the amount of power minorities would have in affecting decisions taken at the center. During the formative years of Sri Lanka's independence, Tamil political organization became subdivided into two basic groups: (1) leadership that represented the interests of the Sri Lankan Tamils, known as the Tamil

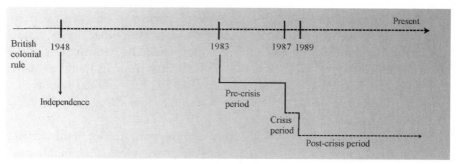

Figure 3.1 The Indo–Sri Lankan Conflict

Congress (which until 1948 had worked closely with the United National Party [UNP]) and (2) the Ceylon Workers Congress (CWC), which represented the interests of Tamil plantation workers who, by 1946, formed over half of the Tamil population of the island. Together, the Tamils formed a large enough electorate to gain representation for their subgroups in the legislature.

Under the leadership of S. J. V. Chelvanayagam, in 1949 a breakaway group of Tamil Congress members formed the Ceylon Tamil State or Federal Party, with the aim of "creating an organization for the attainment of the freedom of the Tamil speaking people of Ceylon" (Kodikara 1982: 195). The Federal Party asserted its interest in four basic issues:

1. Establishment of one or more Tamil linguistic states operating as a federating unit or units enjoying wide autonomous and residuary powers within a federal state in Sri Lanka;

2. Restoration of the Tamil language to its rightful place enjoying absolute parity of status with Sinhala as an official language of Sri Lanka;

3. Conferment of full civil rights to all Tamil speaking people; and

4. Cessation of colonization of traditionally Tamil-speaking areas with Sinhalese people (Kodikara 1982, 1985, 1987, 1989, 1990, 1993).

According to the Federal Party, the call for autonomy (which in 1949 had not become a demand for a separate state) represented a workable scheme because, apart from Indian Tamils concentrated in Kandy and a small percentage of others scattered throughout the island, the bulk of the Tamil population inhabits the northern and eastern provinces.[4] The Federal Party held that the process of British colonization had, among other things, linked the Tamil community, both economically and politically, with the rest of the island (Kodikara 1993). The departure of the British from Sri Lanka signaled to the Federal Party that the Tamils could revert to the political system that existed prior to the arrival of the colonists, in which close links with the Tamils of India had been the norm.

Several acts of the national legislature had the perhaps unintended effect of causing enhanced Tamil solidarity. Most important was the Sinhala-only legislation in 1956—the official language act—which declared Sinhala as the only official language of Ceylon (or Sri Lanka).[5] In the 1970s the radical populist United Front (UF) won a two-thirds majority in parliament, and a 1972 proposal went further by including both language and religion: Sinhala would be considered the sole official language, with Buddhism accorded the "foremost" place in Sri Lanka. This proposal resulted in dissent from all of the federal-level Tamil representatives in the legislature. In that same year, the Federal Party, Tamil Congress, CWC, and two other smaller parties (the Elathamir Ottumai Munani and the All Ceylon Tamil Conference) joined together to create the Tamil United Front in response to perceived hostile legislation. An increase in Sinhalese colonists in Tamil-dominant agricultural areas exacerbated these tensions. In 1975, the leading Tamil organizations came together and formed the Tamil United Liberation Front (TULF) with the aim of obtaining a separate state.

Until the mid-1970s, the issue of Tamil nationalism in Sri Lanka came out in the form of demonstrations and civil uprisings as a response to domination and assimilation efforts by the Sinhalese majority. However, after that time, "the nature of Sri Lankan Tamil nationalism acquired its present-day secessionist dimension" (Kearney 1985 in Taras and Ganguly 2002: 188). In other words, the demand for autonomy evolved into the issue of separation (Taras and Ganguly 2002). Not surprisingly, youth movements proliferated in the second half of the 1970s.

Quotas in university admissions also came along in the 1970s. Sharp discrimination against Tamil university applicants in 1977 substantially reduced the proportion of Tamils in many universities. (While the proportion of Tamils admitted to science-based disciplines reached 35 percent in 1970, it dropped to 19 percent by 1975 [de Silva 1979 in Shastri 1997: 148].) Student riots occurred in the same year. On-campus discrimination played a key role in the rapidly rising militancy of Tamil youth who, affected adversely by the new university admission policy, turned toward tactics that often included indiscriminate violence. University students eventually organized themselves as guerrilla units, most notably, the Liberation Tigers of Tamil Eelam (LTTE), the Eelam People's Revolutionary Liberation Front (EPRLF), The Peoples Liberation Organization of Tamil Eelam (PLOTE), Eelam Revolutionary Organization of Students (EROS), and Tamil Eelam Liberation Organization (TELO).[6]

Factors outside of the government's direct control contributed to the advancement of student militancy.[7] An often-overlooked factor from that era is the world sympathy evoked by riots, deaths, human rights violations, and a growing Tamil refugee problem from 1977 onward. The immediate effect of the violence took the form of terror created among Sri Lankan civilians (especially the Tamils) and a subsequent increase in support from South India for the separatist cause. Like their counterparts in Sri Lanka, South Indian Tamils also had undergone an ethnic resurgence in the 1950s. As will become apparent, their role in the Sri Lankan conflict is primary, and the Sri Lankan government recognized this with a constitutional amendment in 1983 that prohibited support for separation of any kind (Mohan 1985: 297).

3. The Precrisis Period: 25 July 1983 to 4 June 1987

3.1 Indian Intervention—Precrisis through Onset

Decreasing popular support and legitimacy led to increasing use of coercion by the UNP to sustain control of the country. While the government arrested an increasing number of Tamil insurgents, Tamil hostility increased enormously. The early 1980s, therefore, can be characterized as an era of increasing violence and hostility on both sides (Shastri 1997).

Faced with heightened tension and increased violence, the Indian government changed its policy in the same fashion toward Sri Lanka. Although India previously could be called "neutral" (due to its proclaimed policy of noninvolvement), after the early 1980s it became more interventionist in nature. India consistently called for deescalation of the conflict and peaceful resolution. Taras and Ganguly (2002: 191) summarize the Indian perspective, which had the problematic feature of including two conflicting interests: "preservation of Sri Lanka's territorial integrity, sovereignty and unity" and "accommodation of Sri Lankan Tamils' earlier demands for devolution of power and regional autonomy." In mid-1970, the UNP used violence in an effort to maintain control over the community. According to de Silva (in Shastri 1997: 155), despite attempts by the UNP government to represent the ethnic conflict as an internal affair, it became international anyway. The reason for that outcome is obvious;

due to heightened violence, Tamils in Sri Lanka came to believe that they could not handle the issue without outside assistance.

In July 1983, the Indian government chose to become an intermediary between the Sri Lankan Government (UNP) and the TULF. The Indian decision to intervene followed in the wake of postelection riots between Sinhalese and Tamils on 24 and 25 July 1983. At this time the demand for regional autonomy over separation came into play as a tactic by Sri Lanka's Tamil leadership.[8]

Subsequent transition of Tamil demands from regional autonomy to a separate state, along with the beginnings of Sri Lanka's foreign policy crisis on 25 July 1983, can be identified with the material and ideological support that the DMK (Dravida Munnetra Kazhagam) government of Tamil Nadu provided to the separatists and the direct intervention of the Indian government in Sri Lanka's domestic affairs. India's leader, Indira Gandhi, recognized Tamil separatist demands as affecting India's own interests, specifically with regard to the great number of Tamils fleeing to India but also due to the influence that the ethnic conflict had on similar insurgencies in India.[9] The stated interest of India's leaders was to prevent Sri Lanka's internal strife from escalating to a degree that might lead to involvement of extraregional powers (Kodikara 1990, 1993; Taras and Ganguly 2002). At issue was India's concern that the Soviet Union and the United States would become involved. By attempting to isolate the Tamil ethnic issue, India reaffirmed its commitment to Indian Ocean Security as "security manager of South Asia."

3.2 Escalation and Counterinsurgency

During the 1983 riots, Sri Lanka's President Junius Jayewardene sought military assistance from the United States, Britain, Pakistan, and Bangladesh to meet the growing insurgency (V. P. Rao 1988). On 5 August 1983, in a statement designed to placate Sri Lankan concerns, Indira Gandhi addressed the Indian Parliament and asserted that India "does not pose any threat to Sri Lanka nor do we want to interfere in its internal affairs. We want the unity and integrity of Sri Lanka to be preserved" (Parliamentary Debates, Lok Sabha, 5 August 1983, quoted in V. P. Rao 1988: 421). Following Gandhi's speech, the Indian government asserted its regional preeminence by pronouncing the "Indira Doctrine." It said that

> India will neither intervene in the domestic affairs of any states in the region, unless requested to do so, nor tolerate such intervention by any outside power. If external assistance is needed to meet an internal crisis,

states should look first within the region for help. (quoted in C.R.V.R. Rao 1985: 63)

In response to this announcement by the Indian government, Sri Lanka's Jayewardene warned that if Sri Lanka perceived a threat from India, it would turn to the United States, Britain, and others for military aid. Sri Lankan sources revealed that the president did in fact worry about an Indian invasion (Manor and Segal 1985; *Hindu*, 19 August 1983). Yet only several weeks later, Jayewardene agreed to prepare the groundwork for a settlement between the Sri Lankan government and the TULF to be negotiated through the good offices of the Indian government.

Jayewardene's change in strategy occurred because of the discouraging response that came from the Western powers to Sri Lanka's request for military assistance. The United Kingdom and the United States declined Sri Lanka's call for military assistance, and Jayewardene was turned down again by the United States after a visit there in 1984. However, former British Special Air Services (SAS) commandos, who worked for a security organization, called the Keenie Meenie Services, helped train the island's antiterrorist force. Although diplomatic relations with Israel had been severed in 1970, Mossad also assisted Sri Lanka's counterinsurgency training, and Pakistan responded with arms and military training for the Sri Lankan army (V. P. Rao 1988).

Sri Lanka's central concern at this time was Tamil militant activity in India—a fact that the Indian government officially denied until November 1986. Indira Gandhi's reluctance to discourage the Tamil militants had been a major irritant in Indo-Sri Lankan relations (*Globe and Mail*, 22 February 1988). Sri Lankan officials perceived Gandhi to be under pressure from the Indian Tamils. (In fact, India allowed the rebels to build up arsenals of arms in Tamil Nadu, run training camps, and ship military hardware across the Palk straits; retired Indian officers trained the militants in guerrilla warfare [V. P. Rao 1988].) Gandhi had an election coming up in 1985, and Congress preferred an electoral pact with the ruling AIADMK (All India Anna Dravida Munnetra Kazhagan), which hoped to obtain political mileage from the Tamil issue to the point of demanding that the Indian government take direct military action against Sri Lanka. Sri Lanka made it clear that it would not tolerate direct foreign intervention, but India still saw the matter as its concern. Thus, as early as 1983, Sri Lanka's perceived options in dealing with its ethnic conflict became reduced substantially.

Efforts by the Sri Lankan government to control the separatist movement led to a heightening of tension between Sri Lanka and India. For example, in 1984 the Sri Lankan government introduced a surveillance zone to stop the unauthorized movement of people between India and Sri Lanka. In that same year, Sri Lanka detained ten Indian fishing vessels for violating Sri Lankan fishing rights. In response the Indian government mobilized its powerful navy to convince Sri Lanka that detention of Indian citizens would not be worth the risk. The UNP's subsequent prohibition of fishing off the Mannar (northwest) region prompted the outflow of eleven thousand Tamil fishermen to Tamil Nadu (de Silva 1985, 1993).

Rajiv Gandhi succeeded his mother after her assassination in 1985. Gandhi moved swiftly to placate growing discontent among Sri Lanka's decision makers. Among the dissenters, Sri Lanka's then-prime minister, Ranasinghe Premadasa, insisted that if India removed its support, the militant struggle would collapse (*Asiaweek*, 23 November 1986). In response, the Indian government took decisive action to ensure the Sri Lankan government of its honest intentions. On 29 March 1985 the Indian coast guard intercepted a boat carrying guns and explosives to Tamil rebels in Sri Lanka (Kodikara 1987). The Indian government also applied pressure on the government of Tamil Nadu to remove Tamil militants from their training bases. With India taking the diplomatic initiative, two rounds of talks took place at Thimpu, Bhutan, in July and August 1985. The talks included the heads of major militant organizations (the LTTE, TELO, EROS, EPRLF), TULF, PLOTE, and the governments of India and Sri Lanka.

Like those before, the negotiations ended in failure. The talks became stalled, at least in part, because the Sri Lankan government—while advocating peaceful negotiations—had increased its attacks on the Tamil guerrillas. These military measures pushed moderate Tamils into militant organizations. Refusal by the Sri Lankan government to agree to the Tamil demand to merge the Northern and Eastern Provinces proved equally damaging. At that time a great difference existed between the position of Sri Lanka's leaders and a negotiated agreement with the Tamils (*Asiaweek*, 15 July 1986).

Jayewardene once again approached the United States to come to Sri Lanka's aid in solving the ethnic crisis. But the United States responded by informing him that it had cut the annual aid package to Sri Lanka in half, due partly to an effective Tamil lobby in Washington (*Hindu*, 6 June 1986). In voicing his unhappiness with the American response, Jayewardene said, "I am very happy that I have been abandoned. I do not trust a single power" (*South*, September 1987: 36).

On 8 November 1986, in a coordinated move with the Tamil Nadu government and police, the Indian government arrested known militants and their leaders and confiscated their arms and ammunition in a statewide crackdown (*Asiaweek*, 23 November 1986). This response, however, did little to persuade the Sri Lankan government of India's neutrality on the Tamil issue. In fact, the Indian government released those arrested the same day (*Asiaweek*, 23 November 1986).

Also in November of 1986, the South Asian Association for Regional Cooperation (SAARC) met in Bangalore. The major objective of this meeting was to seek a modus vivendi between Tamil insistence on the merger of the Northern and Eastern Provinces and Sinhalese opposition to it. The so-called December 19 Proposals called for administrative linkages between the two provinces and devolution of power to them. Both sides agreed to the proposals. The perception of the Sri Lankan government, however, remained that it would continue to pursue a military solution against the militants while using the proposals as a negotiating position for further talks.

By the beginning of 1987 the dominant Tamil rebel group, the LTTE, began carrying out a plan to take over civil administration in the north, which it already had under its military control. At the same time, the Sri Lankan government imposed a blockade on supplies of fuel and other essential commodities to the Jaffna peninsula while simultaneously picking up military action in the north and east (*Hindu*, 3, 10, 11 February 1987).

Within weeks of the Sri Lankan effort to eliminate the Tamil rebels, the government of India warned the Sri Lankan government against taking further military action against the insurgents. In a message delivered to Jayewardene on 10 February 1987, Gandhi warned that India had suspended its good offices and demanded that Colombo (*a*) lift the economic blockade of Jaffna and (*b*) affirm its commitment to the December 19 proposals. "If these steps were not taken and the military option was continued," Gandhi concluded, the fighting "will be prolonged" and the "situation will escalate" (*Hindu*, 12 February 1987: A1). Jayewardene reacted immediately to this threat. He issued two warnings to the LTTE, suggesting that (*a*) hostilities should cease in the north and the east and (*b*) the lifting of the embargo would be conditional upon observance of a ten-day cease-fire. When the LTTE violated the cease-fire, the Sri Lankan army launched a full-scale military campaign involving over three thousand troops in a land, air, and sea assault on the Jaffna peninsula. At the end of April 1987 the battle for Jaffna had begun. By May, despite the failure to round up the leaders of the LTTE, the Sri Lankan army enjoyed unprecedented success against the Tigers (Pfaffenberger 1988).

3.3 From Precrisis to Crisis

Since the beginning of 1987, intense fighting between Tamil guerrillas and Sri Lankan forces had produced high civilian causalities, mostly from the Tamil side. Some estimates placed the civilian death toll at the end of May 1987 as high as five hundred, prompting Gandhi once again to issue a warning to Jayewardene: "The time to desist from military occupation of Jaffna is now. Later may be too late" (*Hindu,* 29 May 1987: A1). The government of India condemned the government of Sri Lanka's actions, warning that it would not remain an indifferent spectator to the plight of the Tamils in Sri Lanka. Tamil militants inflamed the situation by slaughtering twenty-nine Buddhist monks on their way to an ordination ceremony. Indian newspaper editorials called for an armed invasion of Sri Lanka (Pfaffenberger 1988). During this course of events, the Indian government announced its intention to send relief supplies to the people of Jaffna peninsula. On 4 June 1987, five Indian Air Force supply planes, escorted by Mirage 2000 fighter jets, entered Sri Lanka's airspace and dropped relief supplies in and around Jaffna. The government of Sri Lanka condemned the Indian airdrop, known as Operation Eagle, as an unwarranted assault on Sri Lankan sovereignty and territorial integrity. Relations between Sri Lanka and India had reached the crisis stage.

The decision to seek a negotiated settlement came only after India threatened invasion. It is significant that despite full awareness of India's warnings, Jayewardene pursued a choice that he knew most likely would end in military hostilities. The president acted, at least in part, in response to time constraints—the internal protracted conflict in his view required immediate attention. To do nothing other than submit to Tamil separatist demands would have been, in Jayerwardene's view as well as those of others (particularly Premadasa), suicidal.

Whether the president's choice to seek a military solution against the Tamils was influenced more by pressure from decision makers within his cabinet or by time constraints is a moot point. Significant, however, is that he pursued a military stance vigorously despite repeated warnings from the Indian government and the overwhelming military superiority that backed those threats. Inflexible decision making, the belief in extraregional intervention, and an unwillingness to heed Indian threats suggest a decision-making process greatly influenced and constrained by domestic conflict, an overwhelming desire to resolve the conflict by force, and a belief system that limited, from the outset, the possibility of considering a full range of options.

4. The Crisis Period: 4 June 1987 to 27 July 1989

4.1 Sri Lanka Capitulates to Indian Demands

Within hours of hearing about the airdrop, Jayewardene launched a full-scale diplomatic protest that officially condemned the Indian action. Surprisingly, Colombo neither called for a UN Security Council meeting nor boycotted the SAARC meeting held in July of that year. Instead, Jayewardene, who believed that he had limited options after failing to get Western help against India, signed an accord with Gandhi in Colombo on 29 July 1987. The accord embodied the principles of the December 19 Proposals.[10] The Tamil militants, specifically the LTTE, did not sign the accord but agreed to a cease-fire (Taras and Ganguly 2002).

As when previously faced with Indian threats, Sri Lanka perceived few options. In a 24 September 1987 meeting in Sri Lanka with representatives of the Canadian government, prior to his departure to the Commonwealth Countries Head of Government Meeting (CCHOGM) in Vancouver, President Jayewardene confirmed this view. He pointed out that the terrorists never would have got as far as they did without Indian support. He also said that India's "quasi-invasion" in early June remained totally unjustified—a deep shock that became instrumental to his willingness to sign the accord in the form that he did. It occurred to Jayewardene that India would be coming in and "it was better they come in with him than against him."[11]

The Indo-Sri Lankan Accord represented a major disappointment for both Sri Lankan Tamils and Sinhalese. Despite the fact that the ultimate emphasis was on the territorial integrity of Sri Lanka, the accord stopped short of guaranteeing devolution of authority and the rights sought by the Tamils. Some high-ranking Sinhalese officials also had very deep reservations about the accord, and that remained true throughout the process of negotiation (Taras and Ganguly 2002).

The government of Sri Lanka agreed to the departure of its security forces from the north and east, to solve the Tamil problem through decentralization, and to a referendum on the issue of devolution in the near future (de Silva 1993). For its part, India would provide a sixteen-thousand- to nineteen-thousand-man Indian Peace Keeping Force (IPKF) to whom the Tamil rebels would turn over their weapons. The IPKF also would be responsible for monitoring the cease-fire.

Serious discontent with the accord produced an attempt on Jayewardene's life on 18 August 1987 within the grounds of Sri Lanka's parliament. Speculation at the time lay with the Sinhalese left, possibly the JVP. The attack seemed to galvanize the president's decision making; Jayewardene believed he had little alternative to forging ahead in collaboration with India to end the conflict. Retreat now became unthinkable.

Given the fact that the India had taken over from the Sri Lankan army in the north and east, New Delhi had a surprisingly optimistic view of recent events. For India, unlike Sri Lanka, no time pressure existed to complete the accord. The government of India expected a settlement with the LTTE within six weeks. During that period the IPKF would have departed.

From the Sri Lankan perspective, Indian support for the LTTE, overt or covert, looked like affirmation of the only group capable of forcing Colombo into political compromises. Although the government of India did not support Tamil Eelam (i.e., independence), it could not easily endure assaults on the Sri Lankan Tamil community, which ultimately would compromise its legitimacy within South India. Sri Lanka viewed Indian boldness as guarantor of peace as a step beyond good offices. The Indian decision to take on the LTTE derived from the belief that (a) the Indian Army could meet any LTTE challenges and (b) the LTTE did not have widespread support among the Eastern Province Tamils. The Indian government believed at this time that the Sri Lankan Tamil community still welcomed the IPKF.

By this point in the crisis it had become clear to Jayewardene that the agenda-setting power and creation of a time frame for IPKF withdrawal stood beyond the reach of the Sri Lankan government. Sri Lankan decision making at this time must be considered in light of India's two main foreign policy objectives—reasserting its role as South Asia's security manager and preventing the export of Tamil secession. Until these two objectives had been achieved, Sri Lanka would remain a hostage to Indian political interests.

Lack of cohesive leadership within the Sri Lankan government was emphasized again by its conspicuous absence from negotiations between the Tigers and the IPKF. This absence provoked indignation among Sinhalese nationalists in Jayewardene's cabinet and fueled the fires of widespread Sinhalese discontent against India.

Time pressure on the Sri Lankan government to resolve the domestic crisis became equally significant. The government had to pass the legislation through parliament, provide a Supreme Court ruling on the constitutionality of the Provincial Councils Bill, and hold Provincial Council elections—and all before 31 January 1987. The IPKF was to have withdrawn before this time. Jayewardene's highly personalized decision making, tempered by the assault on his life, cabinet defections, and Sinhalese opposition to the accord, led him to believe that he had to find a political solution because of the Indian government's stated intention of IPKF withdrawal (Samarasinghe and Liyanage 1993).

By late September 1987, India's attitude toward the LTTE had changed only slightly, while that of Sri Lanka showed strains under pressure from Sinhalese extremists. Indian perceptions tended to play down the growing number of clashes between the IPKF and the LTTE. The Indian government cited the psychological difficulties of the LTTE that would stand in the way of converting it to a peacetime role. The Sri Lankan government, on the other hand, found itself increasingly isolated from the Sinhalese people. When the UNP managed to get the Provincial Councils bill through Parliament, a second bomb ripped through a Colombo market, killing thirty-two people, including Gamini Jayasuriya, a member of Parliament who had left the government rather than vote for the accord.

By the beginning of November 1987, the LTTE brought civil administration to a standstill in the northern and eastern provinces by killing one hundred or more members of rival groups. In contrast, the IPKF gave the appearance of being in complete disarray; the Indian government denied allegations of strengthening its peacekeeping contingent while maintaining complete "neutrality."

It should be noted that the accord, as designed, represented an agreement between the governments of Sri Lanka and India. The LTTE, on whose agreement the peaceful transfer to the Provincial Councils hinged, did not sign the agreement. Thus a crucial flaw in the accord became obvious: It depended on a group that did not participate in the peace talks (de Silva 1993). The accord provided only a partial solution to the inherent ethnic problem (Shastri 1997). The IPKF could not succeed in disarming the LTTE and eventually had to fight it.

Both Jayewardene and Gandhi realized that since the LTTE refused to lay down their arms and negotiate, they would have to be eliminated. After obtaining from the Indian government an agreement that its forces would depart quickly after removing the threat of the Tigers, Jayewardene agreed to an increase in the number of IPKF forces on Sri Lankan soil. In a joint press conference held on 9 October 1987, India's defense minister and Jayewardene asserted that "the days of gentle persuasion were over." The amnesty would be lifted from the LTTE, and the IPKF would be increased to twenty thousand troops.

By December 1987 the IPKF became involved in major search and destroy operations in Batticaloa and Mulavattu in northeast Sri Lanka. The IPKF, however, remained incapable of removing the Tigers from Jaffna peninsula and had become involved in a stagnating military operation, at the cost of U.S. $100 million and five hundred dead soldiers (Taras and Ganguly 2002).

4.2 Loss of Autonomy and Internal Cleavage

By this point in the crisis it had become clear to Jayewardene that the agenda-setting power and creation of a time frame for IPKF withdrawal remained beyond the reach of the Sri Lankan government. Sri Lankan decision making at this time must be considered in light of India's two main foreign policy objectives: reasserting its role as South Asia's security manager and preventing the export of Tamil secession. Until these two objectives had been achieved, Sri Lanka would remain a hostage to Indian political interests. While the Sri Lankan government acquiesced to Indian demands, both opposition parties, the SLFP and Sri Lankan Freedom Party, and, more importantly, the JVP, had taken up opposition to the accord and Indian "occupation." This transformation and revival of the JVP invoked a steady increase of anarchy and terrorism in the south and the spectre of a government seemingly helpless to prevent it. As Bruce Matthews from Nova Scotia has pointed out, the JVP, despite its small size (ten thousand active members), determined the political agenda for 1988. All of the universities and most of the schools, many factories, and even Colombo itself (on 12 September) had been shut down by the terrorist activities of the JVP. These attacks represented a major blow to Sri Lankan national security and marked a dangerous phase in the southern campaign to topple the government. Furthermore, at this time the JVP, the SLFP, and the Buddhist monastic order attempted to undermine the possible benefits of the accord and claim it was the source of all Sri Lanka's problems. Both argued that the presence of the Indian army on Sri Lankan soil, along with the perceived fusion of the provinces, constituted the end of the unitary state.

Prolonged Indian presence in Sri Lanka therefore not only conditioned the response patterns of the Sri Lankan government and the JVP, but also contributed to the increasing intensity of hostile internal acts (Samarasinghe and Liyanage 1993). JVP violence influenced not only the perceptions of Sri Lanka's decision makers toward India as the hostile aggressor, but also the gravity of the crisis situation. The unity and fabric of Sri Lankan society, it would seem, faced destruction from within by a force that identified as its main oppressor the Indian government.

In light of these developments the Indo-Sri Lankan accord cannot be viewed as successful in bringing peaceful resolution to the ethnic conflict in Sri Lanka. Like Rupesinghe (1989), over a decade earlier Taras and Ganguly (2002: 201 and 1988) had observed that "it brought about an intensification and transformation of the conflict; the conflict now was not only between the LTTE and the Sri Lankan/Indian forces but also within the Sinhalese community between the JVP and the government." In the early 1990s, the conflict between Sri Lankan Tamils and Muslims in the eastern part of Sri Lanka became part of an already very complex conflict structure. Due to this complexity, regional powers proved incapable of solving the protracted conflict (Taras and Ganguly 2002).

For its part, the Indian government, through various tactics, had succeeded in marginalizing Sri Lankan participation in the north and east and had solid-ified its military position by doing so. The rise to power of President Ranasinghe Premadasa signaled an escalation in verbal hostilities between Sri Lanka and India.[12] For example, at the 10 January 1989 installation ceremo-ny of the president at the nation's most sacred Buddhist shrine, the Temple of the Tooth (in the former Royal Capital of Kandy surrounded by Buddhist monks), Premadasa announced that his priority would be to resolve Sri Lanka's conflicts. He asked the JVP to rejoin the political process. On relations with India he sounded the following nationalist note: "Whatever the cost, I will not surrender an inch of Sri Lankan territory. Whatever the cost I will not surrender a shred of our sovereignty. We should not and will not create situa-tions that provoke or invite intervention" (South, February 1989: 12).

4.3 Renewed Tensions between India and Sri Lanka

Right after his election, President Premadasa announced his intention to ask the Indian government to withdraw "as far as possible" the entire IPKF (now forty-five thousand) from Sri Lanka by 29 July 1989. The president said that "[a]fter July 29, the IPKF has no authority whatsoever over even one inch of my land" (South, February 1989: 12). Significantly, he made the decision without the benefit of cabinet consultation, its rhetoric shaped in order to appease the JVP's demand for IPKF withdrawal and thereby refurbish his nationalist declarations.

Risks associated with this strategy were apparent to Premadasa. A refusal of the Indians to leave within a reasonable time limit would reveal the hollowness of the president's power. Overhasty compliance would thrust the president and the Sri Lankan army on the tender mercies of Tamil and Sinhalese insurgents. Naturally, the government of India became incensed by Premadasa's unilateral decision and argued that it violated the bilateral agreement enshrined in the original accord. For Gandhi the stakes suddenly became higher as well. Giving into Premadasa's unilateral demand would be an embarrassment he could ill afford in an election year. On 7 July 1989 Premadasa reimposed a state of emergency across the nation. The previous order had been lifted in January after being in operation for six years. After two years of being confined to bar-racks, the Sri Lankan army went back on patrol.

4.4 Postcrisis—27 July 1989 to the Present

On 27 July the JVP launched a campaign of protest directed against the fail-ure of the IPKF to comply with Premadasa's order to leave the country by 29

July 1989. On the diplomatic front, Premadasa sent clear signals to India. On 15 July 1989, Sri Lanka's Foreign Minister Wijeratne announced a "misunderstanding" between Sri Lanka and India on the withdrawal issue. Wijeratne said that Premadasa would be flexible on the deadline if India agreed on a phased pullout and gave some assurance on dates, recognized Premadasa as commander in chief, and announced a cessation of hostilities with the LTTE. The Indian government responded by rejecting Premadasa's latter two conditions and responded in turn that the IPKF would not withdraw until the devolution package was in place. In response, Premadasa dropped the second demand, retained the third, and added that India should announce a token withdrawal of troops immediately.

For Premadasa, linking the IPKF withdrawal and granting of greater devolution to the provincial governments did not stand out as the key issue. From his previous statements on devolution, it is clear Premadasa believed that as a sovereign nation, Sri Lanka must not be told how to conduct its parliamentary affairs. In contrast to Premadasa's position, the government of India held that if a devolution package could be devised, then an IPKF withdrawal could take place.

When the cabinet and parliament talks ended on 11 August the president advised his personal envoy, Bradman Weekaroon, to pursue talks in Delhi. They agreed on a timetable and hoped to complete the removal by February 1990 at a rate of fifteen hundred to sixteen hundred personnel per week. The two governments, however, could not agree on withdrawal and implementation of devolution.

After high-level talks in September 1989, an agreement between India and Sri Lanka provided for an observer group consisting of the Sri Lankan army commander and the Indian commander of IPKF to report on violations of the cease-fire and report consequential action. The agreement furthermore specified that there would be a phased handover from the IPKF to Sri Lankan forces in the north and east supervised by Provincial Councils, the government of Sri Lanka, and the government of India.

By the beginning of 1990, the political situation in Sri Lanka stood on shaky ground. The antiaccord sentiment among the Sinhalese opposition remained strong, and India's frequent miscalculations continued to bedevil its military operations in the north and east. Premadasa remained suspicious of Indian intentions. JVP opposition in the south was effectively quelled by February 1990—but not without a cost. Although beginning a phased pullout, Indian troops remained entrenched in the north. Over the next thirteen months of talks in Colombo, Premadasa made significant concessions to the Tigers.

In June 1990, four months after the Indian troops completed their withdrawal, civil war broke out again in the north, and the councils designed to give autonomous government to the Tamils were abolished. By 1991, India now had moved formally out of the picture. India suffered at least one serious side effect from the conflict; Rajiv Gandhi was assassinated on 21 May 1991. Opposition leaders, dedicated to complete Indian withdrawal from the conflict, succeeded him.

Throughout 1991 and 1992 a multiparty parliamentary committee began to consider ways to offer Tamils alternatives to supporting the Tigers. A plan was devised with the proviso that the Northern and Eastern Provinces would not merge. More power would be devolved to the north and the east to protect minority Muslims living in the region. The plan was contingent on Tamil agreement to abandon merging the north and the east. The agreement generated significant hope among the participants for a peaceful solution to the conflict.

President Premadasa's assassination on 1 May 1993, possibly by Tamil Tigers, came as a significant blow to the various initiatives in progress. In less than a two-week period, assassins had erased the country's president and the only other man to challenge him, opposition leader Lalith Athulathmudali. Assassinated on 23 May 1993, Ahulathmudali, a former UNP member, had led a failed impeachment in August 1991 against his rival, accusing the president of abuse of power. He then formed the Democratic United National Front and, under Sri Lanka's council system, could have had power equal to that of the president (*Asiaweek*, 12 May 1993).

In November 1993, LTTE forces seized the government military base close to Jaffna, and only after several days of intense fighting could government forces manage to recover it. Indeed, from 1990 onward, the LTTE gradually increased its power in most of the Jaffna Peninsula, and in 1995 the LTTE seemed to govern Jaffna as a de facto state.

Presidential elections were held in August 1994 and resulted in a coalition of SLFP-led parties coming to power under the leadership of Chandrika Kumaratunga. Later she also won the presidency with 62.3 percent of the vote and committed herself to finding a solution for the problem. In 1995 Kumaratunga promised to devolve some power to the provincial level, and the LTTE agreed to a cease fire. The LTTE, however, insisted on the idea of a separate Tamil state, so the agreement for a cease-fire broke, and clashes between the LTTE and Sri Lankan military started again (Shastri 1997).

Sri Lanka's domestic protracted conflict was sustained by two reinforcing factors. The government was in disarray and leaderless and the Indian government clearly remained unwilling to mediate the conflict. Without either mediation or concerted international effort—and with the LTTE's stubborn-ness—little hope existed that Sri Lanka's conflict would be resolved anytime soon (de Silva and Samarasinghe 1993). According to a MAR Project assess-ment, the LTTE committed to its military campaign over the long term. At the end of 1995, it carried out assaults against military targets and moderate Tamil leaders who favored the president's devolution plan. The Tigers were well equipped, highly disciplined, and determined, so it seemed unlikely that the Tamil separatist campaign would disappear. Low-level violence remained likely, as the Tigers regrouped to continue their struggle (http://www/cidcm.umd.edu/inscr/mar/data/sriindtchro.htm). Unfortunately, it seemed as if terrorism and fighting would continue to be the main characteristics of Sri Lankan politics in the near future.

Talks between the LTTE and the government resumed in January 1995, with a cease-fire declared after a series of talks. Due to differences of opin-ions and agendas between the president and the LTTE's leader, Velleupillai Prabhakaran, talks did not produce a mutually acceptable solution. The peace talks stalled in April 1995 and fighting resumed when the LTTE uni-laterally abrogated the cease-fire by launching an attack against the Sri Lankan army.

In August 1995, as a concrete step toward peace, the government of Sri Lanka proposed a plan for devolution of power. DeVotta (2002) argues that Kumaratunga had for a long time seen the 1978 constitution as a major imped-iment to solving the ethnic problem since it rendered any structural change impossible. Although she sent reform proposals to parliament about a new con-stitutional scheme and new electoral laws, Kumaratunga could not get the response she wanted. The idea behind the proposals was that such change even-tually would provide the two-thirds majority needed to enact constitutional changes and pass devolutionary measures. However, due to opposition from extremist Sinhalese politicians and Buddhist clergy—the Tamil Tigers in partic-ular rejected the proposals as being inadequate—she failed to put together the needed two-thirds majority in parliament. The president abandoned constitu-tional reform proposals and called for new elections (Shastri 2002).

In December 1995, government forces regained control of Jaffna and cleared the peninsula of LTTE fighters. This was the first time for a long time that government forces had claimed control over this area (de Silva 1997). Eventually the LTTE had to withdraw from the city of Jaffna and move to the south. In July 1996 they launched an attack on a Colombo commuter train, which resulted in seventy deaths and significant material damage.

The LTTE continued its activities and organized suicide bombings—for example, a January 1998 assault on Sri Lanka's holiest Buddhist temple that killed thirteen people. In February 2000, the Norwegian government offered to mediate in the peace talks between Kumaratunga's government and the LTTE but that had no discernible impact.

Held in October 2000, the election generated more violence than ever. The People's Alliance (PA) gained 107 seats to the UNP's 89 and two extremist Sinhalese parties, five minority parties, and independent groups captured a total of 29 seats (DeVotta 2002). Since at least 113 seats are necessary for any party to operate as majority in the Parliament, the PA established an alliance with a small minority party, the Sri Lanka Muslim Congress (SLMC). Nevertheless, due to failures in the peace talks and an inability to solve economic problems, the PA lost its credibility, and December 2001 elections produced a victory for the United National Party (UNP) (Shastri 2002). When the president realized that the UNP could not carry a "no confidence" motion to save her minority government from defeat in July 2001, Kumaratunga suspended parliament for two months. This event also contributed to the loss of confidence on her side. Soon after the suspension, the LTTE's attack on the country's only airport and its adjacent air force base destroyed thirteen military and civilian aircraft (DeVotta 2002).

Led by Prime Minister Ranil Wickremesinghe, the new cabinet responded favorably to a unilateral cease-fire declared by the Tigers. On 22 February 2002, with the sponsorship of Norway, both sides signed a permanent cease-fire agreement with the hope of ending the destructive ethnic conflict. A couple of months later the main highways linking the Jaffna peninsula with the rest of Sri Lanka reopened after twelve years.

In September 2002 the first round of talks took place in Thailand, and the Sri Lankan government decided to lift the ban on participation by the Tamil Tigers. Both the government and the Tamil Tigers expressed their optimism and hope for a solution to the conflict. The Tigers dropped their demand for a separate state and opted for regional autonomy within a democratic Sri Lanka. In December 2002, the two sides came to an agreement on the issue of power sharing, and the Tamils committed themselves to autonomy in a federal system within an undivided Sri Lanka. The Sri Lankan government expressed its willingness to give a substantial measure of autonomy to the Tamils in the north and east as long as Sri Lanka remains united as a federal state.

Peace talks, however, stalled in 2003. In July 2004, the first suicide bombing since 2001 took place in Colombo. At the time of this writing, Sri Lanka is one of the countries worst hit by the tsunami in December 2004, with over 45,000 dead, 750,000 displaced, and thousands missing. According to the Indo-Asian News service, on 1 January, President Kamaratunga stated her willingness to shake hands with the Tamil Tigers and thanked India for the help provided in the wake of the tsunami disaster. Despite these recent positive signs in the wake of the natural disaster and some degree of ongoing optimism in the international community, the failure of all past attempts toward a peaceful solution makes it very hard to foresee Sri Lanka's future.

5. Analysis and Propositions

Three stages of the Indo-Sri Lankan crisis relate directly to the stages within the framework. At stage 1, both states exhibited apprehensiveness in formulating foreign policies that would lead to confrontation. Judging from the evidence, this was primarily a result of their ethnically diverse characteristics. Less apparent, especially for Sri Lanka, is the constraining role that institutions were assumed to play in inhibiting ethnically based foreign policies. Even prior to crisis onset, Sinhalese hypernationalism undermined institutional constraints.

Consistent outbidding among Sinhalese politicians occurred at stage 2, whose efforts to build domestic support in light of the presumed threat from India and the Tamils of Sri Lanka led to a kind of belligerence that belies Sri Lanka's small-state status. This is evident in the kinds of speeches given by Sri Lankan leaders, but more concretely, the consistent refusal of Sri Lankan leaders to participate in regional attempts at conflict resolution and their escalation of the conflict in 1987 when the Sri Lankan army was dispatched to the north and began its campaign of terror against Tamil civilians. These last two actions ultimately resulted in a spiraling of tensions between the two states and stage 3 interactions.

At stage 3, neither state was predisposed to using force against the other, this being true especially for India, which easily could have taken formal control of Sri Lanka. Perhaps, facing fewer domestic constraints, it might have done so. As a result, India chose an alternative and ultimately less successful strategy to protect Tamil civilians living in Sri Lanka and to prevent the conflict from spilling over into South India. In sum, the linkages between the various stages of the framework appear to apply to this case with two exceptions. First, it is difficult to determine, from the evidence provided, the exact role that institutions played in foreign policy formation and, second, it is not yet clear if, in fact, high-constraint states are indeed less belligerent. More exactly, India found covert ways of achieving its objectives. This may be true of democratic states in general.

The two-level game perspective finds support when attention is given to

India's own ethnic politics—an important but sometimes neglected aspect of the Sri Lankan conflict. India is an ethnically diverse society that has proved relatively successful in managing ethnic tensions. Political decisions in India rarely have been made without allowing for their differential impact on respective ethnic groups. India's inherited parliamentary structure initially might have seemed unsuitable to such an ethnically diverse society. Preindependence mechanisms had been developed for separating Hindu/Muslims, upper/lower castes, and ethnic minorities; the colonial period itself is a critical factor in explaining the sensitivity of Indian elites to ethnic group demands. For example, the British gave official preference to the Bengali language and Urdu in the north, provided separate concessions to Sikhs and Muslims, and patronized the non-Brahmin movement (Brass 1990).

After independence the Indian government adopted Hindi in an attempt to displace Urdu. The government also adopted pluralist policies in relation to major language and cultural movements. It recognized most of the large language groups, among whom major mobilizations had developed for creation of separate linguistic states (Kohli 1990). The weak status of Hindi in the early years of independence, along with concern over separatist movements among linguistic groups, provided the basis for linguistic reorganization of states. Simultaneously, the Congress Party took measures to insure that linguistic reordering carried out in the mid-1950s would not legitimize separatist demands. Nor would the government tolerate regional demands based upon religious differences (Brecher 1959; Nayar 1966).

Although the Congress government met with considerable success in confronting language issues through linguistic federalism, more recent governments have been less successful in managing the political demands of non-Hindu and tribal minority groups (Nayar 1966; Weiner 1987; Brass 1991). Since the breakup of a unified Congress Party in 1967, India's significant political transformations include a decline in order and authority, erosion of vertical patterns of fealty, a lost capacity to influence the political behavior of communal political parties, the increasing use of force in internal and external affairs, and a disturbing tendency toward patronage democracy as the long-term pattern of conflict management (Kohli 1990; Chandra 2004).

During the period of rapid growth in Tamil militancy in Sri Lanka, the Indian political process experienced a parallel political transformation. The Indian political landscape changed from one dedicated to the principles of unity, order, and secularism—a model of a dominant, strongly centralized, and somewhat autonomous state—to a state dependent on the mobilization of ethnic groups for support at the regional level. India's elites increasingly became constrained by a diverse and clamoring multiethnic population. How India's policy toward its ethnic groups led to a crisis with Sri Lanka is explained by three factors.

First, initial Indian involvement stemmed from the government of Sri Lanka's decision not to extend citizenship to Indian Tamil plantation workers. The government contended that despite their long residence, these workers remained affiliated with their country of origin. By 1964 an estimated 975,000 "stateless" persons resided in the country. Agreements in 1964 and 1974 between the two governments led to the return of many, but not all, of the Tamils to India. The agreement had the net effect of establishing a precedent for future relations with Sri Lanka on the Tamil issue.

The second factor was the delicate political balance between the regional government of Tamil Nadu and the national government of the Congress Party. Since the 1950s, the Congress Party had never been in a position to win the state of Tamil Nadu on its own in an election. The two major Tamil Nadu parties, the All India Anna Dravida Munnetra Kazhagam (AIADMK) and the Dravida Munnetra Kazhagam (DMK), looked to Congress for support. In turn, the Congress Party depended equally on them to consolidate its own position at the state level. Given traditional Tamil Nadu sympathies for the Sri Lankan Tamils, the issue has been important to Congress. For example, Indira Gandhi's astute political maneuvering through the 1970s and early 1980s found her forging alliances first with the DMK and then the AIADMK. From 1980 until her death, Gandhi continued to support the AIADMK and its leader, M. G. Ramachandran, because of his ability to contain the more militant brand of Tamil nationalism espoused by the DMK.

To remain alive in South Indian politics, the Congress Party often found itself being tested on its foreign policy toward Sri Lanka. The conflict in Sri Lanka provided significant political mileage not only for leaders of the AIADMK and the DMK but for Congress as well. For its part, the AIADMK called for active mediation in the Sri Lankan conflict, while the DMK pursued a more hard-line approach. It demanded that the Sri Lankan government grant full autonomy to the Tamils (Sivarajah 1990). Both the AIADMK and the DMK called for some form of Indian intervention, UN mediation, and self-determination for Sri Lankan Tamils. The more moderate AIADMK had to play the ethnic game in order to prevent the DMK from capitalizing on its inaction. For example, Ramachandran pressured the Indian government to issue Indian passports to some of the rebel leaders to facilitate their movement within India and the global community (Khory 1992).

The third factor has been informal linkages between Tamils across the Palk Straits, including economic and military support. The most dramatic example was establishment of rebel training camps in the Tamil Nadu state in South India. Indian former servicemen and members of India's foreign Intelligence Agency frequently provided training (Research and Analysis Wing–RAW) (Khory 1992).

Collectively, these factors amounted to increasing Indian involvement in Sri Lankan domestic affairs. The Indian government perpetuated a public image as an active mediator concerned with finding an agreement acceptable to parties on all sides. Less apparent in the preceding analysis is the complex domestic political game that Congress has been forced to play in order to ensure political longevity and maintain regional preeminence in South India (Taras and Ganguly 2002). Until recently, national leaders have managed the pressures of multiethnic constituencies through an overburdened federal political structure. In that context, South India always played an important role in Indian politics. It is well understood that long-term support from Tamil Nadu, a linguistically defined state, has been crucial to the political longevity of Congress. Thus, at one level, the structure of India's political system would appear to be at odds with a foreign policy based on ethnicity. Raising the salience of ethnicity as a component of its foreign policy could have repercussions for relations with India's other neighbors, most notably Pakistan. The salience of several additional and compounding factors, however, made such policies imperative.

India is a parliamentary democracy and not without success in maintaining appropriate constraints on elected officials (Brass 1990; Kohli 1990). More precisely, India's institutions are designed to prevent any one ethnic group from achieving dominance, although persistence of the caste system and emergence of the Bharata Janata Party are notable exceptions.[13] In principle, the federation scatters power territorially. It decentralizes and allows for autonomy, assigning to different groups the right to decide on domestic issues of concern to them. The central idea behind this approach is to create conditions necessary for permanent conflict resolution between ethnic groups.

Faced with potential losses on the electoral front, India's decision makers inferred that involvement would mean lower net costs. India provided support in two ways, through tacit sponsorship of Tamil insurgents and later direct intervention—all of the time portraying itself as an active and impartial mediator in the conflict. Colombo, as described earlier, lifted the embargo and ceased military operations against the rebels. At the time, political opinion in India insisted that Gandhi must have given the Sri Lankan president the option of accepting the Indian ultimatum or facing an armed Indian invasion. When Gandhi sent IPKF troops to Jaffna in July 1987, Sri Lanka's

President Jayewardene launched a full-scale diplomatic protest that officially condemned the Indian action. Then, however, having become aware of the fact that he had limited options, Jayewardene signed the accord with Gandhi in Colombo on 29 July 1987. India would provide a sixteen-thousand- to nineteen-thousand-man IPKF (later increased to forty thousand) to whom the Tamil rebels would turn over their weapons.

Several basic findings derive from research on this case. These results pertain to commitment, autonomy, domestic costs, and manipulation of perceptions.

Consider Proposition P_1, which concerns commitment to one or more strategies of intervention. The Indo-Sri Lankan case supports this proposition. When a domestic constituency is influential, as in India, leaders indeed do face difficulty in mobilizing an optimal response to an international opportunity. For leaders of democratic societies, risky strategies of intervention, for example, have highly concentrated costs and diffuse benefits. Therefore, even when they share constituents' preferences at the outset, leaders prefer not to have their "hands tied" by constituents (Evans 1993).

India's leaders pursued a variety of strategies to reduce the costs that the conflict imposed on India's domestic political scene. These multiple strategies arose precisely because Congress leaders did not want too close of a connection to any particular constituency (in this case, the AIADMK). In attempting to escape this problem the Indian government explicitly denied any official involvement in aiding the Tamil rebels, all the while pursuing active mediation and other good offices. A survey of events indicates that the Indian government moved from being essentially dovelike (that is, showing explicit disinterest in the conflict in its honest broker role) to becoming an agent of a particular group of interests, namely, South Indian politicians. For India, the domestic costs of not pursuing involvement in Sri Lanka's internal conflict became too high to ignore. In choosing involvement, India's decision makers had to consider the domestic ramifications entailed by regional politics. Faced with potential losses on the electoral front, India's decision makers inferred the costs of involvement to be lower than not being involved at all. They decided to provide support in two ways, initially through tacit backing for the Tamil insurgents and later through direct intervention. During this period, India also attempted to negotiate a peaceful settlement to the conflict (Heraclides 1997). In short, use of different strategies can be traced to India's status as a highly constrained state.

Proposition P_2, which focuses on the preference for nonviolent intervention among ethnically diverse states, also finds support. In this instance, the more clearly Indian regional interests became defined within the Sri Lankan context, the more India's leaders experienced constraints imposed by mobilized regional groups' support for noncoercive strategies. This approach resulted in a strategic dilemma because Indian leaders could not convince Sri Lankan leaders that their hands indeed had been tied by domestic forces. This lack of credibility on the part of India's leaders clearly paralleled a failed peacekeeping accord. The evidence does indicate that India had been constrained in using force against the state of Sri Lanka, but it tried everything short of that in pursuing domestic and international objectives (such as imposing a solution of regional autonomy on the Sri Lankan government).

As mentioned earlier, the separatist demands of Sri Lankan Tamils affected India's interests in two ways: (*a*) Tamils fled to India due to Sri Lankan policies and (*b*) the situation in Sri Lanka influenced ethnic conflict insurgencies in India. The possibility of great power involvement emerged as a major concern. Therefore, India's elites could not allow Sri Lankan aggression against Tamil civilians in the north to go unchecked because that strategy had an impact on politics in India in general and South India in particular. Thus the solution of sending "peacekeeping" troops to Sri Lanka reflected a compromise intended to appease both the Sri Lankan government and South Indian Tamils.

Proposition P_3 focuses on forceful intervention and the concentration of costs and benefits. Forceful intervention is most likely when there are low institutional constraints and limited political resistance among constituents (authoritarian regimes) or generic, all-purpose support from members of the same ethnic group (ethnic group dominance), as is the case for Type I_a states.

When constraints are low or one ethnic group is dominant, as noted in chapter 2, these types of states can show belligerence as third-party interveners. Without internal constraints, elite action is decisive in shaping outcomes, and pursuit of an ethnically oriented foreign policy becomes attractive for leaders. Since elites do not see any significant threat to their power, they move forward.

India, as an ethnically diverse state (i.e., not Type I_a), faced a mixture of constraints and incentives to act since the beginning of the conflict. Use of ethnicity as an issue represented a very risky option for India's leaders. Thus they had to evaluate alternative policies and strategies and then decide what to do. In line with expectations from the typology, India adopted a mild attitude on the issue of Tamil autonomy at first and then tried to mediate between the two sides in Sri Lanka. When good offices and mediation efforts did not produce a peaceful solution, only then did India (as a Type II_b state) decide to intervene.

As noted, however, India's intervention had been "invited." Although it had been coercive, there is no indication that India would have intervened militarily against the Sri Lankan regime if mediation had succeeded. This is because politically constrained but aggressive leaders have a difficult time in sustaining the credibility of their threats. Constituents who see little benefit in the policy will resist any costs to them. By contrast, India's more conciliatory approach created the opportunity for highly effective collusion with Sri Lanka's leader in the interest of "selling" domestic constituents on the desirability of an agreement. This result is consistent with assessments of crisis bargaining that reveal generally disappointing results for intensely confrontational tactics (Leng 1993; Maoz 1997a; Brecher and Wilkenfeld 1997b).

Proposition P_4, which concerns intensifying effects of affinities and cleavage, also finds general support in this case. Lack of control over ethnic insurgents and diasporas helped to generate uncertainty and exacerbate tensions in Sri Lanka. In more general terms, manipulation of foreign perceptions through control of ethnic allies appears to have been an ineffective strategy for India. Efforts by India to conceal its covert support for the Tamil insurgency resulted in loss of credibility in the eyes of both the Sri Lankan government and its supporters, adding fuel to the fire. From an ex ante perspective, the accord between the Sri Lankan and Indian governments was doomed to failure because of domestic interests in each state. A major actor in the conflict, the Tamil rebels, had not signed the accord, and the dispatch of the IPKF evoked only a tepid response. Successful blocking of the accord by Sri Lankan interests presumably had not been anticipated by India's decision makers. With the collapse of the accord and withdrawal of some seventy thousand troops from Sri Lanka, India's leaders had to reevaluate the strategy of covert support for the rebels.

Proposition P_5, which concerns the relative likelihood of ethnic intervention, also finds support from this case. India is characterized as a Type II_b state, that is, high in both institutional constraint and ethnic diversity. India therefore would be expected to adopt *realpolitik* policies in relation to third-party intervention. Not only institutional constraints but also diversity in Indian society reduced the feasibility of a risky foreign policy. The Indian government therefore was very careful in evaluating alternative strategies in order to find the best available option. In other words, the dovish or mild character of Indian foreign policy, which appeared in the form of good offices directed toward the autonomy of ethnic brethren, can be seen as evidence of the importance of domestic sensitivities.

The need for an outcome agreeable to all constituents, or retaining at least a plurality of popular support to maintain political power, kept leaders of India away from ethnic adventurism. Therefore, as expected, Indian intervention took place when strong preferences among the state's ethnic groups existed and important reasons emerged, such as the refugee flow and danger of great power meddling.

To summarize, India's mixed and shifting objectives resulted in the dispatch of "peacekeeping" troops to Sri Lanka. India never was predisposed to using overt force in achieving its geopolitical objectives; it could have taken formal control of Sri Lanka with only a limited effort. Perhaps other leaders, if faced with fewer domestic constraints, might have done so. Instead, the federal government initiated covert support for Tamil rebel movements. Supporting these rebels had considerable domestic ramifications for India's leaders, helping them in their bid to retain political viability in South India. Yet India's decision makers had to be concerned about the conflict spilling back into India. The shift toward a policy of intervention is clearly an extension of India's own domestic communal problems. Sri Lanka's internal strife provided an opportunity for India's leaders to appease South Indian Tamils and generate support at home. Nevertheless, the presumed low-cost approach did not succeed entirely: The influence and power of the Congress Party has been severely eroded at both the state and federal level, India's internal cleavages have worsened, and the army is playing an increasing role in managing domestic political problems (Brass 1990; Heraclides 1997).

6. Conclusions

In conclusion, this chapter has served two purposes. The first was to assess the usefulness of the four variables, and their linkages, in explaining an interstate ethnic conflict in a secessionist setting. The results indicate that ethnic diversity and institutional constraints possess the capacity to explain an elite's decision to become involved in a separatism conflict. The other two variables, affinity and cleavage, also appear to be valid sources of explanation.

The second task of this chapter was to evaluate the propositions from the framework. In the case of India, it appears that domestic and international pressures led an institutionally constrained, ethnically diverse state to explore multiple avenues of conflict management, including mediation. Outbidding, however, ultimately produced confrontation as well.

Less conclusive is whether states such as India are likely to use force. Force appears to be a choice of last resort, when outbidding, cleavages, and the potential for diffusion are very high. Even then, however, force will not necessarily resolve the conflict, especially if multiple interests must be satisfied.

With respect to India's geostrategic interests, the evidence suggests that

India's stated goal of preventing major power involvement was a "red herring." India's primary interests lay in meeting domestic demands. As early as 1983, the United States and other Western states had made it clear they would not come to Sri Lanka's aid, while the declining Soviet Union was not in a position to become involved in an extraregional conflict.

A related conclusion from this analysis is that states with an affective stake in the conflict make poor peacekeepers. Foreign policy objectives work against one another, objectivity will be difficult to maintain, and thus outcomes are likely to be suboptimal. India's peacekeeping effort, which attempted to satisfy multiple interests, ultimately proved to be unsuccessful.

Somalia, 2004. http://www.cia.gov/cia/publications/factbook/

CHAPTER FOUR

Somali Irredentism—
The Pursuit of a "Greater Somalia"

We shall take up arms. Let all perish! We shall take up arms. Let all perish! We shall not delay in recovering our missing parts. We are filled with discontent and fury and shall take up arms. A person robbed of his property wastes no time recovering it. He never enjoys conversation or social entertainments. We shall have no time for gossip and luxurious conversation, but shall take up arms to restore our missing property[1]

1. Introduction: In Pursuit of a "Greater Somalia"

The purpose of this chapter is to examine the interstate dimensions of ethnic conflict in an irredentist setting, namely, Somalia's aspirations for a "Greater Somalia" that would include Djibouti, the North Frontier District (NFD) of Kenya, and all of the Ogaden on Ethiopia's border with Somalia. The division of ethnic Somaliland into five different administrations—Italian Somaliland, British Somaliland, Kenyan Somaliland (NFD under the British administration), French Somaliland (now Djibouti), and Ethiopian Somaliland (Ogaden region under Ethiopian rule)—created feelings of isolation and separation among Somalis. In 1960, Italian and British Somaliland were united as a result of popular insistence and became part of a Somalia republic. However, the rest of Somaliland remained problematic. Since independence, Somalis have made territorial claims based on historical, ethnic, religious, and linguistic aspects. This shaped Somalia's foreign policy extensively after 1960, and an ideal emerged: a single Somali state ruling an entire Somali nation. Somalia, with a five-sided star representing each part of the greater Somali nation, remains a nation in search of a state (Selassie 1980; Laitin and Samatar 1987).

Also known as Western Somalia, the Ogaden consists of two separate areas in eastern Ethiopia. The southeast comprises the Ogaden proper. Here the large majority of people are Somalis of the Ogaden clan, a group closely tied to the Darod clan. The northeast area, known as the Haud, is a key seasonal grazing area for Somalis of the Dir and Darod clans.[2] Djibouti originally existed as a French colony of the overseas territory of the Afars and Issas, while the NFD was and still is a part of Kenya.

To comprehend fully the strength of Somali nationalism, several characteristics of Somalia need to be recognized. First of all, Somalia is exceptional in Africa because nearly everyone living in Somalia is an ethnic Somali and shares a common culture, language, history, and social structure. Second, the clan structure created a belief in a common ancestry as the basis of national solidarity. Third, the role of religion (Islam) is important in reinforcing Somali national solidarity (Selassie 1980).

Political mastery of Somali elites to unite divided clans to pursue irredentist claims is significant. To the extent that external confrontation became a basis for consolidation of power rather than a constraint on action, Somalia's ethnic homogeneity provided an opportunity for irredentism that is unavailable to leaders of most multiethnic societies. For example, since obtaining independence in 1960, Somalia has been involved in seven irredentist-based crises in the region.[3] Among these, the Somalia-Ethiopia conflict stands out as the most violent, protracted, and consequential (Heraclides 1990, 1997).

The Ogaden conflict exhibits a number of complex overlapping issues in which the ethnic features of Ethiopia and Somalia, most notably diaspora and deep-seated cleavage, are fundamental. The most captivating element of the Ethiopian-Somalia conflict is the fact that the two antagonists fall on opposite ends of the demographic spectrum. Ethiopia is a diverse, ethnically segregated state that has experienced no fewer than three significant internal upheavals, the most notable of these being the Eritrean and Tigrayan secessionist struggles, with the Oromo Liberation struggle garnering less external support (Makinda 1992; Heraclides 1997). During the antimonarchical revolution of 1974, armed insurrection occurred in fourteen of Ethiopia's states (see also Brecher and Wilkenfeld et al. 1988). By contrast, in religious and linguistic terms, Somalia is a homogenous state. Its clan-based struggles for identity shift according to external pressures placed upon the country. Approximately 98 percent of its six million people are ethnic Somalis, and almost all are Sunni Muslims. As Laitin and Samatar (1987: 45) observe, "The Somalis are Sunnis, adhering to the Shafiite school of Islamic jurisprudence, and their Islam is characterized by saint veneration, enthusiastic belief in the mystical powers of charismatic roving holy men, and a tenuous measure of allegiance to sufi brotherhoods." By language and history the Somalis are not Arabs; only recently has a relationship formed between the Arab states and Somalia. Clan-based differences are not insignificant. As proof of this point, the MAR Project recently designated the clan Issaq as a distinct minority with Somalia. The Issaq are listed as a disadvantaged "Communal Contender for State Power," defined as culturally distinct peoples, tribes, or clans in heterogenous societies who hold or seek a share in state power.[4]

Until recently, Somali elites have proved successful in mobilizing clans on the basis of a national identity in the face of an external adversary (Makinda 1992). After independence and up to 1990, pan-Somali nationalism served as a unifying and legitimizing principle, and "every Somali leader has been judged by his willingness and ability to pursue the goal of a 'Greater Somalia'" (26). In brief, the idea of a Greater Somalia includes an important political dimension, which is at once internally beneficial and externally divisive (Laitin and Samatar 1987; Saideman 1998b).

Another important aspect of the Ethiopia-Somalia dispute is the regional context within which the conflict unfolded. Suhrke and Noble (1997: 13) suggest that the multiethnic characteristics of African states heighten their feelings of vulnerability, which in turn leads to a restrained policy toward boundary disputes. By extension, African governments pursue restrained policies toward ethnic conflicts in other states. (Saideman [2001: 181–82], however, tests this now-conventional wisdom about vulnerability and, surprisingly, finds no support for the argument concerning inhibition.) Indeed, the multiethnic character of African states stands out as a deeply embedded characteristic of African foreign policy during the Cold War (Collins 1973). The founding Charter of the Organization of African Unity (OAU [now the African Union (AU)]), which upheld the inviolability of borders, reinforced this orientation. Nonetheless, Somalia's continual and contentious conduct in staking claims to Ethiopian territory ran counter to this pattern of institutionalized claims to state sovereignty.

A third dimension of the conflict is the tendency to overemphasize the role played by the superpowers. To be sure, external involvement has tended to exacerbate the conflict. For example, the most extreme phase of the protracted conflict centered on the Ogadeni after the fall of Ethiopia's emperor, Haile Selassie. This period witnessed the transformation of Somalia into an ally of the United States and Ethiopia into a Soviet ally. Western analyses of the conflict stress the importance of U.S. military assistance to Somalia in encouraging territorial claims on Ethiopia's Ogaden and Kenya's Frontier District and in militarization of the region in general.

This view, however, treats the war in the Horn of Africa as an event separate from preceding crises and also underestimates the autonomy of national political forces in the development of local strategies in response to unfolding regional opportunities (Selassie 1984). While superpower military assistance strongly influenced the escalation of tensions in the region, these arms flows represent only a sign of a more significant problem (Selassie 1984). The superpower rivalry did give Somali elites some leverage to obtain substantial economic and military assistance, and that support allowed these leaders to suppress critics and detain opponents by balancing and playing on clan interests and rivalries. However, even after the decline of East-West tensions in the late 1980s, the region experienced three more confrontations between Somalia and its neighbors—all at the hands of Somalia's military leadership.

By the end of the Cold War, external links through which Somali elites maintained power waned considerably. Internally, their hold on power also became significantly weaker due to increased clan rivalries. By the 1990s, historical animosities and clan loyalties had come to dominate political, social, and economic life in Somalia. The loose, segmented, clan-based structure that served Somalia's leaders well during that country's international confrontations had become a significant source of internal divisiveness. By 1992 Somalia faced its own secessionist struggle in the north, namely, with the Isaaq clan, which comprises about 20 percent of Somalia's population. Under the leadership of Abd ar-Rahman Ahmad Ali Tur, the Issaq-dominated Somali National Movement (SNM) proclaimed the breakaway "Republic of Somaliland" on 18 May 1991. Less than one year later, Somalia existed in name only, having succumbed to politically produced human disaster, internecine struggle, "warlordism," and economic collapse.[5]

This analysis will focus on crucial interstate crises or "peak points" in the Somalia-Ethiopia protracted conflict as indicators of a much broader process of interstate ethnic strife and intervention. This approach provides an opportunity to determine the impact of changes in institutional and ethnic constraints on preferences for strategies of intervention and makes it possible to assess the sensitive interplay between irredentist-type conflicts and separatist struggles. Given that Somalia's irredenta also exhibit elements of separatism, specifically in the Ogaden, meaningful conclusions can be drawn from the evolving relationship between these two types of interstate ethnic conflict and the implications therein for internationalized ethnic conflict and intervention (Heraclides 1997).

Figure 4.1 shows a time line for Somali irredentism from independence in 1960 onward. Four crises between Ethiopia and Somalia, which happen to span four decades, are examined. Primary attention is given to the events and decisions leading up to and including the crisis and war of 22 July 1977 to 14 March 1978. Somalia-Ethiopia confrontations preceding the war involved minor clashes along the northern border. Similarly, crises of low intensity fol-

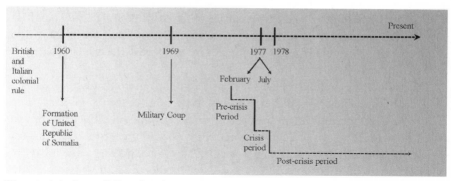

Figure 4.1. Somali Irredentism

lowed on the heels of the war. Although all of these crises resulted in frustration for Somalia's achievement of its objectives, only during the war of 1977–78 did Somalia get close to successfully staking claims to Ethiopian territory. Why that crisis resulted in war is a matter of judgment; it can be explained, in part, by the ethnic and institutional characteristics of the two main protagonists.

Analysis in this chapter unfolds in five further sections. The second section examines the historical and political aspects of the conflict. Political and ethnic determinants of Somali and Ethiopian behavior are weighed, along with contributing effects. The third section analyzes the series of crises from the period of Somali independence up to 1969. Fourth, the relationship between these events and the crisis-war of 1977–78 is clarified, and the implications of those crises for Somalia's deterioration and failure in the 1990s are addressed. Propositions are tested in the fifth section. Sixth, and finally, the accomplishments of the chapter are summarized.

2. Demographic Considerations

2.1 The View from Somalia—Clan Fealty and the National Interest

Somalia, as noted earlier, is one of Africa's most ethnically homogenous states. Somalis speak the same language, follow the same religion, and believe themselves descended from common ancestors. Despite its national homogeneity, Somalia features a multitude of subnational clan-based identities (Saideman 1998a, b). In an attempt to overcome the fractiousness of their clan-based culture, Somali national leaders framed a constitution that made the nationalist struggle the central feature of Somali's political and social history. By all accounts, this strategy succeeded; despite numerous clan divisions, the goal of achieving a Greater Somalia united the vast majority of Somalis for many years.

Traditionally, clans have played two prominent but contradictory roles in Somali politics: They present a compliant and dutiful veneer of political unity in response to external threats, yet revert to dissension when the menace vanishes. Somalia's social and economic activities and political organizations traditionally have arisen from lineage systems based on clans and patrilineal kinship groups. These groups are divided even further into dia-paying groups varying in size from a few hundred to a few thousand (Gorman 1981; Laitin and Samatar 1987; Makinda 1992).

Colonization acted as a catalyst first to the formation, and then to the development, of unity among Somali clans. Colonialism had a significant impact on Somalia. First, during the colonial period, Somalia experienced control by Italy, France, Britain, and Ethiopia. The Italians became the first of the European powers to establish their influence in the area. Ethiopia, which had managed to maintain independence from colonial powers by defeating the Italians in 1896, had long been an important actor in the region. Through a series of dubious political agreements, signed between 1885 and 1935, Ethiopia managed to extract significant portions of Somali territory from the British and Italians. Fearful of Ethiopian designs, Somali clan leaders sided with the British colonists and, under a series of agreements making it a British protectorate, opened the country's borders to British settlement. These agreements later would provide the basis for Somali claims over disputed territory (Sauldie 1987: 17).

Sketched out in 1897, various legal protocols between England and Italy aimed to settle boundaries between respective areas under Italian, Ethiopian, and British control. These mandated boundaries, firmly in place at the turn of the century, did not correspond to demographic reality (Sauldie 1987). Hundreds of thousands of Somali (and mostly nomadic) herdsmen of the Ogadeni clan (a subclan of the Darod family) found themselves under the jurisdiction of Ethiopia. For its part, Ethiopia's leaders assumed that sovereignty over the Somali people was its prerogative, a claim often made in the past (Drysdale 1964).

By the 1920s, Ethiopia, Britain, and Italy had extended their power deep into Somali-held regions. In response, resistance to colonial interference and domination assumed the form of a series of Somali "holy wars" conducted by Sheik Mohammed Abdille Hassan, nicknamed "Mad Mullah" (Drysdale 1964). These campaigns, directed primarily against the British, had the net effect of drawing support from the clans within all of Somalia's regions in the Horn of Africa. The Italians, in search of easy outlets for colonial expansion, provided primary external support for resistance. For Italy, Somali warlords could be viewed as strategic allies in its goal to depose the Ethiopian leader, Haile Selassie I, who had come to power in 1930. With the help of these allies of convenience, a sense of Somali "nationhood" began to develop. In turn, Somali clans set aside traditional animosities to meet the threats from colonial control and short-term exigencies of colonial "divide and rule" policies (Bhardwaj 1979).

2.2 Ethiopian Expansion—the External Threat

The second factor in the construction of Somali unity is the role played by Ethiopian expansionism. The notion of an Ethiopian "state," brimming with myth and tradition, dates back as far as three thousand years. But the history of modern Ethiopia begins with the ascendancy, in 1889, of Menelik II of Shoa (Haile Selassie's father) to the throne of the Ethiopian kingdom. Initially, Ethiopia consisted of a small highland kingdom limited to the Shoan, Tigrayan, and Gonadrin highlands. The rulers of this kingdom were of Christian origin (Coptic) and spoke a language (Amharic) that made them distinct on many counts from the people they ruled and their neighbors. Under Coptic rule, a large mass of territory occupied by Muslim Somali herdsmen did not fall under Ethiopian suzerainty. Over time and through European aid and Ethiopian subterfuge, Menelik managed to consolidate most of these territories (Selassie 1984). The Haud (northern part of the Ogaden) and the Ogaden (proper) territories fell under Ethiopian control.

At this time, most of the Somali population was divided into three distinct regions: the former Italian East African Colonies, Somaliland under British control, and Somali areas in Ethiopia. In 1949, at Somalia's urging, the country had been placed under UN trusteeship with Italy as the administering authority (Drysdale 1964).

Surprisingly, Ethiopian leaders postulated that the Ogaden Somalis would prefer Ethiopian citizenship to secession and first raised the idea of self-determination for all Somalis (Drysdale 1964: 83). The idea of securing self-determination for all of these Somalis came out of the 1947 UN Human Rights Subcommission on the Prevention of Discrimination and Protection of Minorities, associated with the post–World War Two decolonization process (Drysdale 1964). A series of UN Security Council meetings, in which the British proposed uniting all three areas into one state, followed the declaration. The Soviet

Union refused to sponsor the proposal; the Ethiopian Ogaden would have to be excluded (Sauldie 1987; Moynihan 1993). Only conquered, Italian-held territory would be reconstituted within the British protectorate. A bilateral agreement between Britain and Ethiopia reaffirmed Ethiopian control over the Haud region (Drysdale 1964). The final agreement also granted grazing rights to Somali tribes in the Haud. By most accounts, Ethiopian leaders became concerned at this turn of events; the union of the two territories constituted, in their view, a step toward Greater Somalia. An Ethiopian government official expressed his concern in the Voice of Ethiopia: "Ethiopia has fought and will fight, if need be, to preserve her integrity" (quoted in Drysdale 1964: 105). In 1950, Ethiopia claimed forty thousand additional square miles of Italian Somaliland territory (Farer 1976: 81).

By 1957, the decision over what to do with Italian Somaliland fell to the UN General Assembly. When it became clear that the General Assembly would be unable to make a decision because neither party could agree on the terms of reference, Ethiopia rejected the principles of self-determination for the Somali people. In 1959 the fourteenth session of the UN—the last one prior to Somalia's independence—also failed to obtain an agreement from the two parties (Farer 1976; Sauldie 1987: 16–23).

Accordingly, in the period preceding independence, relations between Ethiopia and Somalia became strained. Somalia consisted of some, but not all, of the territory occupied by the Somali people. Above all, its boundary dispute with Ethiopia showed no sign of peaceful resolution. The Ethiopian government continued to see the Somali problem in Ethiopia in terms of territorial integrity for the postcolonial state, not as a matter of the right to self-determination.

2.3 Independence—the Development of Pan-Somali Nationalism

The colonial "divide and rule—unite and depart" policy had a subsequent impact on the strategic choices of the fledgling Somali leadership. When Somalia was granted independence in July 1960, Somali elites faced the difficult prospect of uniting two extremely dissimilar colonies; each had its own colonial language, judicial, and legal systems.[6] In an attempt to surmount these difficulties and maintain the uniqueness of a clan-based culture, Somalia's leaders framed a constitution that stressed Somali nationalist struggle as the defining characteristic of its political and social history.

After independence, foremost among Somalia's foreign policy goals was extension of the boundaries of the new state to include the overlooked Somali communities in Ethiopia's Ogaden region, the French Territory of Afars and

Issas (Djibouti), and Northern Kenya (NFD). Claims against Ethiopia sparked the greatest attraction for Somalia's new leaders; the border between Ethiopia and Somalia never had been delineated clearly, and Somalis in northern Kenya belonged to clans—the Dagoodiya and Harti—not central to the Somali power structure. In contrast, the Darod and Ogadeni clans of the Ogaden belonged to important and influential branches within Somali society.

At independence the constitution of Somalia included eventual realization of a "Greater Somalia" as a key Somalia objective (Sauldie 1987: 17). The constitution held that "the Somali Republic promotes by legal and peaceful means the union of all Somali territories" (Laitin and Samatar 1987: 138). At the same time, the Somalia government published a more aggressive foreign policy document that reiterated the claims to a Greater Somalia. The document also asserted that agreements between Britain and Ethiopia violated previous treaties Britain had signed in 1885 that granted protection to northern Somali tribes (Sauldie 1987). Less than a month before Somalia's independence on July 3, the Ethiopian government announced that upon Somalia's independence, the 1954 agreement no longer would be recognized. The past treaties, conventions, and agreements were ambiguous, confusing, and ineffective, and the Somali case lost much of its edge after the Republic signed, along with thirty-three other African states, the Charter of the OAU in 1963. When the government, under Somali Prime Minister Abdirashid Ali Shermarke, chose to reject the various Anglo-Ethiopian agreements, border clashes broke out between Somali tribesman and Ethiopian forces. This crisis and the ones that would follow can be traced to the inability of the former colonial powers and the international community to develop a coherent and effective policy on the issue of border demarcation in the Horn of Africa. However, the direct causes of these and subsequent conflicts are associated with Somalia's internal political search for national identity and its ongoing quest for democratic and authoritarian forms of political stability.

3. Postindependence Confrontations

3.1 The Politics of Irredenta

Faced with potentially debilitating domestic divisions, Somalia's leaders set about framing a coherent foreign policy to reclaim Somali territory, in the belief that such action would be the best way to achieve internal unity. Somalia's leaders pursued this goal on two fronts: through diplomatic channels like the UN and the OAU and via covert support for secessionist movements in areas adjacent to the Somalia Republic. The linkage between Somalia's political and ethnic configuration and its belligerent activity is central to understanding these strategies. The most notable aspect of this connection is the relationship between Somalia's institutional structure and its confrontational policies. For example, Somalia's postindependence experimentation with democracy resulted in a series of limited border clashes with its neighbors. In contrast, confrontations with Ethiopia after the rise to power of the Somali military in 1969 took on a decidedly more aggressive tone (Saideman 1998b).

Somalia's political system's chief weakness, by some accounts, was clan-based domestic politics. This informal system, paradoxically, found expression in a unitary constitution. Although it was formally a liberal democracy, kinship ties remained the means for marshaling entire clans that sometimes numbered hundreds of thousands. This was not without its problems; prestige, usually accorded with age and rank, became an impediment to the government's stated goals of regional equality, development, and modernization. Overrepresentation of southern Somalis in the government compounded this problem (Laitin and Samatar 1987). Political parties formed along regional clan cleavages, which complicated the national unity issue. Since independence, southern clans had occupied most of the senior government posts, including senior positions in the military (Makinda 1992).

Among the three regions contested by Somalia—Ogaden, Djibouti, and the North Frontier District in Kenya—the latter two provided seemingly inferior opportunities to achieve reunification on the diplomatic and military front. The French occupied a firm position in Djibouti, and France had a strong regional ally in Kenya (Farer 1976: 81–88; Bhardwaj 1979). Confrontation with Djibouti would mean, in effect, a conflict with incomparable French political and military resources. In the event of war, the vastly underequipped Somali army no doubt would be defeated, with its elected leaders facing the consequences.

Ethiopia, at the same time, experienced political turmoil. Provocative and potentially destructive policies, now directed toward Muslims in the Ogaden, reinforced assimilationist policies, most notably promotion of Amharic cultural integrity to elevate the political and social structure of Ethiopia's Christian community to a national requirement in the 1950s (Farer 1976: 82–83). Furthermore, Ethiopia had a parliament but no political parties through which Somali frustrations could be vented. A failed coup against Selassie in 1960 indirectly strengthened Somalia's hand (Farer 1976; Henze 1991). Somalia's regional objectives focused on exploiting the weaknesses of Ethiopia first and Kenya second. After repeated diplomatic failure to bring to the world's attention the complexities of their dilemma, Somalia's leaders diverted their energies to help liberate the Somali regions. Initially, Ethiopia had military superiority, which meant that, at best, Somali clansmen (often interspersed with Somali guerrillas) could harass Ethiopian troops but not defeat them. The Somali government, in turn, provided sanctuary and support for the Ogaden "freedom fighters" (members of the West Somali Liberation Front [WSLF]). These initial Somali intrusions amounted to brief probes, intended to determine Ethiopian military weaknesses and bolster support for the government at home.

3.2 Postindependence Interactions

In December 1960, the WSLF, essentially guerrillas trained and supported by Somali forces, surrounded an Ethiopian police garrison and launched an attack. Ethiopia responded to the threat to territory with mobilization of its military units and air force. Faced with superior forces, the guerrillas had to withdraw. At the same time, Somalia protested the mobilization to Ethiopia and appealed to the All-African People's Conference (the precursor to the OAU which was established in 1963). Somalia chose not to acquiesce to Ethiopian threats to discontinue its efforts toward irredentism (Brecher and Wilkenfeld et al. 1988). Clashes and sporadic violence along the border continued into 1961 (Farer 1976).

In its decision on the issue, the All-African People's Conference of 1961 voted heavily in favor of Ethiopia and made efforts to obtain a settlement between the two states. Despite these and subsequent efforts, clashes between WSLF guerrillas and Ethiopian forces continued over the course of the next several years.

3.3 Crisis in Kenya—Exploring Opportunities in the Horn of Africa

The postindependence crisis with Ethiopia moderated Somalia's relations with its neighbors. With the Ethiopian mishap still on their minds, Somali leaders turned to the situation in Kenya. In Kenya, a British fact-finding mission of October 1962 found that 87 per cent of the 400,000 Somalis living in Kenya's North Frontier District (NFD) favored union with Somalia (Sauldie 1987: 25). For its part, Kenya used counterinsurgency techniques borrowed from the British and restricted the movements of potentially rebellious nomads through "population centers" (Farer 1976: 80). Worried that Somalia would invade the NFD, Kenya's newly elected leader, Jomo Kenyatta, placed his troops on full alert and declared a state of emergency.

On 29 December 1964, Kenya sealed its border with Somalia. Ethiopia, worried about the implications Somali success would have for its own border dispute, pursued and obtained a secret mutual defense treaty with Kenya (Sauldie 1987: 27).

Somalia could do little to respond, apart from providing sanctuary for the insurgents. It soon became clear that as long as Kenya's ethnic leaders in Nairobi remained united on the Somali question, the Somalis in the NFD never would manage to secede on their own. To assist the secessionists, Somalia would need new weapons. It looked first to China and then the Soviet Union for support.

Kenya requested in February 1964 that the dispute be mediated by the OAU. The process ended without resolution. On 4 March 1964, Kenya held elections, and this time the Somali secessionists agreed to participate in exchange for some degree of local autonomy. By mid-1967, a Zambian initiative to mediate the ongoing conflict succeeded in obtaining a temporary halt to hostilities when Kenyan and Somali leaders promised to cease provocative acts and restore normal relations (Brecher and Wilkenfeld et al. 1988). This did not mark the end of the strife—on the diplomatic front, the conflict over Somalis in the NFD continued into the 1980s, and a Somali presence in Kenya continues to be a force for destabilization (Sauldie 1987: 26).

3.4 Crisis in the Ogaden—Prelude to Change

By 1964, three significant internal and external changes had taken place in the region. First, Somalia's democratic leaders faced increasing pressure from political opponents to resolve the Greater Somalia question. Much of the parliamentary debate on the issue consisted of rhetorical belligerence to outbid Somali opponents and identify those with questionable loyalty. But genuine concern also existed for the plight of Somalis in the Ogaden (Farer 1976). As early as 1963, the inhabitants of the Ogaden had come out in open revolt against the Ethiopian government (Sauldie 1987). Second, in this period the Soviet Union made a substantial military gesture to Somalia. The offer included arms and training designed to equip a twenty-thousand-strong army, possibly for use against Ethiopia, which had been receiving military aid and equipment from the United States. Third, and finally, a new government had been elected in Somalia. Its leaders adopted an openly aggressive stance in pressing Somali claims. The new government's President Abdirazak, Haji Hussein (1964–67), a key opponent of Shermarke, achieved election based on a promise to resolve the Ogaden problem. With Soviet armaments in hand, he resolved to do so through a combination of force and diplomacy (Sauldie 1987).

Accordingly, Somalia triggered a crisis for Ethiopia on 7 February 1964, when its military forces carried out a mass attack on the Ethiopian frontier post at Tog Wajeleh. Ethiopia responded through resistance at the border and called for an immediate meeting of the OAU (Brecher and Wilkenfeld et al. 1988). Ethiopian retaliation on the eighth and the subsequent military action on Somali territory triggered a crisis for Somalia. On the ninth, Abdirazak responded by declaring a state of emergency throughout Somalia. Through dispatches sent to the OAU, Abdirazak accused Ethiopia of penetration into Somali territory. Somalia perceived correctly that OAU members would continue to support the Ethiopian claims.

Somalia immediately requested a meeting of the Security Council, contingent on whether the OAU could end the border dispute (Brecher and Wilkenfeld et al. 1988). Secretary-General U Thant appealed to the parties to settle the dispute peacefully. A cease-fire was agreed upon on 16 February but did not hold. The crisis ended on 30 March 1964, with a formal agreement for a cease-fire achieved through the good offices of the Sudan. The antagonists established a joint border commission that favored the status quo. No changes were to be made to the existing border. Ethiopia once again had succeeded in preventing Somalia's irredentist objectives from bearing fruit.

3.5 Political Transformation and Reconciliation

After four years of independence and three international crises, Somalia's irredentist goals had been crushed soundly in both political and military terms. Somalia had failed to capture favorable attention from either the world or even Africa for the Somali people's situation. African leaders consistently aligned themselves behind Kenya's Kenyatta and Ethiopia's Selassie. Furthermore, the government's irredentist objectives earned the country a reputation as a regional misfit and troublemaker. Apart from its ties with the Soviet Union and the Arab states, Somalia had become increasingly isolated in the diplomatic sphere.

Still, Somalia's leaders stood committed firmly to a Greater Somalia. Their choice of tactics, however, changed significantly. Somalia's leaders realized that it would be futile to press their irredentist claims in light of objections from both the OAU and the UN. Instead, Somalia decided that secessionist movements with the goal of "self-determination," rather than unification, would be nurtured. Both the UN and the OAU recognized self-determination as a legitimate basis for struggle, so the Somali leadership hoped that strategy would prove more successful on the diplomatic front.

Somalia would continue to pursue its irredentist goals, but with covert support hidden behind the authenticity of "anticolonial" struggle. Although Somalia's support was axiomatic, its leaders continued to deny direct involvement in what it viewed as domestic "struggles for liberation." For example, amid the hostilities with Ethiopia in 1964, the OAU passed a resolution reconfirming the colonial boundaries. In response, the Somali National Assembly passed unanimously its own resolution, declaring that the OAU stance "shall not bind the Somali Government" and that it sought a resolution of the conflict through "peaceful means" (Laitin and Samatar 1987: 138). For three more years, border disputes periodically erupted. For instance, in 1966, about 1,750 Somalis were killed on the border between Kenya and Somalia. With the return of Shermarke as president in 1967, Somalia's aggressive foreign policy reversed abruptly.

When once again elected president of the Republic of Somalia in June 1967, Shermarke chose Mohammed Ibrahim Egal, a member of the Issaq clan and more evenhanded in approach, as prime minister. Egal sought a rapprochement with Ethiopia as best he could with the limited means available to him. At this time the Arab states, which had been firm supporters of Somali objectives, were defeated in the Arab-Israeli Six Day War of June 1967 and could not be relied upon for support. The Kremlin, as well, adopted a more distant approach to the conflict after the June war and could not be counted on for support in the event of armed conflict. The closure of the Suez Canal also threatened Somalia's economy. Finally, U.S. aid to Somalia remained contingent on obtaining a multilateral arrangement with its neighbors. Thus a temporary reconciliation with Ethiopia and Kenya would have to be arranged (Sauldie 1987: 28).

Under OAU auspices, a series of meetings occurred throughout 1967 and 1968. At these meetings Somalia agreed to end hostilities on the Kenyan border and restore friendly relations with Kenya. This agreement included reopening diplomatic relations, encouraging growth and trade, and discussing the possibility of a larger East African federation comprising Somalia, Kenya, Sudan, Ethiopia, and Djibouti (Sauldie 1987: 29). The concept of an East African Federation, however, would not be considered seriously for another ten years (Sauldie 1987).

Relations with Ethiopia, by contrast, remained less promising because of Selassie's insistence on maintaining assimilationist policies in the Ogaden. Violent encounters between Ethiopian security forces and WSLF forces continued through the rest of the decade and into the 1970s (Saideman 1998b).

In sum, between 1964 and 1967 the Horn of Africa experienced turmoil. Somalia confronted Kenya, Ethiopia, and France, but its irredentist efforts proved unsuccessful.

4. Confrontation as State-Building

4.1 The War Within

Any hope of reconciliation with Ethiopia through democratic means came to an end on 15 October 1969, when a coup toppled the Somali government. In the coup, Shermarke was assassinated, and leadership of the government under Egal was replaced by a Supreme Revolutionary Council headed by Major General Mohammed Siad Barre (later President Barre). Barre nationalized the economy, banned political parties, and suspended the constitution. Kibble (2001) argues that all of these actions, including the emergence of socialism, nationalism, and centralization of power, principally served the purpose of overcoming problems originating from clanism and backwardness. A political machine under Barre's leadership, called the Somali Revolutionary Socialist Party (SRSP), was established in 1976. For the purposes of the present inquiry, the importance of this political transformation is threefold.

First, the rise to power of the Somali military meant the temporary cessation of any form of peaceful resolution of the conflict between Ethiopia and Somalia. Barre's generals, also his clan allies, pressed for a military solution to the issue. Earlier defeat at the hands of the Ethiopians had led to an upsurge of clan antagonisms within the army as each group looked for scapegoats to explain its past failures (Makinda 1992). Barre proved to be an astute political player and knew that pan-Somali nationalism would provide the appropriate vehicle for assuaging the military's concerns. Indeed, Barre had risen through the ranks of the army on the basis of his nationalist and regional ambitions, and like the leaders before him (except Egal), he belonged to the Darod clan and had strong ties to the Ogaden. In times of domestic turmoil, Barre proved successful in pitting one clan against another. Alliances and interests became aligned according to clan lineages, and to ensure allegiance the army recruited heavily from Ogadenis.

Second, Somalia changed internally in ways that would have implications for later rounds of irredentism. Originally, the aggressive policy of arming

Somalia derived from the need to reunite the clans and satisfy nationalist ambitions. Now militarization moved toward becoming a means for internal repression. Initially, the foreign policy plan worked. By the mid-1970s, social cohesion within Somalia had improved. Clan differences continued, but the government's effective handling of the threat of a 1973 famine muzzled many critics (Gorman 1981). Even when dissent emerged, Somalia's new military government remained relatively insulated. As mentioned earlier, Barre, operating through the SRSP, maintained an autocratic, centralized system that tried to replace clan loyalties with revolutionary allegiance to the nation through "scientific socialism" (Makinda 1992). Additionally, the autocratic nature of the regime resulted in abuses of human rights and oppressive behavior. The military emerged as the most powerful institution (Kibble 2001).

Barre's ascent to power is significant for a third reason related to this study: relations with the Soviet Union and its Arab allies (notably the United Arab Republic) became stronger than ever. This was due less to Barre's council's stated goal of scientific socialism than to the decreasing amounts of financial aid the Somali government had been receiving from the West. (For example, in the early 1960s, Somali received aid packages from Britain and the United States equivalent to $8 million annually. This paled in comparison to the $32 million offered by the Soviet Union. The European Community remained a donor through the 1970s [Farer 1976: 98].) Despite a population one-seventh the size of Ethiopia and far fewer resources, the quality of Somalia's armed forces now matched or exceeded those of Ethiopia. Although Ethiopia had a larger army and a more advanced air force in absolute terms, at least half of its armed forces had to be used against the growing secessionist threat in Eritrea (Gorman 1981). Within this context, the combination of advantageous external opportunities and internal pressures produced Somalia's decision to step up support for the WSLF.

It also is important to note that the United States long had been an important ally of the Selassie regime after World War Two. In part, the United States had tried to fill the vacuum left by the departure of the British and Italians by supporting Ethiopia as a regional force and linchpin for anchoring American policy in the Horn of Africa. This took the form of military and economic aid, along with use of naval and air facilities. Neglect by the U.S. government of Ethiopia's internal conflicts indicated how much the policies of the United States became guided by external factors, most notably confrontation with the Soviet Union. The decision in 1973 to end Ethiopia's relations with its longtime ally Israel complicated the situation but also served as an indicator of changes yet to come (Selassie 1984). In sum, the period under

Siad Barre, up to 1976, can be characterized as years of seemingly quiet diplomacy building up to action.

Somalia joined the Arab League in 1973. This amounted to a major political feat for a country whose inhabitants, although Muslim, were neither Arab nor spoke Arabic. Prospects for financial aid from OPEC members increased markedly. President Barre also was made chair of the OAU in 1974 and therefore became able to influence more African leaders in that way (Sauldie 1987: 38). Under Barre, détente on Africa's Horn was clearly a calm before the storm (Laitin and Samatar 1987). The buildup culminated in the violence of 1977.

4.2 The Precrisis Period—21 February to 22 July 1977

After more than a decade of independence, Somalia had emerged on the regional scene as an influential and relatively cohesive state, whereas its chief enemy, Ethiopia, faced collapse from within. Into this matrix of political changes entered a propitious combination of opportunities for Somalia's leaders. In 1974, Selassie was deposed, and in his place a military revolutionary council known as the Dergue came to power. In 1977, Mengistu Haile Mariam emerged as the leader of the Dergue, after eliminating many rivals (Selassie 1984). The coup effectively produced two geopolitical transformations in the region.

Realignment of regional and international forces stood as the first result of the military coup. Although both sides now inclined toward Moscow—Somalia more than Ethiopia—that fact could not induce either of them to seek out and obtain a negotiated solution to their problems. The leaders of these two countries had more skill as fighters than negotiators. If anything, the rivalry between Ethiopia and Somalia increased in intensity because Somalia, the traditional ally of the Soviet Union, now believed that Ethiopia was gaining financial and military support at its expense. On 27 May 1977, Somalia warned the Soviet Union that increasing aid to Ethiopia would endanger Somalia's relations with all Soviet-bloc countries.

The second effect of the military's rise in Ethiopia was its influence over the WSLF. With Ethiopian collapse imminent, the WSLF decided to increase its efforts. Since independence, the Somalis of the Ogaden had fought for reunification with Somalia, but, over time, the WSLF leaders developed an independent organizational capacity and became less convinced that reunification would be the best choice for them. From the WSLF perspective, the general weakness of the Ethiopian government and brutally repressive acts directed against Ethiopian minorities made an independent WSLF-led state both desirable and plausible. By the time of the Ethiopian coup, considerable bitterness existed among Somali rebels over the question of unconditional union with Somalia (Gorman 1981). Barre responded to these threats by reorganizing the WSLF; its efforts would be coordinated with those of the Somali regular army. In effect, this meant permitting regular troops to "resign" and join the WSLF. Such efforts not only brought the WSLF back on an irredentist course but also ensured its loyalty to Barre (Laitin and Samatar 1987). Furthermore, around this time the idea began to circulate that potentially large oil reserves existed beneath the surface of the Ogaden, which provided an additional incentive for reclaiming the territory (Sauldie 1987).

The impact of revolutions in Ethiopia and Somalia should be mentioned at least briefly. Selassie (1980) argues that Somalia's revolution took place due to internal social and political events. As noted above, the failure of Western-style democracy, public welfare, and social justice led Barre to reject Western-style parliamentary democracy and replace it with a "revolutionary democracy that aimed both at representation and self-government" (117). In Ethiopia, by way of contrast, antidemocratic behavior of the Mengistu regime reflected "feudal values that he and his group internalized under the old system." In Somalia, however, "the legacy of a 'pastoral democracy' enriched the revolution." Thus the collision between those two regimes regarding Ogaden might be viewed as much as "a result of the incompatibility of the two sets of values as of conflicting territorial claims" (117).

By early 1977, reorganized WSLF forces took advantage of the movement of Ethiopian troops from the Ogaden to Eritrea. The Eritrean conflict approached crisis dimensions. On 21 February 1977, hostilities broke out in the disputed Ogaden frontier. Somalia denied involvement, asserting that it had "always advocated the peaceful settlement of problems of any nature" (Legum and Lee 1979: 69). Simultaneously, the Republic of Djibouti faced impending independence, and Somalia accused Ethiopia of planning an invasion of Djibouti. By May 1977, Ethiopia blamed "Somalia trained infiltrators for attacks on the Addis-Ababa-Djibouti railway" (69). In mid-June the WSLF reported that it had killed 352 Ethiopian soldiers and captured 176 in a skirmish in the mountains near Harar. Several days later, on 19 June, after the capture of several small towns in the Ogaden, Ethiopia had yet to react to what already seemed in evidence: Somalia's forces, not just the WSLF, had been carrying out these attacks.

By most accounts, WSLF forces carried out initial attacks on Ethiopian territory as a prelude to major war. The WSLF succeeded in destroying railway bridges, capturing water holes, and laying siege to small towns. The incursion had the net effect of discouraging the Western powers, staunch allies of Kenya, from supporting Somalia. With a break in relations with the Soviet Union now imminent, Barre no longer could bank on Western support as well.

These actions against the Ethiopian regime, by Somali accounts, had been perpetrated by the WSLF. However, Barre, not the WSLF, made the subsequent decision to escalate the conflict to full-scale interstate war (Laitin and Samatar 1987: 141). On 22 July 1977, Somalia's armed forces mounted a full-scale attack on the Ogaden, thus triggering a foreign policy crisis for Ethiopia.

4.3 Crisis and War in the Ogaden—22 July 1977 to 14 March 1978

On 23 July 1977, Ethiopia claimed that an all-out Somali attack had been launched against its territory. Although Somalia continued to deny involvement (a deception maintained until 13 February 1978, when Somalia openly committed its regular forces), U.S. spy satellites later confirmed "this was no simple desert skirmish on the order of previous Ethiopia-Somali confrontations" (Legum and Lee 1979: 32). Ethiopia responded in two ways: First, Ethiopian representatives appealed to the UN and again to the OAU to halt the fighting in the Horn of Africa. Second, Ethiopia's leader, Mengistu, appealed for external military assistance. Romania, East Germany, and Czechoslovakia shipped arms to Ethiopia. In addition, Greek mercenaries reportedly came to the aid of Ethiopia (Sauldie 1987: 48), while Vietnamese delegations arranged sale of U.S. war surplus equipment, and Israeli pilots allegedly flew in spare parts and ammunition for Ethiopia's American-made equipment (Legum and Lee 1979: 33).

On 24 August, renewed efforts at mediation by the OAU again ended in frustration; this time the Somali delegation refused to join in because representatives of the WSLF had not been allowed to participate. The OAU secretary-general, William Eteki Mboumoua, announced that the OAU did not recognize the WSLF as an African liberation movement. The Somali delegation then accused the OAU of "ignoring the major interest on which the OAU Charter is based . . . the liberation of African territories still under colonial domination and oppression." Tanks, aircraft, and army battalions were in evidence, although it is difficult to reconstruct the exact numbers involved (Legum and Lee 1979: 70).

Throughout October, the WSLF, now fully supported by Somali troops, tanks, and aircraft, increased in size to twenty thousand men. Around this time, the Soviet Union withdrew its support for Somalia. In turn, the Soviet

Union now provided Ethiopia with "defensive weapons to protect her revolution" (Legum and Lee 1979: 71, 72; Sauldie 1987: 51). This infusion of support marked the turning point in the war and the end of relations between Somalia and the Soviet Union. On 12 November, Mogadishu revoked the Friendship treaty and expelled all Soviet advisers from the capital.

Somali forces, in their desperate attempt to capture Harar, had become overstretched. As a result, Somali supply lines now lay open to air attack from Ethiopian MIG fighters. Ethiopia also bombarded northern Somali cities. In response, in late January 1978, Somalia protested to the OAU and called for the organization to condemn the Soviet Union and Cuba and other Warsaw Pact countries for their interference. The call for support also served as a plea to the Western powers, notably the United States, who had remained silent during this surprising turn of events. The United States remained concerned about what it perceived as an alarming level of Soviet presence in the region and set about cautiously trying to resolve the issue. U.S. President Jimmy Carter began to devise a means of preventing a possible invasion of Somalia. He did so, belatedly, by channeling U.S. military aid to Somalia through the latter's Middle East allies, notably Egypt (Legum and Lee 1979). This support, however, came well after Ethiopian success in the Ogaden. Carter also called on both sides to end the conflict peacefully.

Given Somalia's weakness, the Soviet-orchestrated (both Soviet and Cuban) counterattack to regain the lost territories was predictable and swift. On 5 March 1978, Jijiga became the first major city to be recaptured by Ethiopian forces. By then, most Somali forces had been driven back or had undertaken "tactical withdrawals" to their points of origin prior to the war. One-third of the Somali forces reportedly were killed.

On 9 March, Mogadishu broadcast a statement: "The big powers have suggested that the problem of the Horn of Africa be solved peacefully and that all foreign troops withdraw, and that Somalia withdraw her units, at the same time promising that the rights of Western Somalia will be safeguarded, the Central Committee of the Somali Revolutionary Socialist Party has decided that Somali units be withdrawn" (Legum and Lee 1979: 35). On 15 March the Barre regime announced that all of its regular forces had been withdrawn and that it would accept a cease-fire. In response, the Dergue refused to accept a cease-fire until Somalia (a) publicly renounced for all time any claims to the Ogaden, Kenya, and Djibouti and (b) confirmed with the OAU and the UN that it recognized the international border between Ethiopia and Somalia (Sauldie 1987: 55).

Although Somalia's army had been defeated in the battle, the WSLF had not surrendered and refused to accept the cease-fire. WSLF leader Abdullah

Hassan Mohammed defiantly announced that "the masses will continue to wage war until complete success, no matter how long or how many sacrifices it takes" (Legum and Lee 1979: 35). Despite this braggadocio, the war was over (Heraclides 1997).

This war proved to be important for both the warring parties and outsiders. While the Ethiopian government perceived the developments in terms of a war of aggression and violation of its territorial integrity, Somalia regarded the strife as a by-product of the idea of the right of self-determination and regaining lost territories. Most African governments perceived Somalia as the aggressor state. The failure of OAU and UN mediation between Somalia and Ethiopia created a political vacuum that led, in turn, to outside intervention by Cuba and the Soviet Union (Selassie 1980).

4.4 Postwar Phase and After—15 March 1978 to the Present

Several important changes occurred during the immediate postwar period. The United States, although never openly committed to the WSLF, tried to strengthen its relations with Mogadishu. In March 1978, Washington renewed its economic development programs and began discussions about future military aid to Somalia. In return, the United States obtained access to Somali ports and airfields in early 1979. This occurred against a backdrop of regional events that encompassed a Treaty of Friendship between Ethiopia and the Soviet Union and an appeal from Djibouti for help to defend itself against an alleged Ethiopian plot to overthrow its government (Selassie 1984). Not only the defeat but also the coup attempted by a conservative-leaning Arab group transformed Somalia's internal situation. Specifically, three major changes can be traced to the coup attempt.

First, the coup attempt signaled serious dissatisfaction among various clans with the postwar turn of events and thereby threatened the Barre regime. Officers of the Majerteen clan, who had led the failed coup, sought refuge in Ethiopia. They subsequently formed the Somali Salvation Democratic Front (SSDF). The onset of Somalia's spiral into disintegration clearly is linked to this failed coup.

Second, a new Somali constitution formally renounced all claims to the Ogaden and instead stated support for the liberation of Somali "territories under colonial oppression" (Selassie 1984). This change in orientation had the net effect of establishing a basis for détente with Ethiopia and undermined any legitimacy the Barre regime may have had with clans who still dreamed of a united Greater Somalia. By the late 1980s, opposition to the Barre regime broke along clan lines.

Third, Somalia experienced another foreign policy crisis, from 5 December 1980 to 29 June 1981. During this crisis, Ethiopia threatened Somalia with invasion unless it agreed formally to cease support for the WSLF (Brecher and Wilkenfeld et al. 1988).

By mid-1981 it became clear that Barre no longer had control of the WSLF and other political groups within Somalia. For example, on 30 June 1982, in an alliance of convenience with the Ethiopian Dergue, the SSDF attempted another coup against Barre's government and created a new foreign policy crisis for Somalia. Fighting ensued and Somali forces infiltrated deep inside Ethiopian territory and attacked a town a hundred kilometers from the border (Henze 1991). In response, the SSDF, almost certainly with Ethiopian support, took control of two border towns. Again as a consequence of internal challenges to the Barre regime, relations between Ethiopia and Somalia flared up. A foreign policy crisis began for Somalia on 12 February 1987 and ended two months later in April 1987. Border skirmishes of that nature continued sporadically for the next several years until Somalia formally withdrew its forces from Ethiopian territory and signed a peace accord with Ethiopia in 1988. The accord called for demilitarization of the common border. This proclamation effectively amounted to Somalia's renunciation of its claims to the Ogaden region. Immediately after the accord was signed, civil war broke out in the north as the Somali nationalist movement started to fight for the independence of Somaliland. Barre repressed the civilian population, but also agreed to work on a new constitution and emphasized UN-monitored, multiparty elections to be held in February 1991. A constitutional review process got underway but, in late 1990, already weakened severely by clan conflict, Barre's support collapsed. In January 1991, Barre's militia admitted defeat and his Darod party, the Somali National Front (SNF), was toppled from power, which in turn forced Barre to flee the country. Into this vacuum entered a coalition of the United Somalia Congress (USC), the Somalia National Movement (SNM), and the Somalia Patriotic Movement (SPM), who together deposed the leader and replaced him with a "national salvation committee" (*Globe and Mail,* 13 February 1993). In May 1991, Somaliland in the northwest declared unilateral independence; however, it still lacks formal international recognition. According to Kibble (2001:12), the declaration of independence responded to the regime's "record of lack of power sharing, corruption, abuses of human rights and autocracy."

For several reasons, Barre's defeat merely accelerated the disintegration of Somalia.[7] First, the opposition forces had only one thing in common: the defeat of Barre. Barre had managed to stay in power because of the inherent weakness and disunity of his opponents. With few allies, Barre was no match for these clans when they united against him. Second, when Barre was overthrown, the Hawiye-led but severely divided USC immediately assumed power. The USC deeply opposed the SNM and SPM. Under its leader, General Aideed, the USC automatically assumed power and made a unilateral appointment of an interim president without consulting the other groups.

During November 1991 the most intense fighting since the fall of Barre broke out in the capital. The forces that occupied Mogadishu and overthrew President Barre split into two groups under warlords Ali Mahdi Mohammed and Mohammed Farah Aideed. Fighting persisted in Mogadishu and spread throughout Somalia, with heavily armed elements controlling various parts of the country. Ensuing struggles reflected clan-based politics at its most basic level. In the absence of any pretense to institutions, the struggle for survival and power became determined by weapons and clan alliances.

It is important to note that despite Somalia's being a unitary republic, it effectively had two administrations—one in the northwest (Somaliland) and the other in the northeast (Puntland). All other places (and even Somaliland from 1994 till 1996) suffered from human right abuses and fighting. Many cities, including much of Mogadishu itself, were destroyed and shortages of food were severe. Somalis suffered from famine, and, according to various estimates, one to two million Somalis either became displaced internally or refugees (Kibble 2001).

Due to the intensity of the conflict between the clans, in 1992 the United States sent a peacekeeping force (Operation Restore Hope) to restore order and safeguard relief supplies. Given the humanitarian challenge posed by clan warfare, the UN secretary-general concluded that airlift operations—already being carried out by the World Food Programme (WFP) and the UN Children's Fund (UNICEF), as well as by the ICRC—needed to be enhanced substantially, with priority given to central and southern Somalia. In addition, a "preventive zone" on the Kenya-Somali border was established for special deliveries of food and seed, in an attempt to reduce famine-induced population movements. The secretary-general concluded that the UN did not have the capability to command and control an enforcement operation of the size required. He concluded that no alternative existed other than to resort to the enforcement provisions under chapter VII of the UN Charter.

Efforts to find agreement among the leaders of the fifteen Somali political movements began in 1993. On 27 March 1993, these leaders signed an Agreement of the First Session of the Conference of National Reconciliation in Somalia. All of the participants, including representatives of women's and community organizations, as well as elders and scholars, unanimously endorsed the agreement. The parties resolved to put an end to armed conflict in Somali and reconcile their differences through peaceful means. They reaffirmed their commitment to comply fully with the cease-fire agreement signed in Addis Ababa in January 1993, which had included the handing over of all weapons and ammunition to UNITAF and UNOSOM II. This ceasefire proved to be short-lived.

From June until October 1993, the United States launched a military offensive against General Aideed in Mogadishu. On 3 October 1993, U.S. Rangers launched an operation in south Mogadishu aimed at capturing a number of key aides of General Aideed (suspected in subsequent attacks on UN personnel and facilities). The operation succeeded in apprehending twenty-four suspects, including two key aides to General Aideed. During the course of the operation, Aideed's headquarters were destroyed, but Somali militiamen shot down two U.S. helicopters using automatic weapons and rocket-propelled grenades (Sloyan, "Mission in Somalia," *Newsday*, 7 December, 1993; Bowden 1999).

In 1994 the United States withdrew all of its forces from Somalia and in March 1995 the remaining UN peacekeeping force, which had tried to continue providing aid and mediating, also withdrew. After the departure of UNOSOM II, the country still had no effective, functioning government, no organized civilian police force, and no disciplined national armed forces.

In general, the UN's success remained limited to ending the famine and the sporadic return of refugees and displaced persons. It failed to provide resolution or reconciliation between the warring sides. Clashes between clans have continued since 1995, and Somalia remains one of the poorest countries in the world according to the human development index, with an average life expectancy of forty-one to forty-three years and a mortality rate for children under five of more than 25 percent (Kibble 2001).

Muhammad Aideed died from gunshot wounds in August 1996. Aideed's son, Hussein Muhammad Aideed, replaced him. The younger Aideed boycotted the Ethiopian government-sponsored reconciliation conference in November of that year. In November 1997, clan leaders met in Cairo and decided to set up a national government and constituent assembly. They failed, however, to come up with an acceptable power-sharing agreement. With no central government, renewed famine created intense problems for Somalis; insecurity and interclan violence continued, especially in central and southern Somalia, throughout 1999. Aideed's forces continued to control the large area south of Mogadishu.

On 2 May 2000, with the initiative of the Djibouti government, the Somalia National Peace Conference brought the clan leaders and senior figures together to end years of civil war and form a new government. On 26

August 2000, the Transitional National Assembly (TNA) was formed and elected on the basis of clan participation. Abdulkassim Salad Hassan became the new president of Somalia. In October he appointed Ali Khalif Gelayadh, a former minister of industry under Siad Barre, as prime minister. In April 2001 the Somali Restoration and Reconciliation Council (SRRC), basically a group of southern clans opposed to the transitional government, formed in Ethiopia. The SRRC announced its aim: to establish a rival national government. The interim government has been on duty since 2000, although it should be noted that some groups claimed that they remain outside of this Djibouti-sponsored peace process.

Fighting continued to take place in the south, and referendum results proved that many in Somaliland support the idea of independence from the rest of Somalia. Due to a vote of no-confidence on 28 October 2001, the prime minister and his cabinet were replaced by Hassan Abshir Farah on 11 November 2001. In addition to this, in that same month, the United States decided to freeze the funds of the main remittance bank, and the largest employer, al-Barakat, due to suspected links with Al-Qaeda.

In April 2002 the Rahanweyn Resistance Army (RRA) in the southwest unilaterally declared autonomy for six districts in the region. After Somaliland in the northwest and Puntland in the northeast, the "Southwest Sate of Somalia" became the third region in Somalia that declared its independence. Warring groups and the transitional government agreed to sign a cease-fire so hostilities would end for the duration of peace talks in October 2002. Dahir Riyale Kahin was elected as the first president of breakaway Somaliland in April 2003.

At the beginning of 2004, warlords and politicians reached an agreement on forming a new parliament. They agreed on the principle of equal representation of the four main clans and some minority groups. In October, Somalia's transitional parliament elected Abdullahi Yusuf as the new president, with a mandate to restore order in the country after thirteen years of civil war. Although this does not mean that the war is over, it is a big step forward. Somalia has been without a functional central government since warlords ousted Mohamed Siad Barre in 1991 and turned the country into clan-based fiefdoms. Two governments have been formed since 1991, but neither could manage to establish control across the country. On 12 December, Somalia's parliament passed a vote of no-confidence against the government of Prime Minister Mohammed Ali Gedi and his cabinet and dissolved his government. However, two days later, President Abdullahi Yusuf reappointed Gedi as the prime minister, and on 24 December, Gedi managed to obtain parliament's approval.

Most recently, the Somali coast has been hit by the deadly tsunami of 26 December 2004 and approximately 50,000 people have been displaced. More than 140 people are reported dead. At the time of writing, the Somali people are trying to heal their wounds and hope that their government will function effectively and bring peace to a war-torn country.

5. Analysis and Propositions

In terms of the framework, the three stages proceeded as follows.

At stage 1 both states exhibited apprehensiveness in formulating belligerent foreign policies that could lead to confrontation. Based on the evidence, this resulted primarily from Ethiopia's ethnically diverse demography and Somalia's weak status as a new state. Nevertheless, at the outset Somali leaders did rely on the issue of a Greater Somalia as the basis for acquiring domestic support.

During stage 2 the presence of high levels of affinity and cleavage within Ethiopia provided an opportunity for Somalia to initiate a conflict. The persistence of cleavages provided recurring opportunities for Somalia to escalate the conflict.

Finally, at stage 3, each state had become organized to use force against the other. This is true especially for Somalia, which, after Barre came to power, set about acquiring arms. Perhaps with fewer domestic constraints and his control of the military, Barre could use force. In response, Ethiopia was intransigent, which, as expected, ultimately resulted in war. Ethiopia's internal divisions prevented it from doing more than simply defending itself. The last three crises ultimately result from Somali internal divisiveness, with interactions that led to policies of moderation for both sides. In other words, weakened by internal pressures, the leaders of both states became either unable or unwilling to reescalate the conflict to war once again.

Somalia's homogeneity presents a challenge to commonly accepted interpretations of ethnicity. Under the "subjective" definition provided by Barth (1969), along with more "objective" versions (Rothschild 1981), clan-based divisions are sufficient to constitute differences among ethnic groups. Thus, at one level, each clan constitutes a distinct ethnic group while, at another level, the Somali peoples also make up a distinct ethnic group (Saideman 1998b). This apparent contradiction is not really one at all; it merely underscores the instrumentalist and situational features common to processes of ethnic mobilization within Somalia (Olzak and Nagel 1986).

Indeed, the unfavorable implications of a clan-based society are significant. Many scholars have noted that the basic characteristic of such a society is its *inherent instability*. Depending on the nature and context of a particular political matter (Laitin and Samatar 1987: 158), "segments of a clan unify temporarily, to deal with an imminent emergency only to splinter off into antagonistic sub-segments when the emergency abates." In this context, the idea of a Greater Somalia held advantages for Somali leaders in state-building and developing personal power. Consider, by way of contrast, the multiethnic nature of Ethiopia. Ethiopia's diversity appears to have heightened its sense of vulnerability, which led to its support for creation of the OAU Charter and a search for external allies, both designed primarily to restrain Somali adventurism. Also consistent with Laitin and Samatar's (1987) assessment of segmented societies is that repeated foreign policy failure proved to be divisive internally.

For purposes of brevity, interactions between Somalia and Ethiopia provide the main focus for this analysis. Somalia's relations with Ethiopia, however, also appear to have influenced its interactions with other states. Notable in this context are the two far more restrained interstate crises between Kenya and Somalia. The more limited nature of that conflict can be explained, in part, by Kenya's multiethnic character and moderate levels of institutional constraint.

Five propositions are tested, as in the other case studies. These propositions relate to strategies of intervention, autonomy, domestic costs, the role of affinities and cleavage, and the typology, respectively.

Proposition P_1 pertains to the commitment to multiple strategies of intervention. The limited period of Somali democracy allows for some comparison. Evidence indicates that political parties did compete to be the best representatives of the Somali interest, the most intensely symbolic being pan-Somali irredentist movements. Leaders competed on the basis of their nationalist credentials, and the public judged them that way. Legitimacy derived, at least in part, from achieving the goal of uniting all Somalis, and in turn this had implications for clan-based unity. The system proved particularly effective during the democratic phase, when political leaders obtained a "balance of power" among the clans that reduced the need to pursue foreign policy objectives to obtain internal unity. When this power balance fell out of synch, largely because Barre recruited heavily from his clan-group, uniting the clans through external confrontation became more of a necessity. The unfortunate aspect of this approach is that, eventually, the process of achieving clan-based unity, which served Somalia during its first decade of independence, became the basis for undermining its fragile institutional structure.

Institutions did moderate the Somali inclination for intervention in the early years. All of the interstate crises during this period primarily took the form of border skirmishes. Despite the low intensity of these cases, Somalia might have been expected to show greater efforts at managing the potential for crisis escalation. Instead, Somalia set about accumulating weapons to reclaim the territory by force. Prior to crisis onset, Somali nationalism caused consistent outbidding among politicians. Thus, Somalia constituted a threat to Ethiopia from the outset. The threat is evident in attempts at finding both a military and negotiated solution to the Ogaden problem prior to Somalia's independence. The former action, which included support for the WSLF and confrontations with other states, resulted in a spiraling of tensions between the two states.

Could a difference between mass and elite preferences account for the more restrained Somali foreign policy? Based on the evidence presented so far, it appears that escalation of the crises, which had occurred under Somali democracy, reflected elite efforts to shore up a succession of weak governments. Over time, each succeeding crisis became more intense as leaders built upon pan-Somali nationalism for political gains. More specifically, where executive aims and constituency desires are fundamental to the choice of strategy, then a forceful interventionist policy may emerge if (and only if) constituency desires do not undercut support for leaders and internal cohesion. Consistent with this view, Waller (1992: 43) argues that:

> one source of a political regime's legitimacy in territorial states is conquest. Yet as such states grow larger they encounter other states, hence increasing the cost of expansion. As these costs increase so does the probability of . . . foreign policy failure. The primary outcome of foreign policy failure is the delegitimation of the regime in power at the time of the foreign policy failure. Delegitimation creates an opening in the political process for opposing factions.

Proposition P$_2$ focuses on a preference for nonviolent interventions by ethnically diverse states. Although Somalia's demographic characteristics do not permit a full evaluation of this proposition, it is worth pointing out ways in which Somalia's behavior is consistent with the assumptions underlying the proposition. According to conflict linkage theory, when a state beset by internal strife enters into a conflict with another state, internal coherence is expected to increase because those within the state will put aside their differences in order to pursue the higher goal of national security (Wilkenfeld 1973). A conflict at its origins, such as domestic unrest threatening an insecure government, can be transformed and possibly even intensified at an interstate level. Consistent with this idea, Coser (1956; see also Rummel 1963; Wilkenfeld 1973) developed the idea of cohesion through conflict: war becomes the opportunity for a state ridden with antagonisms to overcome them by uniting against an external enemy. The conflict linkage perspective suggests that Somalia's leaders would pursue a strategy of confrontation as long as benefits clearly outweighed costs. Toward the end of Somalia's experiment with democracy, a period in which clan divisions became more salient, the country began to experience levels of domestic disorder that surpassed the threshold for which externalization of conflict would be conducive for cohesion.

After the 1969 coup, elite preferences for confrontation faced even fewer domestic barriers. Only military and clan divisions constrained Somali elites. In response to that situation, Barre proved effective in recruiting heavily from his own clan group and packing the military with clan-friendly officers. Barre also succeeded in developing pan-Somali nationalism as a hallmark of the country's collective struggle. Indeed, the only formal constraint on Somali belligerence then became OAU condemnation—until Barre's selection as head of that organization. In sum, Somalia's clan divisiveness and militarization show a strong correlation, and that connection is manifested in at least three ways.

First, as noted previously, the constitutionally embedded idea of pan-Somali nationalism served as an important defining characteristic of Somalia's identity. A succession of failures to realize this goal led to a loss of legitimacy for popularly elected governments. The army then became a custodian of the national interest.

Second, compared with the multiethnic states of sub-Saharan Africa, Somalia experienced fewer coups. In most African states the pivotal role of the military is due to fear of an unstable ethnic situation. Military coups occur most often in societies that exhibit porous ethnic-military boundaries. In Somalia's case, the recruitment of specific clans into the military led to their overrepresentation and resulting breakdown of the military along clan lines.

Third, the aborted coup of 1978 indicated that elites had become dissatisfied with the Barre regime, but dissent had not yet trickled down to the masses, because the Barre regime maintained a monopoly on power and had stepped up repressive acts. As Muller and Weede (1990: 627) have argued, extremely brutal authorities can discourage all forms of group resistance. When the army and militia began to break up along clan-based lines in 1988, competition among clans no longer was restricted to clan leaders.

Proposition P_3 concerns forceful intervention and the concentration of costs and benefits. Forceful intervention is most likely when political resistance among constituents is low (i.e., authoritarian regimes) and generic, all-purpose support exists from members of the same ethnic group (i.e., ethnic group dominance), as for Type I_a states. The proposition finds support in the latter stages of the protracted conflict. Before the war of 1977, Somalia's international opportunities presented themselves on three fronts: a favorable military balance with Ethiopia, a supportive ally in the WSLF, and a war in Eritrea. Although there may be other reasons for the sustained conflict between the two states, including U.S.-Soviet rivalry and military aid from the superpowers to both states, at least three internal conflicts erupted within Ethiopia, and these events facilitated repeated Somali attempts at territorial retrieval. When cleavages also appeared in Somalia's fragile clan structure in the 1980s, two more crises occurred between the two states.

Proposition P_4 concerns the heightening effects of affinities and cleavage. It also finds general support in this case. Like the Sinhalese in the previous chapter, Somalis consider themselves a distinct ethnic group. For this reason, Somalia's affinities with other states generally are low. However, the presence of Somalis outside of Somalia provided the incentive for staking claims to territory. An important aspect of the dynamics of this claim is the varying importance Somali elites have attached to different regions. For example, the Ogadeni and Darod of the Ogaden are central to the power structure of Somali politics, whereas the Somalis of Kenya and Djibouti are less so. This fact shapes the interests of Somali leaders who derive support from specific clans. Leaders of clans with a strong link to the Ogaden (e.g., Barre) have shown a greater interest in irredentism than those from clans without this level of affinity (e.g., Egal).

The extent to which a state mobilizes social resources to mount a credible campaign to assist ethnic brethren is arguably as much a function of strong preferences for the issue at stake as of capabilities. Indeed, transnational ethnic linkages can create extreme preferences that compensate for a deficiency in capabilities. It is clear from the evidence that some Somali elites became concerned about the plight of Somalis in the Ogaden, and this link led to direct support for the WSLF. This backing increased internal divisions within Ethiopia, which provided additional incentives for future invasion. The central concern in this instance is whether states are able to regulate protracted conflicts when affinities are so strong.

Evidence shows that rules developed for facilitating cooperation between the two states became too one-sided in favor of Ethiopia. In other words, Ethiopia could impose internal assimilationist policies on Somalis in the Ogaden and also manipulate international rules (e.g., OAU Charter) in its favor. Guarantees for the safety of the Somali minority in Ethiopia proved insufficient to prevent Somali elites from making an issue of their plight and then taking actions to address it. The decision by Barre to fully support the WSLF in the early 1970s signaled the potential for future interstate conflict. However, Barre's clan stood out among the groups with the greatest ties to the Ogaden, and he recruited heavily from the Darod clan.

The perceived security issue of the Ogadenis became a symbol for creation of a Somali ethnic identity that leaders showed skill at manipulating. It also became a source of tension between the two states. The combination of increasing tensions and an uncompromising Somali worldview made finding a cooperative solution difficult. As a result, the one-time perceived problem of security for Somalis in the Ogaden became a very real issue of interstate security—one that proved difficult to deescalate.

Evidence also indicates that as Ethiopian cleavages increased, Somalia continued to press its advantage. The main issue, here as above, is that Ethiopia constituted a threat to Somalia from the outset because of its historical claims to the Ogaden. One implication of this linkage is that conventional safeguards, such as the ability of the African community to control both Ethiopian and Somali belligerence, could be expected to fail (Saideman 1998a, b). For example, both Djibouti and Kenya expressed an understandable reluctance to become involved in the issue. Only after several crises and wars did an alliance between Ethiopia and Kenya emerge.

Proposition P_5 focuses on the relative likelihood of intervention. In the typology presented in figure 2.1, Somalia would be classified as an ethnically dominant, constrained Type II_a state until the 1969 coup against the democratic government. Under the regime of General Barre, Somalia became an ethnically dominant, low-constraint, or Type I_a, state.

In general, Somalia's foreign policy tends to confirm the predictions based on the typology. During the early 1960s, in a high-constraint, ethnically dominant state, Somali leaders had to be sensitive about the support of their constituencies. They therefore could not easily pursue belligerent, revanchist policies that would jeopardize the national economy and potentially eliminate key trading partners and outside aid. To appeal to both elements within the international community and nationalist sentiments of their constituents, Somali leaders provided covert assistance to their coethnics over the border while publicly renouncing the goal of a greater Somalia. In short, Somalia's inconsistent stance during this time is largely in accord with the framework's expectations—namely, the state practiced sporadic interventionism.

After the coup in 1969, however, the situation changed dramatically. Somalia became a low-constraint state, and, in line with expectations, its military government supported more bellicose policies vis-à-vis coethnics in neighboring states. General Barre openly committed Somali troops to support the secessionist movement in Ethiopia. By early 1977, Somali secessionist forces engaged in a war with Ethiopian troops. UN and OAU threats did not work against the military regime, which did not care about either mass support or external criticism. Given the homogeneity of the society, an ethnically oriented foreign policy became the optimal strategy.

6. Conclusions

The goal of this chapter was to examine the interstate dimensions of ethnic conflict and the impact of institutions and ethnic constraints on intervention in the case of Somalia. The chapter started with historical and political aspects of the conflict involving Somalia and Ethiopia over the Ogaden region. These developments led to the 1977–78 war that along with the conflicts afterward have been analyzed in depth. Five propositions have been evaluated in light of historical developments, with generally favorable results.

Judging from Somali behavior, ethnically dominant states will formulate ethnically oriented foreign policies and will do so much earlier compared to high-constraint, diverse states when confronted by a perceived security issue. In this case, the plight of the Somalis in the Ogaden created a structural security dilemma for both states that was very difficult to resolve within the parameters of existing international norms and rules and a single crisis. Convergence of mass and elite aspirations on the issue of a Greater Somalia appears to have compounded the problem. This may indicate the skillfulness with which Somali leaders could manipulate mass sentiment. It is possible that interparty policies during the democratic phase did not differ on the issue of a Greater Somalia and therefore intransigence rather than compromise was more likely. Thus, within ethnically dominant, institutionally constrained states (i.e., Somalia before 1969), elites appear to show greater solidarity on foreign policy issues, including decisions to use force.

Levels of cleavage and affinity appear to have an impact on protractedness and future escalation. Combining this evidence with that of the preceding chapter, it appears that high-constraint states of both the diverse and dominant variety are not as immune to using force as expected. However, the elites of these states appear to favor support for insurgency movements rather than direct state-to-state confrontation.

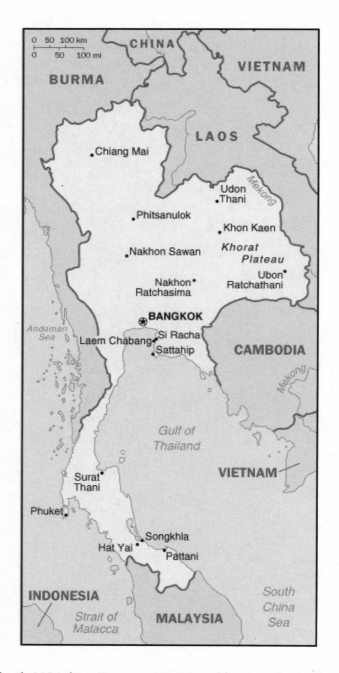

Thailand, 2004. http://www.cia.gov/cia/publications/factbook/

CHAPTER FIVE

Thai Malay Separatism:
Managing Interstate Ethnic Conflict

> The southern region of Thailand is a demarcation line between the
> Buddhist mainland and the Malay-Muslim world of Southeast Asia. Thus
> the centrifugal forces that are manifest in the case of the Muslim-Malays
> of South Thailand can, at the same time, be viewed as a result of the cen-
> tripetal tendency of the Malay geo-cultural phenomenon. The ethnic ties,
> cultural links and historical roots are exerting themselves, in defiance of
> political boundaries superficially imposed on them. (Pitsuwan 1985: 259)

1. Introduction: Managing Interstate Ethnic Conflict, or the Pursuit of the Stag

The purpose of this chapter is to evaluate the factors that contribute to the
effective management of interstate ethnic crises. This objective will be accom-
plished by assessing the framework on the basis of a case study of the Thai
Malay struggle for autonomy, centered in the southern Thai provinces of
Patani and Yala.[1] As the section heading suggests, the case will show similarities to Rousseau's famous story of the stag hunt, which often is used to
explore strategic interactions. The implication is that Thailand and Malaysia
selected mutual cooperation in pursuit of the stag (opting for a joint effort to
protect themselves from a mutual threat from communism) instead of defect-
ing to pursue the "hare" (support for ethnic kin).

Next to the Moro of the Philippines, the Malay of Thailand represent one
of Southeast Asia's most vocal and least assimilated Muslim minorities.
Consistent with the preceding assessments of interstate ethnic conflict, the
Thai Malay struggle shows strains of both separatism and irredentism. On
the one hand, the Thai Malay developed their separatist tendencies in close
association with extraregional support as well as by emulating patterns of
politicization that existed within Southeast Asia's larger Islamic community
(Che Man 1990; Chaiwat 1993). On the other hand, elements of irredentism

are evident in the way in which some of Malaysia's more strident regional leaders approached the Thai Malay issue; calls for reunification, intervention, and rebellion became common in the early and middle stages of the conflict.[2] Despite deep-seated ethnic cleavages and affinities, a history of minority repression and assimilation, along with long periods of mutual mistrust, frictions between Malaysia and Thailand, at least on this issue, have been minimized in three important ways (May 1990).

First, according to Saideman (1997), ethnic discord often can be reduced by a focus on more extensive threats to state security. The Thai Malay case is no exception. To be sure, growth of a communist threat within the region had the side effect of generating space within which Thai Malay separatists could function. But the communist insurgency assumed paramount importance in inducing Malaysia and Thailand to set aside their differences to face the higher threat. Indeed, extensive cooperative efforts to manage the shared threat of a communist insurgency offset disagreements between Thailand and Malaysia over the issue of Thai Malay autonomy.

Second, and related to the first point, despite strong transborder ethnic ties, a perceived mutual vulnerability on regional and development-related security issues served as a source of cooperation between the two states. Existing perspectives on the interstate dimensions of ethnic conflict tend to underemphasize alternative security threats as a basis for interstate cooperation (Heraclides 1991; Gurr 1993; Van Evera 1994). Yet the common interests of both Thailand and Malaysia in building regional stability, coupled with a desire for domestic economic growth, served as counterweights to interstate tensions that otherwise might have developed out of the Thai Malay issue (May 1990). In addition to various state-to-state agreements, protocols, and treaties, Thailand's efforts in the 1980s and 1990s to enhance basic minority rights and guarantees through regional development programs reduced the overall intensity of the conflict to a manageable level (de Silva et al. 1988).

Third, consistent with Heraclides' findings (1990, 1991), minority movements usually require more than affective support to prosper and grow. In particular, when the foundations of international support are seen by the majority population to be both vulnerable and controversial, separatist aspirations of a minority will be more difficult to sustain. This seems to be true for the Thai Malay, who have been on the receiving end of economic, cultural, and political support from wealthy but politically moderate Arab states. On the one hand, the net effect of this activity has been to raise awareness of the political situation of the Thai Malay and to develop a consciousness of a shared destiny among them. On the other hand, political challenges to various Thai regimes did not generate commensurate international efforts in providing critical levels of military support to the minority challenge. With time, the latter point weighed more heavily.

Even at the height of the Thai Malay movement and despite a current resurgence in violence in Patani province, political action seldom took the form of full-scale organized violence, and when it did, that violence clearly depended on material sustenance from leadership pools within the communist movement. In fact, since the mid-1950s, when Thai Malay separatism entered a phase of heightened politicization and regional irredentist aspirations intensified, the southern provinces of Thailand became identified with violence—not just Thai Malay, but communist inspired as well (Che Man 1990; Chaiwat 1993).[3]

The general pattern of association appears to be as follows: during the 1960s and 1970s, cooperative efforts in response to the regional threat posed by communism reduced friction between the two states over the issue of Thai Malay autonomy. The threat of a communist insurgency acted as both the catalyst for cooperation between Thailand and Malaysia and for a vigorous Thai Malay political movement. When the communist insurgency reached its zenith, confrontation between the two states remained at a minimum. As that threat subsided, so too did the Thai Malay insurgency, which derived much of its material and logistical support from the communists.

Five additional sections make up this chapter. The next section traces the evolution of Thai Malay separatism over a five-decade period from inception to the present. In the third part of the chapter, the roles of domestic and international factors are presented and assessed. The fourth section is devoted to an examination of two near crisis periods. In the fifth part, the propositions are evaluated. The sixth and final section concludes with directions for future research.

2.   Thailand's Malay Community: Politics on the Periphery

2.1 The Roots of Separatism—Ethnic Cleavage

Figure 5.1 provides a timeline for Thai Malay separatism from the establishment of a constitutional democracy in 1932 to the present period. During the formative years of Thai Malay separatism, Thailand exhibited high levels of ethnic cleavage.[4] Among the various underlying causes for high levels of cleavage within Thailand, the first and most important has always been that the Malay see themselves as a small, repressed religious minority within a

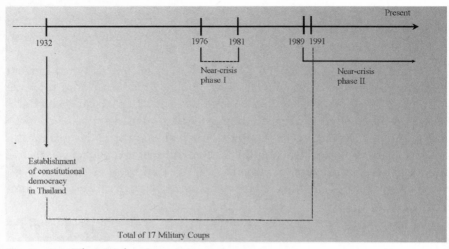

Figure 5.1. Thai Malay Separatism

Buddhist-dominated Thailand. Measured against the spectrum of states ranging from diversity to complete ethnic homogeneity, Thailand's ethnic composition reflects a moderately diverse society but one governed by Buddhists of
Thai descent. According to ethnolinguistic criteria, the Thai constitute 60
percent of the population and the Lao-related people another 25 percent.
Estimates of the total Thai Malay population range from 1.4 million to 1.5
million, which is slightly less than 4 percent of Thailand's total population of
60 million (The higher estimates usually come from the separatists while the
lower figures are provided by Thai government sources). The remainder
includes hill tribes in the north, ethnic Chinese, Thai Muslims, and (not
counting the ongoing influx of refugees from Vietnam and Cambodia) communities of Vietnamese, Hmuong, and Khmer along the Thai border (Suhrke
1981).[5]

Despite this diversity, however, there is a great deal of religious homogeneity among most of these ethnic groups, which has served to isolate the
Thai Malay even more.[6] When measured in terms of religious identity, for
example, the Buddhists occupy a dominant position in excess of 95 percent
of the population. Muslims constitute the largest religious minority.
Language, by contrast, tends to crosscut the religious dominance of Thai
Buddhists so that Thailand is a more ethnically diverse country than its religious composition would indicate. However, within the four southern
provinces of Patani, Narathiwat, Satul, and Yala, where they are most heavily concentrated, the Malay form the dominant ethnic group (Suhrke 1989).[7]

The second cause of ethnic cleavage relates to the political and economic aspirations of the Thai Malay. A number of theories have been put forward to account for the rise of political divisiveness in the Patani region, including variations on the themes of relative deprivation (Brown 1988), religious revivalism (Chaiwat 1993), historical materialism (Forbes 1989), statism (McVey 1984), and core-periphery relations (Pitsuwan 1985; Suhrke 1989; Rumley and Minghi 1991). In reality, several related factors, including socio-cultural and economic conditions, have produced an ethnic consciousness among the Malay-speaking Muslims in Thailand.

Thai Malay have tended to remain in the province where they were born; net migration to Buddhist-dominant provinces tends to be very low for Malay Muslims (Suhrke 1989). Therefore, the Malay are a geographically concentrated group straddling the border of Malaysia and Thailand (Rumley and Minghi 1991). As Suhrke (1989) has shown, most Malay within the region come from rural smallholder farms or coastal fishing villages. They traditionally have dominated rural rice production, rubber tapping, and cash crop production sectors in Patani. In contrast, the Buddhist population of these provinces, which includes Thai as well as Thai Chinese, is predominately urban and mobile (Anurugsa 1984). Historically, the Malay have been underrepresented in the civil service as well as the private sector, so urban-rural lines of cleavage between Malay and non-Malay are reinforced by divisions in income, language, and religion. This economic and political balance remained relatively unchanged at least since the 1950s (Brown 1988; Suhrke 1989). In the 1980s and 1990s, available aggregate data indicated that the Thai Malay occupied the lowest economic rung among the three ethnic groups in the region, although Yala province does constitute an exception because of its large-scale rubber production and tin reserve. Until recently, rural poverty in the south has been the highest in Thailand, and it is in the poorest of these provinces, namely Patani, where Malay separatism has been most vociferous and resilient (Suhrke 1989).

Demographic and economic characteristics explain, in part, the development of Malay ethnic consciousness. A third factor, Thai national development policies, also is noteworthy. Successive Thai regimes have approached the Muslim issue from two perspectives: implementation of policies toward all Thai Muslims and specific policies directed toward the Thai Malay. Since the late 1950s, the central government's policy toward Thai Muslims has been relatively flexible. More recently, sporadic efforts by Thai regimes to recognize religious freedoms for Muslims in the constitution at both national and provincial levels have eased tensions between Muslim minorities and Buddhists (Forbes 1982; Suhrke 1989). These policies recognize the fact that, in aggregate, the population of Muslims in Thailand is nearly double that of the Malay. In an overall sense, Bangkok's treatment of the Malay has been less consistent, ranging from policies of forced assimilation during the 1930s and 1940s to political repression in the 1950s, minority rights recognition in the 1970s, and regional autonomy in the 1980s and 1990s.

Little doubt exists that Thai repression against Thai Malay political and religious leaders played a fundamental role in establishing and broadening international political linkages. In the early formative years of the Thai Malay movement, the search for international security guarantees in response to Thai repression assumed two forms. First, Thai Malay leaders sought annexation to preindependence Malaya in the hope that ethnic allies would support them in their struggle (de Silva et al. 1988; May 1990). Second, the Thai Malay also looked to the international community for recognition and legitimacy. For example, when the military-nationalist government of Pibul Songkhram came to power (for the second time) in 1948, Thai Malay leaders demanded that the fledgling UN give them recognition as a repressed minority. Fearful that the nationalist and authoritarian policies of Phibul would eliminate their religious and political power, Malay religious leaders sent a petition to the UN requesting that the three provinces of Patani, Yala, and Narathiwat be allowed to secede and join the newly constituted Federation of Malaya (Forbes 1982; Thomas 1989). Indeed, efforts at unification with Malaysia had been pursued since 1902, when Thailand's King Chulalongkorn (Rama V) formally annexed the three southern provinces (Gopinath 1991).[8]

Conditions for internationalization became riper still when the Pibul regime suppressed the appeal and jailed the leaders of the reunification movement (Forbes 1982). In response to the crackdown, leading Thai Malay religious leaders (mostly wealthy and conservative) fled to Kelantan province in the northern part of what then was called West Malaya. Using Kelantan as a base of operations, Thai Malay leaders slowly cultivated links between themselves and supporters in West Malaya as well as within the international community.

Political pressures applied by an aloof but concerned British government (who still controlled Malaya and had concerns about regional escalation) had already resulted in a slight relaxation of tensions between Thailand's central government and Malay elites. For example, after several Thai Malay dissidents were jailed, the British government called on Bangkok to provide "a just solution of Patani's case" but made no effort to mediate or provide good offices for a negotiated solution or even to recognize the legitimacy of the Thai Malay movement within the confines of UN definitions of minority self-determination (Jones 1948: 4–5). Thereafter the government abandoned efforts at forcible assimilation in favor of an uneasy combination of accommodation and integration strategies that included dropping compulsory attendance at Thai primary schools and promotion of the use of Thai over the Malay language (Brown 1988; May 1990; for further details see Thomas 1989 and Forbes 1989).

Despite directives from UN Security Council members to cease and desist, successive Thai regimes continued to pursue expansionist and centralizing policies. These included elimination of minority language access in education and dismissal of local councils in matters of education and religious practice. These centralizing efforts had been aimed primarily toward building Thai national identity, with an emphasis on strengthening the observance of Buddhist religious practice in minority areas and enhancing the use of Thai language in Thailand's border regions (Yegar 2002).

To be sure, these policies did have the immediate effect of stalling the Malay movement in Thailand, but several important and unintended consequences ensued. On the one hand, nationalist policies served to undermine the legitimacy of local Malay elites, especially political leaders who had been shown to be powerless against Bangkok's heavy hand. On the other hand, by design, nationalization diminished opportunities for moderation and dialogue between the two contending loci of power: the central government and Patani province. Some Thai Malay believed that without quick acquisition of local autonomy guarantees, the Thai Malay would be forced to pursue alternative, and potentially more violent, paths to autonomy (D. Brown 1988; May 1990).

Nationalization, in sum, affected the Thai Malay movement in three fundamental ways. First, more Thai Malay began to see themselves as leaders of a marginalized community within someone else's homeland (Suhrke 1989). As a consequence, the Thai Malay, especially those who already had fled to Kelantan, believed reunification with Malaya to be the only way to ensure the survival of the Thai Malay language and culture.

Second, nationalization coincided with and perhaps precipitated an irrevocable erosion of the traditional authority structures of the Thai Malay political and religious elites. Thai centralization hastened this process considerably, but challenges from younger, generally better-educated Thai Malay (i.e., those who would be most likely to suffer under Thai discrimination in the private and public sectors) also served to undermine the traditional authority structure. Thai Malay could no longer be convinced that those who fled to Malaya would be capable of directing the group's interests and began to form alternative and often more radical bases of support in Patani. The main distinction between the leaders of these two groups can be understood in terms of their divergent strategies. The less educated and older separatists favored an independent sultanate, while the younger students favored an autonomous republic (Gopinath 1991).

Third, the broadening of leadership across territorial boundaries meant that alternative bases of support for the Thai Malay movement, including those traditionally associated with the Malay regional movement, fast became main sources of moral and material support. The most important of these linkages, to be discussed below, concerned the Islamic community in Southeast Asia and in the Middle East. In effect, because the Thai Malay nationalist movement became larger, with more diverse (and potentially contending) interests, it drew other countries into the process of ethnic minority struggle. This process took place at a distance, but also more directly within Malaysia through transnational linkages, population transfers, and increasing financial and ideological support from benefactors beyond the Malaya peninsula.

2.2 Ethnic Affinity—Spanning the Border

During the decades between World War Two and 1960, Malay elites in Thailand focused primarily on irredentist strategies rather than secessionist goals. (Gurr [1993: 21] uses the term "secession" as intended here: "to signify any strong tendency within an identity group to attain greater political autonomy.") Leaders pursued reunification with the Malay Peninsula rather than independence or autonomy. Territorial redemption related directly to the ongoing plans to create a federated Malaysia consisting of West Malaya, Sabah, Sarawak, Brunei, and Singapore. The assimilationist policies of the government, initiated during the war and continued under the leadership of Pibul Songkhram, played a crucial role in intensifying feelings of resentment within the Muslim population toward the government and in strengthening the resistance of Malay Muslims to the central government (Yegar 2002).

Most Malay elites in the southern border regions of Thailand pursued unification with a federated Malaysia to ensure the constant flow of material support from wealthy expatriates in Kelantan province. As Suhrke (1977) notes, Kelantan is an obvious source of support for other reasons: a shared dialect, religion, and history. Kelantan is one of the most orthodox states in Malaysia, and orthodoxy, according to Suhrke, implies special interest in a condition in which fellow Muslims are governed by non-Muslims.

The net political effect of cross-border involvement led to the formation of the Gambungan Melayu Patani Raya (Association of Malay of Greater

Patani, GAMPAR). GAMPAR was one of the first nationalist Muslim groups to emerge after the Second World War and served as the forerunner of the separatist underground movements that developed in later periods (Yegar 2002). It had the specific goal of uniting all Malay Muslims living in Thailand and Malaya (Gopinath 1991). Leaders of GAMPAR designed the pan-Malay doctrine during the Pibul regime. The party's related objectives included improvement in living standards, education, and cultural awareness. Leadership was assumed by the Malay Muslim religious and royal exiles living in Malaya. A second populist organization—the Patani People's Movement (PPM)—was also established at this time (Gopinath 137).

Unfortunately for those Thai Malay bent on the idea of a pan-Malay state, Indonesia's confrontation (i.e., *konfrontasi*) with Malaysia from 1963 to 1965 undermined the credibility of the pan-Malay movement in general and reclamation of Thai territory in particular. This is because Indonesia's more strident interpretation of Malay nationalism was consistent with GAMPAR's own stated objectives, and to that extent, Indonesia would be willing to play "big brother" by providing support to the Thai Malay movement. Indonesia's open hand to GAMPAR, not surprisingly, became a source of irritation to both Thailand and Malaysia. Indonesia's leaders, however, also preferred not to see postindependence Malaysia expand beyond its current borders. Therefore, they would support the Thai Malay movement up to a point, but not at the expense of larger geopolitical concerns. Indeed, Indonesia had already confronted Malaysia over that country's claims to Sabah and Sarawak and had backed down. In fact, Indonesia's confrontational policies failed to generate much support for its irredentist claims within West Malaya itself, let alone within southern Thailand.

The net short-term effect was to deny GAMPAR the crucial political legitimacy it required from a leading Malay state and a radical one at that. In addition, GAMPAR's connection with the *konfrontasi* did not help its relationship with the Malaysian government. By default, GAMPAR had to seek out and build on support from the politically isolated ethnic brethren of Kelantan province in Malaysia, an otherwise inauspicious beginning for a fledgling movement that laid bold claims to reuniting all Malay in Southeast Asia. Thus, for the Thai Malay, the political dilemma became double-edged.

On the one hand, open support from Malaysia's federal government could not be counted on. From the perspective of Malaysia's leaders in Kuala Lumpur, the Thai Malay constituted a troublesome fringe minority, neither sizable enough to warrant a firmer course of action nor small enough to be ignored. Thus, Malaysia's new government had an interest in the Thai Malay situation, but one tempered by the realities of time and demography. In addition to these two obvious factors, Kuala Lumpur did not share Kelantan's enthusiasm for another reason: other Malay did not broadly share the particularist affinities between Kelantan and the Thai Malay (Farouk 1984).

On the other hand, although the Malay have not always constituted a numerical majority, since 1969 they have enjoyed special constitutional and political privileges as *bumiputra* (sons of the soil) in Malaysia.[9] Although Malaysia is constitutionally a Muslim state to the extent that Islam is the official religion, in reality the society is highly diverse. No province within Malaysia has been more vociferous in supporting the rights of the *bumiputra* than Kelantan. To be sure, the development of a pro-Malay and staunchly Islamic province on their southern border had a powerful demonstration effect on Malay elites in the Patani region. For example, in 1969, the leader of the Pan Malayan Islamic Party (PMIP or PAS) openly discussed the prospect of an alternative Malay nation—comprising the Malay states of Malaysia and those of southern Thailand "should Malaysia collapse as a country" (Farouk 1984: 245). Kelantan was (and is) the home of Malaysia's political conservatives, with PAS as the primary political instrument through which these leaders expressed their views on the Thai Malay issue. PAS ruled Kelantan from 1959 until 1978 and returned to power in the late 1980s.

While in opposition during 1970, Datuk Seri Mohammed Asri, a senior official in Malaysia's National Front cabinet and later leader of Kelantan, described the struggle against Thai rule as a "holy one" that merited support from Muslims the world over (Pitsuwan 1988a, 1988b). Later, while serving as chief minister for Religious Affairs in the United Malay National Organization, he also commented that "the request for autonomy with specific conditions for the four provinces as put forward by the freedom front seem credible if well received."[10] In essence, Malaysia regarded the Thai Malay and their Kelantan connections as a radical fringe that mainstream Malay leadership would not accept but also could not overlook. Malaysia faced an ongoing communist insurgency and looked to Thailand for support, and the probability of Thai Malay success became even less likely.

3. The Key Actors in the Conflict, the Separatist Movements, and Linkages

After the formation of GAMPAR it became evident that neither the international community nor the newly established Malay Federation would support reunification openly. However, links between Thai Malay leaders and Kelantan province remained strong. Tensions between traditional elites (who favored unification with West Malaya) and younger, more progressive Malay students within GAMPAR (who pursued separatist goals) began to undermine the effectiveness and unity of the Malay nationalist movement. Not until Malay leaders traded in the strategy of irredentism for autonomy across the board did the nationalist movement regain its lost momentum (Farouk 1984; Pitsuwan 1988a).

According to Yegar (2002), in 1963–64 a severe problem emerged when guerrilla units of the Malay People's Liberation Army (MPLA)—the military arm of the Communist Party of Malaysia—organized a recruitment campaign among Muslims in southern Thailand. This had the purpose of reinforcing their rebellion against the Malay governments. However, due to lack of empathy between the Malay Muslims and the Chinese Marxists, cooperation did not come into being (Yegar 2002).

Several distinct separatist organizations emerged on Thailand's political map by the mid-1960s, with each group featuring different goals, leadership, and strategies. They therefore could not unite within one institution, and fragmentation prevented their success. Although approximately twenty separatist bodies existed in the early 1970s, the number declined sharply in the latter part of that decade. By 1981, only five remained active, with three being notable (Yegar 2002; see also Anurugsa 1984). The first, the Barisan Revolusi Nasional (BRN), formed in Kelantan in 1960 under the leadership of Tengku Abdul Jalal. It obtained support mainly from educated young Muslims and intellectuals who had studied abroad (Yegar 2002). A creation of conservative Malay Muslim leadership, the BRN initially espoused pan-Malay objectives. The BRN was not merely a separatist movement. It also had Pan-Malay aspirations and therefore aimed to remove the four Muslim provinces from Thailand and then, if successful, incorporate them into a wider state within the Malaysian Federation (Gopinath 1991).[11] BRN leaders favored creation of a new state that would combine socialism and Malay nationalism with Islamic principles. Its leaders initially had important affiliations with the Communist Party of Malaya (CPM) and later with radical states in the Middle East.

The BRN was the one Thai Malay organization most heavily affected by *konfrontasi* and its aftermath. In essence, confrontation raised questions within Islamic Southeast Asia about Malaysia's foreign policy orientation, especially its relations with Britain and other Western powers. For example, Indonesian support for the Thai Muslim movement had both ideological and ethnic foundations, that is, to liberate those Malay unfortunate enough to be ruled by conservative, "Old Established Force" governments (Suhrke and Noble 1977: 207). In 1965, Thai Malay leaders who supported Indonesia's confrontational and Islamic worldview split from the BRN and formed the Partai Revolusi Nasional (PARNAS). Throughout the decade and into the 1970s, PARNAS operated in unison with the Communist Party of Malaya (CPM).

Conservative Islamic elites formed the Barisan Nasional Pembebasan Patani (National Liberation front of Patani, BNPP). Founded by Tunku Mayhiddin, the BNPP developed in liaison with traditional and religious elites living in Kelantan, although much of its support consisted of financial transfers from overseas Malay students in Saudi Arabia, Egypt, and Pakistan (May 1990). By 1991, the BNPP, which had become marginalized, remained an Islamic organization, and its political objectives still included the unlikely goal of liberation of all Muslims, including the Thai Malay, and establishment of a sovereign state of Patani (Gopinath 1991). The BNPP maintains close relations with the Islamic Secretariat, the Arab League, and the Palestine Liberation Organization. At its height, the BNPP claimed a guerrilla force of three thousand mostly trained in Libya, with weapons obtained from Indochina after the U.S. withdrawal from Vietnam (Gopinath 1991).

A third group, the Patani United Liberation Organization (PULO), was established in 1967. The PULO became the largest and most influential of the various Muslim militant separatist organizations that operated in Southern Thailand since the 1960s—mainly because of material support from Libya and Syria and ideological backing from Malaysia and Saudi Arabia. (Little is known of the two remaining groups, the Sabilallah [the way of God], which emerged in the late 1970s, and the Patani Islamic Nationalities Revolutionary Party, which came into being in 1980 or 1981.) The Patani United Liberation Army (PULA) conducted military actions on behalf of the PULO. Although the PULO began as a loosely organized insurgency movement and not a political organization, it evolved over time. Twenty years later, the PULO had become Thai Malay's most internationally active and violent separatist group (Gopinath 1991). The PULO continues to rely on external support, without which it could not persist.[12] For example, during its heyday, the leadership of the PULO was centered in Mecca, with much of the recruitment of members carried out from there (Thomas 1989).

While the BNPP is a religious and conservative organization and the BRN represented pan-Malay interests, PULO existed primarily as a militant insurgency movement. In the mid-1970s, efforts took place to create an organization that could represent all (or most) of the separate bodies by bringing them under an umbrella-type structure. Although BNPP and PULO agreed to cooperate and coordinate their military actions, this fell short of a fully unified approach. Together, these organizations, in particular the BRN and

PULO, applied pressure on the government in Bangkok. In concert with the CPM, they would pose a considerable obstacle to cooperation between Thailand and Malaysia.

With the emergence of three significant separatist movements on its southern flank, the government in Bangkok began to look for diplomatic support from both Indonesia and Malaysia for its own activities against the Thai Malay separatists (Pitsuwan 1988b). Indeed, at one point, sensing an opportunity, Thailand's Prime Minister Kriangasak Chomanand personally sought out and obtained Malaysian and Indonesian support for Thailand to contain the Malay separatist elements (*National Security Council Document on Policy toward the Malay Muslims, 1978:* 14; Pitsuwan 1988b). Signals from Malaysia remained ambiguous at best. At times it became difficult to deduce the exact message Kuala Lumpur was trying to convey to Bangkok. On the one hand, the government of Malaysia distanced itself from the Thai Malay issue. On the other hand, Malaysia's Islamic community expressed solidarity with the Thai Malay. For example, Seri Abdul Aziz bin Zain, vice president of the Muslim Welfare Organization of Malaysia, was quoted in 1977 as saying that "the Malay in South Thailand had nourished a resentment to what they considered the forcible incorporation of their homeland into Thai-speaking Buddhist Thailand" (Pitsuwan 1988b: 341).

On balance, consolidation of power under UMNO brought the Thai Malay question into comparative perspective. Development of a vigorous government policy to improve the economic well-being of all *bumiputra* through strategies of economic and political rebalancing had become the main platform of the UMNO after the 1969 emergency. These policies, collectively known as the New Economic Policy (NEP), aimed primarily at bringing the Malay peoples into the modernizing, commercial, industrial, and educational sectors of Malaysian society, an area long dominated by Malaysian Chinese. The effect the NEP had on the Thai Malay expatriates who had become political activists in Malaysia represented an important consequence. The NEP and its pro-Malay emphasis induced many Malay to support conservative, pro-Malay opposition parties. Parties such as PAS attempted to make political gains by emphasizing the Thai Malay problem to an even greater extent than did official government channels. In general, these policies appeared insufficient to either decrease hostilities or raise the standard of living in the southern provinces (Yegar 2002).

Dovetailing of platforms between the UMNO and its Islamic party opposition in the north became the net effect; the UMNO government rarely renounced the PAS position publicly. Malaysia's leaders knew that pan-Malay sentiment remained popular with voters in that region. For example, a 1977 poll of Malaysian attitudes toward the Muslim problem in southern Thailand indicated that a majority supported a policy of active Malaysian governmental intervention in favor of the Malay Muslims (Gopinath 1991: 139). Thus, official relations between Thailand and Malaysia in the 1970s, although cordial, remained influenced heavily by regional politics. Thai Malay leaders tried to make political gains within Malaysia, where their ideas were well received.

Indonesia's clear approach to the Thai Malay issue contrasted with Malaysian ambiguity. In quid pro quo fashion, Indonesia moved to support Bangkok precisely because it also faced separatist problems. In fact, Sukarno's initial policy of support for the Thai Malay did not persist after Suharto came to power in 1965. Separatist movements in East Timor, West Papua, Aceh, and the South Molluccas, among others, ensured that the Suharto government would be extremely sensitive to pursuing an aggressive ethnically based foreign policy, for fear of obvious repercussions at home. As Indonesian Foreign Minister Adam Malik said when he returned from the Islamic Conference at Kuala Lumpur in 1974, "We cannot have a separate state for every minority in a country" (Suhrke 1977: 207). Two effects ensued. First, to the extent that each recognized a potential internal threat to political stability, the bonds between and among the governments of Indonesia, Malaysia, and Thailand became stronger. Second, Thai Malay separatists would have to look further abroad for support.

Rising Islamic nationalism in other parts of the world at this time (notably the Sudan, Philippines, Pakistan, Iran, and India) inspired local Thai Malay elites to look to the Middle East and North Africa, the centers of backing for Islamic movements worldwide. Initially, their cause became known through international awareness and human rights monitoring (Gopinath 1991). For example, Malay Muslims in exile (mostly in Saudi Arabia) and students in Saudi Arabia proved to be instrumental in organizing international opposition to Thai policy. Separatist meetings were held during the Haj season (Farouk 1984), and Saudi Arabia, Libya, and Syria primarily provided training for PULO leaders (Chaiwat 1991).

Muslim religious organizations also served as sources of support for the Thai Malay (Farouk 1984). Initially, the Conference of Islamic Foreign Ministers held disparate views about the Patani issue. Formally, the conference excluded communiqués that referred to the problem (Suhrke 1977). Informally, however, subjects of discussion included imposing an oil embargo against Thailand (Gopinath 1991) and the problem of Muslim minorities all over the world (Gopinath 1991; Chaiwat 1991). By the 1980s, the issue of Patani became an important item on the agenda of the Islamic Summit

Conference, and the PULO received considerable financial support from the Muslim World League (Saudi Arabia's official government organ for rendering assistance to Muslims around the world). The 1990s witnessed a warming of relations between Thailand and the states of the Middle East, with the possible exclusion of Iran and Iraq. Instances of social, educational, and religious assistance also have been documented (Gopinath 1991).

Finally, it is important to include China and Vietnam as potential sources of support for the Thai Malay cause when both countries were flexing their internationalist muscles in the 1970s. Both countries became involved in the region because the Communist Party of Thailand (CPT) and the CPM engaged actively in supporting various elements of the Patani separatist movement. (Of the two parties, the CPM has been by far the most active; for its part the Communist Party of Thailand had become a spent force by the 1970s.) In the atmosphere of ideological confrontation between the then-communist bloc of Indochina (Vietnam, Laos, and Kampuchea) and the ASEAN states, the Malay insurgents and the CPM (and to a lesser extent the CPT) held particular interest for all regional actors. Both became effective weapons in destabilizing national governments and subverting the positive effects of intra-ASEAN relations. In 1948, the revolt of communists in Malaysia started and the Malaysian government termed this situation an "emergency." When this period ended in 1960, remnants of the CPM units started to establish camps on the Thai part of the border, areas well suited to them due to the nature of the terrain and jungles. These developments and Thailand's apathy regarding communist penetration upset Malaysia: "It appeared that there was an unspoken understanding between the CPM and the Thai authorities in which the communists concentrated their actions only against Malaysia and did not attack Thai targets or incite the Malay population in the south" (Yegar 2002: 155). Under these circumstances, the government of Thailand acted slowly and carefully in cooperating with Malaysia because "as long as the organization existed, it posed a potential threat to Malaysia, in consequence of which Malaysia would refrain from aiding Muslim separatists" (156).

After the mid-1960s, Thai policy started to change because the government began to worry about cooperation between the CPM and the CPT: "The Thai government feared that not only the CPM of Malaya but also the underground Thai communists would exploit separatist tendencies in the south" (Yegar 2002: 156). Anxiety also existed about potential cooperation between the communists and the Malay Muslims. Indeed, despite communist efforts, Malay Muslims rejected that ideology and kept their distance. However, it is reported that an exchange of information and a supply of arms continued to take place between communists and Malay Muslims. Communist fighters crossed the border often due to its unsettled nature and an absence of agreement between Thai and Malaysian forces in the frontier area.

When the conflict in Indochina culminated in Vietnam's intervention in Cambodia in 1978 and the subsequent Sino-Vietnam war of 1979, the struggle to exert influence over the whole of Southeast Asia led these states to seek allies on the Malay Peninsula (Pitsuwan 1985). How this process generated near crises for Malaysia and Thailand is the subject of the next section.

4. The Regional Threat

4.1 Malaysia's Ethnic Politics—Divided Interests before the Emergency

Although the primary focus of this chapter is on Thailand's internal cleavage as a source for interstate ethnic conflict, Malaysia's domestic ethnic politics influenced its foreign policies in two ways.

First, as noted, with the belief that Malaysia's pro-Malay orientation eventually would include them, Thai Malay separatists stepped up their activities against the Thai central government. The threats, however, had the effect of stimulating collaboration between the two governments.

Second, the anticommunist stance of successive Malaysian governments had distinct anti-Chinese overtones (Suhrke 1977). Malaysia's pro-West foreign policy emanated largely from the internal threat posed by a large Chinese communist community. The CPM was primarily a Chinese organization, and since the Chinese constituted a significant proportion of Malaysia's population, the government could not tolerate infiltration of the CPM into Malaysia through Thailand. The Chinese minority clearly had a firm hand in influencing Malaysia's foreign policy. Malaysia had, for example, consistently declined to join SEATO (South East Asian Treaty Organization) because its Chinese leaders saw the organization as essentially a U.S. device designed to contain China. Relations between Thailand and Malaysia, however, remained generally good in spite of Malaysia's reluctance to join SEATO (Thomas 1977).

Malaysia's 1969 communal riots provided the catalyst for renewed Thai Malay–CPM collaboration and a positive shift in relations between Bangkok and Kuala Lumpur. Sensing an opportunity to exploit a weakened Malaysian regime, the CPM stepped up its infiltration along the border. As a result, the

Malaysian and Thai governments established joint formal border operations. Since 1952, the year the CPM established its base of operations in the jungle along the Thai border, there had been small-scale, joint border operations. However, during the 1969 Malaysian emergency, a Thai Malaysian Communist Suppression Command was established to conduct joint operations against terrorists in the border provinces. In the same year the Thai government placed the four southern provinces under martial law.

Potential linkages between the PULO and communist insurgents also created concerns for the Thai government. With PULO activities connected explicitly to those of the CPM in the southern region, the Thai government acted to suppress quickly any hint of Malay insurgency (Alpern 1974). In turn, support for the rebels in the form of arms shipments from Kelantan ensured a growth in the militancy of these movements. Although the CPM posed a more serious threat to Thai-Malaysian relations at this time, the separatist movement remained a constant source of irritation between Bangkok and Kuala Lumpur. For several reasons, both the Thai and Malaysian governments had reason to fear a CPM–Thai Malay alliance (Thomas 1977).

For the Malaysian government of the day, a communist insurgency movement operating out of southern Thailand represented a considerable deterrent to its plans for the political unity of disparate ethnic groups within the Malaysia Federation (Thomas 1977). The Thai government, on the other hand, could not risk losing favor with Malaysia's leaders by neglecting the CPM, for fear that the Malay card would be used against it. Mutual insecurity in these two separate issue-areas led to a convergence of interests between the two governments.

Thai leaders remained convinced that as long as a communist threat to Malaysian political stability existed, formal support for Thai Malay separatism would remain at low levels. In turn, any confrontation between Thailand and Malaysia would be to the CPM's gain, and thus the communists' strategy had been precisely to inflame existing conflict (Suhrke 1977). For example, on 7 March 1970, Thai and Malaysian military units established a new border agreement that would allow "hot pursuit" in each other's territory. Two years later, in May 1972, a joint Thai Malaysian border command was established in a further effort to suppress transborder movements of the CPM and PULO. A coup d'état in Bangkok later that year brought a staunchly anticommunist government to power which, in an unprecedented move, showed willingness to allow Malaysian forces to expand their area of operation into southern Thailand.[13]

Both governments knew that Malaysia's extraterritorial activity could not be delinked easily from its suppressed irredentist goals. While there is no proof that by the 1980s Kuala Lumpur had designs on Patani (or any other southern province for that matter), evidence exists that fringe elements within Kelantan as well as PAS continued to advocate reunification and offered open support to Thai Malay rebels. Furthermore, Thai nationalists also began to grumble about threats to sovereignty. They could not reconcile the need for Malaysian troops on Thai soil with Thai security needs and the fact that their government remained incapable of confronting both the Thai Malay and CPM issues without Malaysia's support. To deal with this dilemma, both governments came to the conclusion that eradication of the CPM could lead, in theory, to a decline in the activities of the Thai Malay insurgents, who had relied extensively on the communists for logistical and material support. As a result, in 1977 a massive joint operation began against the CPM. At that time, the Malaysian government tried to reassure the Thai government that it had suppressed all claims to southern Thailand (Pitsuwan 1985: 175).

4.2 Near Crisis, Phase I—1976 to 1981

Under the agreement of 1970, Malaysian troops could enter Thai areas in hot pursuit of the CPM, but Thai forces could not enter Malaysia in pursuit of Malay insurgents, a fact that led Thai nationalists to protest against the government (Anurugsa 1984). In their efforts to eliminate the CPM, Malaysian forces often had crossed the Thai border. One such incident served to trigger a series of threats and counterthreats between Bangkok and Kuala Lumpur.

When Malaysian security forces suspected Thai officials of helping communist guerrillas find refuge, they engaged in a unilateral "cleanup" and indiscriminately killed, wounded, and arrested Thai citizens (mostly of Chinese origin) without Thai consent and lingered on Thai soil for another fourteen days during May 1976. The Thai government accused Kuala Lumpur of "showing no trust and displaying an unfriendly attitude toward their Thai hosts" and asked for withdrawal of Malaysia's peace force from the region (*Foreign Relations Committee Report*, 11 June 1976). In response, the Malaysian Home Affairs Minister Tan Sri Ghazali Shafie asserted that "[t]o protect our national interests and indeed our survival, we will have to regard that part of Thailand as hostile and the ramifications of such an attitude must not only be understood but accepted by all" (*Far Eastern Economic Review*, 18 June 1976: 11). Under pressure from Bangkok to withdraw by January 1980, the Malaysian field forces had stepped up their operations against the CPM (*Asiaweek*, 2 May 1980, cited in Pitsuwan 1985). They forced the communist insurgents to disband into small units and cede their long-established sanctuaries in Narathiwat and Yala. As a result of this action, Malay Muslims, including elements of and sympathizers with the PULO, moved in to fill the vacuum.

Malaysia and Thailand had different priorities among the various threats that they faced in Phase I. For Thailand the main problem was Muslim separatism, with the communist threat in second place. However, for Malaysia the most important goal was to suppress communism. Therefore, as long as Malaysia had the communist problem, "it would not jeopardize its interests by supporting Muslim separatists" (Yegar 2002: 158).

Concomitantly, the PULO initiated several near crises against the Thai government. They began with a series of internal violent acts culminating in an exchange of threats between Bangkok and Kuala Lumpur. Several interrelated events took place between 1976 and 1981 (Chaiwat 1987). At least one event constituted a threat to the Thai regime but did not lead to a foreign policy crisis for Thailand. A bomb attack during the royal visit to Yala province on 22 September 1977 is believed to have been linked indirectly to the downfall of Thanin Kraivixien's administration (Forbes 1982, 1989).[14] The attempt to assassinate the king and his royal family led to resignation of the prime minister in the same year (Anurugsa 1984). Another sixteen violent minor acts occurred over the same period. In all, twenty-one acts of violence resulted in at least 221 civilian casualties, although the Thai government reported higher figures (Chaiwat 1987). All of these acts occurred in Yala province, with separatist rebels involved in each of the major incidents being connected to the PULO (Chaiwat 1987; see also Forbes 1989 and the MAR Project).

Three emerging patterns can be ascertained from the above-noted twenty-one events. First, the terrorists showed the willingness to attack and kill Thai Buddhist civilians, a notable change in tactics. Second, efforts by the PULO to extend the campaign to Bangkok became extensive. A third discernible pattern took the form of a growing threat of transnational terrorist attacks, including foreign government targets in Thailand and Thai government targets in other countries (Forbes 1982, 1989). Within the series of events, four violent acts stand out:

1. 22 September 1977—a bombing undertaken by members of the PULO, Sabilallah, and Black December during the royal visit to Podoks in Yala province (47 casualties, no deaths reported);

2. 14 December 1977—a holdup/shooting of a local casino (18 casualties, 10 deaths reported);

3. 6 October 1979—a bombing of a railway station in Yala (9 casualties, no deaths reported);

4. 21 February 1981—a shooting of travelers on a road in Yala (25 casualties, 15 deaths reported).

One obvious question arises: Why did this period witness an increase in violent tactics? Several patterns stand out. The more notable of these patterns is the parallel course of events relating to the activities of the CPM, most significantly a rise in its activities and a subsequent decline around the same time. The behavior of the CPM provides the first clue as to why the Malay separatist insurgency also peaked and then declined during this period.

With respect to the first point, the CPM, working alongside the PULO, found that they could generate a great deal of political instability and violence in the region (Anurugsa 1984).[15] When the Thai military took control of the southern area, protest and violence became the preferred path to liberation, followed by equally oppressive governmental measures and more PULO violence (Pitsuwan 1985, 1988a).

Violent confrontations between PULO and Thai forces ensued in 1980 when Malaysian forces withdrew and Thai forces tried to round up both CPM and PULO leaders. Muslim villagers, caught in the crossfire, fled to nearby Kelantan and Kedah. At the height of the confrontation an estimated 1,178 people took refuge in "refugee camps" inside Malaysia and vowed not to return until their safety could be guaranteed (Pitsuwan 1988b). For its part, Malaysia's UMNO leaders said that the "refugees would not be returned against their wish and Malaysia would provide them shelter on purely humanitarian grounds" (338). From Bangkok, charges ensued that the Malaysian authorities had encouraged elements of the PULO to strike at CPM base areas because the latter had informed the Thai authorities of their activities and movements (*Far Eastern Economic Review,* 9 October 1981: 12).

In September 1981 the Thai government attempted to settle the refugee issue with Kuala Lumpur. As a gesture of friendship and "a favor to an ASEAN neighbor" the Malaysian government decided to absorb the refugees, as had been done previously. The near crisis wound down with an offer of general amnesty to members of the CPM in 1984. In December 1989 an accord between Thailand, Malaysia, and the CPM formally ended the CPM's forty-year struggle (*Straits Times,* 28 September 1991). The communist threat diminished considerably along the border after CPM leaders agreed to lay down their arms in return for Malaysian financial compensation and rehabilitation. One thousand members of the disbanded units decided to settle down in Thailand (*Straits Times,* 11 February 1993). With the removal of the CPM from the scene, the activities of the Malay separatist movement also declined in scope and violence, at least until 1989. In that year a series of internal events triggered a second near crisis for Thailand. In contrast to the first, this conflict featured full cooperation between Malaysia and Thailand.

4.3 Near Crisis, Phase II—1989 to the Present

After the demise of the CPM, both the Thai and Malaysian governments could give full attention to the Thai Malay dispute. The year 1989 marked renewed attempts by the popularly elected Chat Thai government to resolve, with the assistance of Kuala Lumpur, the PULO insurgency in the southern provinces. Under pressure from opposition parties to resolve the question amicably and have the army withdraw from the region, Bangkok devised an economic plan called the Hardpan Barau (New Hope). The plan was implemented as a strategy for development of tourism, the southern seaboards, and a coastal industrial zone. The goal was to strengthen the regional economy and defuse tensions between the Malay and Thai communities (*Asiaweek,* 21 April 1989). The year 1989 became noteworthy for another reason. It marked a brief revival of violent activities in the Patani region. Throughout the year, what then were believed to be Thai Malay rebels carried out attacks on non-Malay teachers, random bombings, and kidnappings.

These significant events signaled a change in direction among the Thai Malay leadership. The source of this change could be traced to a minority Shi'ia sect with considerable Middle East international connections. From the end of 1988 onward, Iran became especially active among Shi'ite Muslims in the south. For example, as part of the New Hope plan, the government chose to restore a mosque in Yala province. Between 23 October 1989 and 3 June 1990, followers of the Shi'ia leader, Sorayuth Sakunasantisart, protested the use of government money to renovate the mosque in a series of marches, speeches, and mass prayers (Chaiwat 1993).

Given that the dissidents came from a Shi'ia core group, Thai sources believed the preceding events and violence in 1989 to be promulgated with the assistance of the Iranian embassy in Bangkok (Chaiwat 1993). The PULO was not implicated in the attacks, which signified a significant realignment in Muslim minority politics in Thailand. A new pan-Muslim movement under Shi'ia leadership included not only disgruntled Malay of the southern provinces but also the non-Malay Muslims centered around Bangkok. Thai Malay autonomy now became of secondary importance relative to the larger issue of Muslim religious revivalism.

This transformation in leadership is important because of the realignment of international interests in the conflict. A significant shift occurred from Saudi Arabia to Iran as the primary external focal point of support. The Gulf War did much to hasten this process. At the beginning of the crisis, many Muslims were pro-Saudi because the country was the biggest sponsor of Thai Malay students. After the war, these students viewed Saudi Arabia as a "tool" of the United States in its efforts to destroy Muslims. According to one source, hundreds of young men crossed the border to Malaysia to link up with the fundamentalists there, in an effort to serve with Iraq (*Straits Times,* 22 February 1991).

These events concerned Thai officials because of their potentially broader impact on national security. The Kruzai event, a violent protest by Muslim groups at a Buddhist temple, became significant because of its implications for an Islamic resurgence independent of traditional Thai Malay political interests (Gopinath 1991; Chaiwat 1993). The fact that the PULO was not involved in the demonstrations also is significant. In fact, in the past decade, PULO guerrilla activity in Thailand and along the border had declined to almost nothing. By 1991 PULO membership disintegrated into several small factions—their movement was finished (*Straits Times,* 28 September, 4 October 1991).

Kuala Lumpur and Bangkok, in an effort to bring the issue to a close, formalized a joint bid to suppress the rebels in 1991. Malaysia agreed to seal the border to the rebels. Even Kelantan's PAS government proved willing to cooperate, calling the matter a concern between Bangkok and Kuala Lumpur. With the Kelantan government siding against the rebels, the potential for interstate conflict diminished significantly. Finally, cooperation between the Thai and Malaysian governments had been obtained with perceived gains on all fronts except one. The internal threat posed by the radical leaders of Thailand's Shi'ia community remained in place.[16]

Indeed, in the spring of 1994, a series of bombings occurred, and PULO members with Shi'ia sect connections in Iran and Pakistan claimed responsibility. These bombings occurred mostly in popular tourist areas (U.S. Task Force on Terrorism and Unconventional Warfare 1998; MAR Project). From 1997 onward, the issue of Malaysian support increased in importance. The Malaysian government started a campaign against Thai insurgent leaders. Cooperation against the separatists took place because Malaysia did not want to jeopardize the emerging Malaysia-Thailand-Indonesia "growth triangle."[17] Collaboration resulted in success and led to the arrest of four core PULO leaders in 1998.

After this event, many militants participated in the government's rehabilitation program while some leaders as well as their followers fled the country. However, these events have not been sufficient to bring an end to armed separatism in southern Thailand. Isolated, small-scale incidents continue to occur. For example, on 11 July 2000, the BBC reported that two policemen had been killed in the south, near the Malaysian border. The interior minister claimed, however, that "it must be a bandit group but not terrorists" and linked violence to the issue of drug trafficking. Past events make it clear that Thailand's policy is firm: granting autonomy to Muslims is unacceptable. Cultural differences between Muslims and Thais, however, persist. In 1998 the Minorities at Risk Project concluded that the Thai Malay movement remained active but highly fragmented in organization and capability:

> The factionalization of the Muslim separatist movement and the limited nature of their support raises questions about the ability of the groups to launch a large-scale campaign for autonomy or even independence. Recent campaigns by the groups to forcibly obtain funds from locals in the southern region are likely to alienate many Muslims. Finally, Malaysia's decision to take a strong stand toward actions by Thai separatists living in Malaysia could reduce external support for the separatist movement. (http://www.bsos.umd.edu/cidcm/mar/thamusl.htm, 4 October 1998)

Violence in the southern provinces has increased since September 11, 2001. The PULO claim lives lost at the hands of the Thai government numbering in the hundreds and thousands displaced. Support for the PULO continues to emanate from Islamic organizations in the Middle East. From January through March 2004, separatist activities and attacks continued throughout southern Thailand. Martial law was declared by the government in the affected areas including the provinces of Narathiwat, Patani, and Yala. In April of 2004 more than a hundred suspected Islamic militants were killed in clashes with security forces in southern Thailand. In October 2004, seventy-eight Muslim protestors died in trucks, many from suffocation, while in military custody after being arrested at a demonstration outside a police station in Narathiwat province. Government officials claimed that the deaths were not intended, but feelings continued to run high after the incident. In short, the separatist movement continues, but on a smaller scale than in the 1980s as a result of the government's efforts to improve integration and development. So far, the Thai government has not been able to resolve the troubles in the south.

Our analysis now turns to an assessment of the key explanatory variables used in this study. The two main actors, Thailand and Malaysia, are examined on the four dimensions: ethnic composition, institutional constraint, ethnic cleavage, and ethnic affinity.

5. Analysis and Propositions

Three distinct stages of interaction took place between Malaysia and Thailand, each marked by peaks and valleys of conflict and cooperation.

The first stage featured general receptiveness to the plight of the Thai Malay from specific groups within West Malaya, but a general lack of response from extraregional sources and the Malaysian government. Conservative and radical Malay political organizations formed with the specific goal of being incorporated into West Malaya. Their politicization increased under the centralization policies of the military-nationalist regimes of succeeding Thai governments. In the years before Malaysia's independence, the international community failed to adequately resolve the issue of Malay irredentism and Thai minority rights. For example, the United Nations would not recognize the inclusion of Patani province into a greater Malay state.

After Malaysia obtained formal independence, the second stage of interactions ensued. The Thai Malay conflict became a vigorous political issue in the context of Indonesian "confrontation" and growing concern about communist activities in Malaysia and Thailand. Initially, the leaders of both states were wary that their internal threats could be used against them by the other, as they often had been. For example, the CPM obtained sanctuary in southern Thailand, while the Malaysian government rarely denounced the support that Kelantan province continued to provide to the Thai Malay separatists. Around this time, the strategy of Thai Malay elites transformed; their irredentist goal changed to demands for greater autonomy and a separate state independent of both Malaysia and Thailand. Levels of violence increased, new movements formed, and support spread to the Middle East. Although the means of achieving it took various forms, the organizations covered the political spectrum from left to right and generally supported outright independence. The radical PULO emerged on the scene as the leading insurgent group and cooperated with the CPM in efforts to challenge both state-centers. Ethnic cleavage came to the fore.

The heightened sense of perceived difference between the Thai Buddhist community and Thailand's minorities is not difficult to explain. As in Sri Lanka, the Thai Buddhists constitute a distinct ethnic group with low linguistic or cultural affinities to groups within the region. This sense of perceived difference clearly became linked to a virulent form of Thai military-nationalism during the 1930s and 1940s. After the nationalist revolution of 1932, the Thai government undertook a program of assimilating its minorities. Under the military rule of Phibul Songkhram (1938 to 1957, with a break from 1944 to 1947), the government attempted to assimilate forcibly the Thai Malay. Thai Buddhist laws displaced Shar'ia law in the areas of marriage, dress, and diet. Forbes (1982: 1059) argues that the period marks the onset of Malay separatist sentiment. Each successive wave of Thai political centralization brought with it rebellion among the Malay elite, who had the primary goal of reestablishing authority in the region. Most government officials, at least until 1975, were Thai Buddhists; hence the dominance of Thais in the political sector. After violence in the Patani region during the mid-1970s, the first of several steps took place to alleviate the problem through, for example, appointment of a southern Muslim as governor of Patani. The penetration of the state into areas of education is particularly notable because it caused a shift in the pattern of separatist leadership from traditional Islamic leaders to Patani youth increasingly conscious of stiff competition for jobs (Thomas 1989: 75).[18]

When Malaysia's own internal threat led to the 1969 emergency, the two states arranged for peaceful comanagement of their internal problems. In turn, Thailand's military leaders did not exploit Malaysia's internal turmoil. In fact, Malaysia would be allowed hot pursuit of the CPM into Thai territory, while Malaysia would make efforts to prevent the flow of material and peoples between Kelantan province and Patani.

As the fallout from the 1969 emergency faded, renewed threats, posed by potential Vietnamese expansion into the region, became a source of concern for both governments and, in fact, all ASEAN states. During the latter half of this second stage, conflict between Thailand and Malaysia also reached a peak and focused on the sovereignty of both states. Thailand accused Malaysia of being overzealous in its pursuit of the CPM into Thai territory. Malaysian leaders countered by providing refuge for Thai Malay dissidents. It appears that even alliances designed as a means for preventing interstate ethnic conflict are sensitive to issues connected to sovereignty and transborder relations. Nevertheless, careful and coordinated government efforts, which combined military and police actions with social and economic policies, had succeeded in reducing the level of both the Thai Malay and communist insurgencies.

The third phase entailed a decline in the CPM threat and with it the Thai Malay insurgency. After the events of 1989, the PULO's original leadership also admitted defeat, replaced by new Shi'ia leaders. This transition in leadership signaled that a different kind of political movement had gained ground, one that neither Thailand nor Malaysia has proved fully capable of thwarting.

Interestingly enough, Thailand's short-lived, democratically elected government proved slightly better than the subsequent military regime in managing these tensions. The collapse of communism in Southeast Asia may be associated with the decline of class-oriented ethnic struggle and its replacement by more fundamentalist orientations. Perhaps this is because communism in Southeast Asia always had an ethnic as well as ideological character.

Largely because of the low intensity of conflict between the two states, the Thai Malay case offers a somewhat different environment within which to test the propositions. For example, Proposition P_1 focuses on the commitment of a constrained state to different strategies of intervention. Over time, Malaysian leaders developed a consistent and restrained policy of support for the Thai Malay. Although ethnic cleavage within Thailand provided an occasion for Malaysian leaders to maximize their domestic political fortunes, this did not occur. In the case of Malaysia, a diverse ethnic makeup, in combination with the threat from a communist insurgency, appears to have dampened support for the Thai Malay. Except for sporadic and ultimately unsuccessful overtures by the leaders of Kelantan province, ethnic affinities alone proved to be an insufficient justification for direct interstate conflict.

Thailand's nationalist policies, designed at first to assimilate and then integrate the Muslim community, brought the issue of Thai Malay separatism into comparative perspective. Initially, the government tried to prevent forcibly the Thai Malay from exercising control over their education, language use, and local politics. The Malay of Malaysia, by contrast, succeeded in implementing policies (i.e., NEP) that worked to their political advantage. Thus tensions between Thailand and Malaysia came from primarily domestic sources. Malaysia's NEP policy aggravated the conflict in Patani by accentuating differences between Thai Malay and Thai Buddhists. Thailand's pro-Thai, centralist policies made the situation even more intense.

By the mid-1980s, Thailand developed policies to improve the conditions of the Thai Malay so that neither a separate state nor union within Malaysia would be attractive. Horowitz (1985), among others, suggests that Thai military intervention and economic performance are related directly; a second link, connected to perceptions of internal threats, also seems to exist. For example, when the communist and Thai Malay insurgencies reached their zenith, so too did the perceived need for internal security. The lack of constraints on the leaders led to policies of unchecked assimilation. As internal threats subsided, the conditions that brought military intervention also declined. Within the past decade, effort continues toward military "civilianization," but democratization remains low.

Proposition P_2, which focuses on the relationship between diversity and pacific strategies, is supported. Evidence indicates that Malaysia's leaders deliberately set about to reduce the impact of the Thai Malay situation on their political fortunes. An important moderating effect on Malaysian nationalism in the northern provinces of West Malaysia is the country's overall multiethnic character. Territorial distinctiveness among the Malay within Malaysia is at only a moderate level, while the Chinese and the Indians are even more scattered. (This fact makes separatism a remote prospect in West Malaysia, at least for Malaysia's minorities, but this is not true for East Malaysia in relation to the federation as a whole [Suhrke and Noble 1977: 207].) Malaysia's leaders always have walked a fine line between advancing the interests of their ethnic group and reducing the negative impact of that policy on Thai-Malaysian relations. Consequently, various aspects appear in Malaysian foreign policy. Formally, Malaysian leaders have persisted in finding cooperative solutions to the conflict because West Malaysia's multiethnic character makes support for Thai Malay self-determination politically inappropriate. Malaysia until recently has been forced to consider the ramifications of such support for its other internal threat—the CPM. Informally, various Malay leaders at the national and regional level have expressed support for the Thai Malay. Material and political support from Kelantan province are noteworthy in that context.

The precise role of the Malaysian government in the resurgence of Islamic fundamentalism among the Thai Malay is less conclusive. Given that the Malaysian government persuaded the leaders of Kelantan province to reduce support for the Thai Malay, it appears that Malaysia's leaders are wary of Islamic fundamentalism. This caution may be due to the challenges that the Islamic revival poses to Malaysia's policies of economic and political restructuring. In recent years, Malaysia's leaders have distanced themselves politically from radical Islamic movements. In the Thai Malay case, the more clearly international interests become defined, the less Malaysia's leaders are constrained by mobilized interest groups and by personal investments in the strategy.

With respect to the book's framework, we argued earlier that involuntary defection, a problem for constrained, diverse states, can be reduced if the elites of these states perceive cooperation to be in their interest. For example, Kelantan represented Malaysia's potential rationale for involuntary defection.

Kelantan's support for the Thai Malay might have caused Malaysia to renege on its reciprocal agreements with Thailand. Pressure applied on Kelantan leaders, possibly along with the offering of incentives, eventually resulted in their tacit withdrawal from the issue. Malaysia, an ethnically diverse state, already tilted toward finding a cooperative solution. An alliance structure based on a shared threat enhanced the attractiveness of cooperation between Thailand and Malaysia and reduced the ethnically based security dilemma.

Several decisions suggest that Thai leaders made the Patani conflict an important component of their foreign policy. Their policies might have exacerbated tensions in the region had Malaysia's leaders responded to them in a more confrontational way. By way of contrast, Malaysia's leaders relied extensively on their working relationship with Indonesia and other ASEAN partners as a means of moderating the potential conflict. For Thailand, this included monitoring and controlling the situation in Patani province, in concert with the government in Kuala Lumpur, and seeking assurances from Malaysia and Indonesia that they would not interfere directly in the Patani conflict. Bangkok also sought and obtained support and cooperative measures from moderate states in the Middle East (e.g., Saudi Arabia) to help reduce economic and political cleavages within the southern provinces. Thai elites also showed no aversion to using Thai nationalist sentiment to their advantage. To many Thai nationalists, the right of hot pursuit granted to Malaysia symbolized the weakness of the Thai government and represented an infringement on the country's sovereignty. In general, however, the additional threat of a communist insurgency in both states moderated tensions between them. Cooperative efforts to manage that conflict, within the framework of formal alliances (ASEAN) and border agreements, had positive spillover effects for cooperation on the Thai Malay issue (May 1990).

Proposition P_3 focuses on forceful intervention and concentration of costs and benefits. According to this proposition, forceful intervention becomes more likely when there is low political resistance among constituents, particularly within ethnically dominant states. Force did not become a component of Malaysia's foreign policy against Thailand, so indirectly the proposition finds support. The evidence indicates that threats to use force, other than those directed toward the CPM, were exceptional. If, in fact, Malaysia directly supported the PULO, then that must be taken as a more subtle indicator of its willingness to use force. The evidence provided here indicates that Kelantan, not the Malaysian government, provided assistance to the rebels.

It is important to note that the greatest potential for violent interstate conflict occurred during the formation of the Malaysia Federation in 1962, when Indonesia's confrontational policies resulted in a crisis between the two states but not war (Brecher and Wilkenfeld et al. 1988). After the post-1969 emergency, relations between Malaysia and Thailand also appeared to be on a shaky footing but steadily improved into the 1980s and 1990s.

While Kelantan province supported Thai Malay self-determination, the government in Kuala Lumpur had reasons to adopt a more moderate policy. Even the proposed Federation of Malaysia plan to incorporate the Federation of Malaya (West Malaysia, Brunei, Sabah, Sarawak, and Singapore) would have worked to the disadvantage of the Thai Malay cause. The plan would have made the new federation even more multiethnic in nature. When Singapore went its own way after federation in 1965, Malaysia's ethnic political situation remained an uneasy balance between its Chinese minority and Malay.

Proposition P_4 is concerned with the role of high affinities and cleavage in exacerbating tensions between states. There is little doubt that uncertainty over rogue elements within Kelantan played a role in aggravating tensions between the two states. Lack of state control over ethnic insurgents also generated uncertainty and influenced the foreign policy strategies of key decision makers. In Malaysia's case, elected leaders proved to be sensitive to the interests of their constituents, even when these interests lay beyond its borders. However, an alternative security arrangement reduced the scope, salience, and intensity of the transborder ethnic confrontation.

Regional frameworks, developed to confront the communist threat, provided a vital and important framework in this context for cooperation between Thailand and Malaysia. At least two aborted crises are in evidence. Had the basis for cooperation been much weaker, the two states may have been less willing to put aside their differences over the Thai Malay issue. The role of transnational ethnic affinities within the cooperation/conflict continuum is significant. These linkages can create either benefits (through aid and trade) or insecurity (support for insurgencies).

Ideological linkages, for the most part, have emanated from extraregional actors, although of course Kelantan also played an important role. Evidence indicates that while these linkages constrained relations between Thailand and Malaysia, they did not prove enervating. Both states eventually could find cooperative solutions to the conflict despite perceived and real ethnically based security threats.

The answer as to why identity politics in Thailand has not resulted in an outright protracted communally based civil war that afflicts, for example, Sri Lanka, relates only partially to the fact that the minority group is far smaller with limited access to resources within the region.[19] It is conceivable that had Thai Malay ethnic strife been *the* salient security issue, conflict between

Thailand and Malaysia would have been much greater in scope and intensity. Indeed, the evidence suggests that a durable form of cooperation between states can be maintained even after the original basis for cooperation dissipates. Efforts to reduce the effects of transborder ethnic insurgencies can be successful under specific circumstances.

The collapse of communism in the region led to an important crossroads for Thailand and Malaysia. Thai authoritarianism dampened both the communist and Thai Malay insurgencies. If Thailand should become a true democratic society, alternative paths to resolving the Thai Malay and the larger Thai Muslim issue will have to be developed (de Silva et al. 1988). By addressing the Thai Malay economic situation, recent Thai governments have initiated the process of reducing disparities between the Thai Malay community and the rest of Thailand. Similarly, a more open and "permissive" Thai society also will have to find ways in which to engender toleration among Thai Buddhists for a new wave of Islamic fundamentalism in the region.

Proposition P_5 focuses on the relative likelihood of intervention among our ideal type states. In the typology from figure 2.1, Malaysia would classify as an ethnically diverse, high-constraint state, or Type II_b. Type II_b states generally adopt a relatively mild position on the autonomy of ethnic kin and try to intervene by using various moderating strategies. Ethnic interventions, therefore, take place only after careful calculation of multiple constraints and when there are strong, even overwhelming preferences among the state's ethnic groups or where a general consensus exists for involvement abroad. Thus a foreign policy based on ethnicity remains unlikely as long as elites can withstand the pressures of ethnic outbidding. Malaysia's foreign policy tends to confirm the predictions based on this typology. Malaysia's diverse constituency, and federalist institutions, decreased the probability of a risky foreign policy and increased its cooperative and towards the end "dovelike" actions. In short, Malaysia's foreign policy toward Thailand confirms the framework's expectations, namely, that the state practiced realpolitik policies.

Intervention always seemed a poor option for Malaysia not just because of ethnic diversity and institutional constraints but also due to the communist threat in the region, which forced leaders to behave prudently in advancing the interests of their constituencies. Although ethnic affinity has played some role in Malaysia's relations with Thailand, high costs and risks prevent those affinities from determining government policy.

To recapitulate, evidence from this case study and the two previous cases indicates that diversity plays a direct role in restraining state adventurism and in moderating ethnically based security dilemmas. Equally important is the nature of, and perceptions about, the ethnic threat. Under certain conditions, both sides will sense mutual vulnerability and seek out cooperation despite potentially debilitating ethnic affinities and cleavages. For example, in the previous two chapters the states involved interacted within formal but weak regional security regimes (SAARC for India and Sri Lanka, the OAU for Ethiopia and Somalia). Neither of these organizations succeeded in preventing the outbreak of interstate ethnic crisis (and war). A key difference in the Thai Malay case is that cooperation emerged out of a second, very real threat to both antagonists: communism in southeast Asia and potential Vietnamese expansion. For Sri Lanka and Ethiopia, in contrast, ethnic conflicts *defined* and shaped perceptions of India and Somalia as their chief external antagonists and main sources of insecurity.[20]

6. Conclusions

This chapter has examined the interstate dimensions of ethnic conflict in a separatist setting. The Thai Malay case is different from the other cases examined so far because of the relatively low intensity of conflict between Thailand and Malaysia and the absence of a clearly defined foreign policy crisis. The chapter summarized the evolution of Thai Malay separatism and the role of domestic and international factors in that process, which included two near crises. Historical evidence from the case study, in turn, offered general support for the propositions. In brief, three implications can be culled from this conclusion.

First, it appears that a durable form of cooperation can be maintained even after the original threat has dissipated and when the perceived threat is low. Efforts to reduce defection among states seeking to support ethnic groups in other states can be successful under specific circumstances. An alliance structure, even an informal one, enhanced the attractiveness of cooperation and reduced the ethnically based security dilemma. Since ethnically diverse, constrained states already are oriented toward finding cooperative solutions (a point made in chapter 2), the key issue is finding ways in which to restrain less diverse or institutionally unconstrained states. One way, as suggested in this study, is to pursue internal change toward greater diversity and increase the strength of political institutions. In addition, external mechanisms, cooperative agreements, and formal alliances can and do assist in reducing conflict between states who share ethnic kin. For example, the ASEAN states of Southeast Asia are now reevaluating their relationship with nonmember states.

Second, the elites of minority groups who actually benefit from conflict but foresee only interstate cooperation will be forced, as a consequence, to pursue alternative strategies that will undoubtedly involve extraregional support. The evidence for this conclusion is the three stages of strategy and leadership change adopted by the Thai Malay. The first stage was irredentist and political in nature. Regional actors played an important role in perpetuating the conflict. That strategy succumbed to cooperative agreements between the two states and the reduced mutual salience of ethnically based insecurities. In the second stage, new radical leaders pursued separatist and more violent strategies. These second-generation leaders looked farther abroad for support among conservative and radical Arab states. Initially that strategy proved unsuccessful, but gains eventually ensued on several fronts. Thai Malay leaders did obtain a greater degree of economic and political independence. In the third stage, yet to be concluded, a third generation of leaders emerged, seeking increased religious autonomy for Thai Muslims using an even more radical fundamentalist approach.

It remains to be seen whether the growth of Islamic fundamentalism will take root among the Thai Malay and become a source of renewed insecurity for both Malaysia and Thailand. Much of what happens next will depend on the ability of the Thai regime to convey the perception to the Malay of Malaysia and to the world that the country is capable of providing legitimate and tolerant leadership.

The third implication of this case is that extraregional actors are extremely important sources of support for marginalized ethnic minorities. International support directly influences changes in minority leadership pools and strategies. These may be evolving at a much faster pace than the coping mechanisms of the state-center. States that face such internal and external threats to security may become more common in the post-9/11 era. Moderate elites may come to believe that their own security is threatened and consequently take action to shore up their support or, alternatively, give way to more radical leaders who are more effective in motivating their followers.

The former Yugoslavia, 1945–1990. http://www.nytimes.com/
specials/bosnia/context/balkans-political.GIF.html

CHAPTER SIX

The Breakup of Yugoslavia and Its Immediate Aftermath

> Yugoslavia's communists tried for more than forty years to "solve" the national question. . . . [U]ltimately they failed. But their failure was not so much a failure of confederalism, but rather a failure of the concept of limited democracy, of the idea that democracy can emerge out of one-party rule. (Ramet 1992a: 279)

1. Introduction: To Balkanize Is to Europeanize

Yugoslavia is just one of the many places in which international boundaries do not coincide with those of ethnic groups. With the exception of Slovenia—which had a 90 percent Slovene population—all other states from the former Yugoslavia are quite mixed. The federal structure created in 1945 made it certain that the largest and most scattered nation, the Serbs, would not be given a sufficiently large republic to enable them to dominate others: "Equality among six republics was used to mobilize support among these national groups for the communist party and its leaders" (Pavkovic 2000: 51). However, ultimately even this strategy could not save the country from disaster.

Two dominant schools of thought exist on the causes of the Balkans war. The popular view asserts that the collapse of the Yugoslav state in 1991 reflected a general trend in post–Cold War politics. According to this explanation, ethnic antagonisms grew, prospered, and took on numerous characteristics—institutional, political, economic, and cultural—when confronted with the simultaneous tasks of political and economic liberalization. This argument is expressed effectively by Cohen (1992: 371): "[H]istorically, the potential for ethnic and religious based violence in the Balkans has been most evident during periods of regime crisis and breakdown (for example the last phase of Ottoman control leading to the Balkan wars, the final throes of Hapsburg rule and the collapse and dismemberment of the Yugoslav state in 1941)."

Less widely held is the view that sees purpose rather than inevitability in the crisis. The Yugoslav conflict did not represent a direct and certain outcome of the collapse of the Eastern Bloc countries. Nor did the origins of the conflict begin with centuries-old hatreds (Kaufman 2001). On the contrary, Yugoslavia's destruction began as late as the 1980s, with the rise to power of nationalist (as opposed to communist) leaders; the process of ethnic group polarization seems to have started as recently as fifteen years ago (Ramet 1991a; Saideman 1997). From this less common perspective, most recently advanced by Gagnon (1992, 1994, 1994/1995) and Saideman (1997), Serbian territorial and ethnic ambitions constitute a response to both domestic and international opportunities (see, in particular, Gagnon 1994, 1994/1995).

Why, despite the appearance of democratic transition, did Serbia's leaders behave in such divisive ways? Political participation and opportunities in Yugoslavia realigned quickly along narrow bands of ethnic identity (Midlarsky 1997). Coupled with the deliberate suppression of nonethnic issues and unfolding opportunities, the policy options narrowed systematically, which led to interethnic confrontation, crisis, and war.

This chapter assesses the extent to which domestic and international factors conditioned the behavior of key actors in the Balkans conflict, with a principal focus on Serbian and Croatian involvement and some attention to the Slovene and Bosnian cases as well.

The Yugoslavia case is significant for two reasons. First, like the Thai Malay case, elements of both secessionism and irredentism are present. However, the relationship between these types of ethnic strife is the inverse of the Thai Malay case. Whereas irredentist impulses eventually gave way to separatism in the case of the Southeast Asian conflict, separatism sensu stricto (secession), heralded by the breakup of the Yugoslav federation, was followed by efforts at territorial retrieval on the part of Serbian and Croatian regimes. Second, in terms of ethnic diversity, institutional constraints, cleavage, and affinity, the main components of the framework, the Yugoslav case is significantly different. The Balkan conflict provides an opportunity to examine ethnically based security issues from the opposite end of the theoretical spectrum, namely, from the perspective of a Type I_a state.

As described in chapter 2, Type I_a states have low institutional constraints and a dominant ethnic group. Elites therefore can mobilize the population through manipulation of group symbols in order to pursue foreign policy goals. Foreign and domestic policies are designed to appeal to the dominant ethnic group, but not in a way that would threaten the power base of elites. Since elites are unconstrained, they tend not to worry about the ramifications of policy choices. Therefore, Type I_a is associated with *belligerence* in figure 2.1.

After this introduction, the analysis is carried out in five additional parts.

In the second section, the historical background to the current conflict is presented. The third section is an analysis of the precrisis period, including key decisions taken. The fourth section examines the crisis period and focuses on the three "theaters"—Slovenia, Croatia, and Bosnia. The fifth section conveys the analysis and tests the propositions. Conclusions are offered in the sixth and final section.

Faced with the task of disentangling several distinct theater-based crises, namely, the secessionist crises of Slovenia and Croatia and Bosnian irredentism/secessionism, one simplifying procedure is adopted. To provide an account that maintains the continuity, flow, and contextual integrity of the entire Yugoslav crisis, each of the theater-based components will be treated as a separate but integral series of events in the larger Yugoslavian conflict. Phases and periods specific to each crisis will be disaggregated for purposes of clarity, although some events occurred simultaneously.

For two reasons, this analysis addresses the component parts of the individual crises and wars within the broader framework of interstate ethnic conflict. First, at a theoretical level it is important to see how aspects of the framework relate to varying combinations of opportunities and constraints as presented in each specific conflict. Second, the Yugoslav crisis started a civil war, albeit a complex one, which turned into an interstate conflict when Slovenia, Croatia, and Bosnia became de facto states, processes that occurred while conflicts got underway in each crisis theater. In this sense, the war in Yugoslavia began as a civil war—a foreign policy crisis for Yugoslavia—but escalated to an interstate ethnic conflict (i.e., an international crisis) as each of its republics declared independence (Ramet 1992b; Riga 1992).

2. History and Background to the Crisis:
   The Panther and the Lynx

Figure 6.1 shows a time line for the Yugoslav conflict that begins with the end of World War II and carries through to the present. Tito maintained cohesion within Yugoslavia through the idea of "panslavism," which had both domestic and international imperatives. Throughout the 1950s, Tito worked very hard to create Yugoslav national unity by reducing the rights of the republics while simultaneously increasing power at the center. This artificially created unity of the South Slavs was the main reason behind the coherent internal structure in Yugoslavia for a long time. Union served to insulate the region from outside interference and promised a harmonious vision of the future that was better and more peaceful than before.

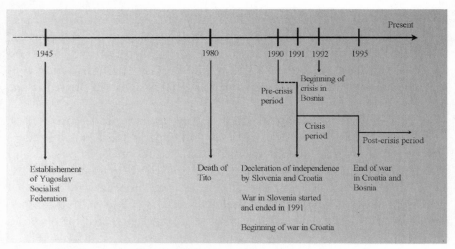

Figure 6.1. The Yugoslavia Conflict

As the epigraph to this chapter observes, while ethnic nationalism provided the foundation for Yugoslav politics, socialism continued to exist as a closed system in which an elite bureaucracy strictly controlled public opinion and ideology, and the country never developed a tradition of legitimate democratic rule of the kind that would permit the cultural and social emergence of a Yugoslav, as opposed to particularist, elite (Flere 1991). In brief, Yugoslav politics always reflected a monopoly over certain institutions by specific ethnic groups, which fits the definition of a "patronage democracy" from Chandra (2004: 6): "a democracy in which the state monopolizes access to jobs and services, *and* in which elected officials have discretion in the implementation of laws allocating the jobs and services at the disposal of the state."

Particular identities and competing visions of the future among Yugoslavia's various ethnic groups developed most significantly during the decade immediately after Tito's death in 1980. The confederal structures instituted under his power gradually ceded more and more power to the republics. Subsequent inability of the leaders of these republics to develop a national policy consensus can be traced to the rise to power of Serb nationalist leaders and the failure of the other republics to pursue policies that would balance this domination (Midlarsky 1997). Reformists, who held firmly to the view that the constitution and economy could be restructured along existing political arrangements, became discredited by their failure to respond effectively to Yugoslavia's economic collapse. These leaders could match neither the populist appeal of ethnic leaders nor their political visions that promised for Croatians and Slovenians a potentially greater role in the Western economic system, and for Serbs the opportunity to control the destiny of the South Slav peoples (Glenny 1992c).

Balancing against competing claims had been effective in the past, largely because the communist leaders of the republics had a common interest in cooperation to ensure their preservation. Mainstream elements in the elite succumbed to leaders with more narrowly defined interests. The inherent problem in this arrangement, as Lake and Rothchild (1996, 1998) observe, is that the potential for intransigence among leaders whose power derives from ethnic sensibilities is very high. At some point there are, at least for the leaders, greater benefits to be had in whittling away at a decentralized structure than maintaining it. As the Yugoslav case exemplifies, these perceptions do not always converge at once; Serbia showed reluctance to embrace change, with Croatia and Slovenia clearly more open to it.

The failure of Yugoslavia's leaders to preserve national unity in the post-communist state can be attributed to the presence of several significant factors, which included (a) a society that was never fully integrated, retaining instead a basic segmentary quality and lacking the infrastructure of a civil society; (b) the existence of socially separate and culturally different systems throughout the republics and provinces; and (c) widespread economic disparities between the republics. It would be erroneous, at the same time, to attribute the sources of the conflict to any single structural factor without paying heed to the political ambitions of specific ethnic leaders.

Yugoslavia's ethnic configuration had ramifications not only for its viability as a state but also at the level of the various republics and provinces. These historical, demographic, and political antecedents are all important components of the ongoing conflict. Each is considered in turn.[1]

2.1 The Battlefield of History

Observers of Yugoslav politics note that processes of integration and disintegration tend to be cyclical. On the one hand, successive efforts by Serbian leaders to bring a unified Yugoslavia under Serbian control take place. On the other hand, different groups, mainly the Croatians, always seek autonomy from the Serb-dominated center. Quests for majority status and protection of minority rights have been dominant features of Yugoslavia's political terrain; these tendencies emerge with the Ottoman and Hapsburg Empires and development of Catholicism and a common language (Cohen 1992; *Globe and Mail*, 19 June 1993).[2]

Yugoslavian territory fell under Habsburg rule in the thirteenth century. In the fourteenth century, the Ottoman Empire began to conquer the southern and eastern parts. For a long time fighting continued over this Balkan land. Until the eighteenth century the Ottoman Empire extended its boundaries against the Habsburgs and basically dominated the area. However, after the eighteenth century, the Habsburg Empire started to regain its power, and with the Ottoman Empire already in decline, they recaptured some areas. During the First World War, both the Ottoman and Habsburg empires (known as Austria-Hungary after 1867) collapsed. Germany and Russia lost territory and gained new forms of government as a result of the war. In the center of Europe, small independent states started to emerge. When the national council of Slovenes, Croats, and Serbs declared the independence of the State of Slovenes, Croats, and Serbs from Austria-Hungary, Yugoslavia became one of these independent states (Pavkovic 2000; Rogel 1998).

Northern regions of Croatia and Slovenia, which fell under Austrian and Hungarian control, adopted Roman Catholicism and the Latin alphabet. When the southern regions—Serbia, Bosnia-Herzegovina, Montenegro, and Macedonia—came under the Byzantine and later Turkish Ottoman empires, they converted to Orthodox Christianity—or in some cases Islam—and started to use the Cyrillic alphabet (Banac 1984). Composed of distinct religions, these two main groups are as different as the panther and the lynx (West 1941). Although they practice different creeds, Croats, Serbs, and Muslims share a common language, Serbo-Croatian, brought about by the unifying efforts of the Austro-Hungarian Empire.

Waves of external control impacted upon on these disparate pockets of regional nationalities in two ways. First, the collapse of the Ottoman Empire at the end of the nineteenth century effectively created "oases" of Muslim communities within the southern half of Yugoslavia. Second, the Yugoslav dream of a Slavic state, elaborated mainly by Croatian intellectuals at the beginning of the nineteenth century, took hold (Cohen 1992, 1993). Both the Serbs and the Croats saw each other as oppressed brothers. They believed that the two main religious groups, after throwing off imperial shackles in the late-nineteenth and early- twentieth centuries, could rediscover their commonality and live together under one national roof. The Tsarist Russian Empire strongly supported the unity of Slavic groups. In the course of its dealings with the then-major powers, Russia also attempted to superimpose "panslavism" over Yugoslavia (Stavrou 1976). However, the idea of a union of South Slav peoples attracted little popular support except from the Serbs, the largest among them, who regarded inclusion of the Croats, the Slovenes, and the Macedonians within the borders of an expanded state as fulfillment of their destiny (Stavrou 1976).

As mentioned earlier, in 1918 a unified Yugoslav state, which brought together several South Slav and non-Slav ethnic groups, was created. Serbia annexed Bosnia-Herzegovina in that same year. At that point, the Versailles Treaty established Yugoslavia's borders, but the state did not adopt the name of Yugoslavia until 1929, retaining instead the official name, "the Kingdom of Serbs, Croats and Slovenes" (Stavrou 1976: 137). Belgrade became the capital of the new Yugoslav state. Under the auspices of a constitutional monarchy and unitary government, Yugoslavia fell under Serbian control.

The Second World War ended with the victory of the communist party in Yugoslavia. In addition, Yugoslavia became a federation of six republics—Croatia, Macedonia, Serbia, Slovenia, Montenegro, Bosnia-Herzegovina—and two autonomous units—Kosovo and Vojvodina (both in Serbia). The war also intensified underlying ethnic tensions. The primary ongoing problems reflect wartime atrocities perpetrated among the Serbian and Croatian communities. In 1941, after invading Yugoslavia, Germany set up a puppet regime in Croatia under Ante Pavelic, head of the fascist Ustase, which herded Jews, Gypsies, and Serbs into concentration camps. In retribution, royalist Serbian guerrillas, known as Chetniks, destroyed Croatian villages. Serbia already had lost a quarter of its population in the First World War and an estimated half million more during World War Two (Ramet 1992b).

Yugoslavia's ethnic demography by the end of the Second World War became more or less fixed in composition. Ethnically diverse parts of Croatia and Bosnia served as illustrations of peaceful coexistence.[3] When Tito broke off the provinces of Vojvodina and Kosovo from the Republic of Serbia and drew new federal boundaries that left millions of Serbs outside its rule, Serbian angst increased. The Serbs then maintained their status as the most numerous ethnic group in Yugoslavia (36 percent of the entire population) but never formed an absolute majority (Flere 1991).[4] They comprised a majority within Serbia (65 percent) itself but not in the province of Kosovo, for example (only 13 percent), where in recent years their numbers have diminished rapidly.[5]

2.2 The Politics of Presecessionist Yugoslavia

Under Tito, the son of Croat and Slovene parents, Yugoslavia emerged as a federation of six reasonably equal republics. Despite its federal nature, Yugoslavia became more centralized than ever under his rule. Disputes often arose concerning ethnic policy and the methods for advancing ethnic group interests. For example, the Tito version of liberalized communism endorsed regional but not political pluralism (Ramet 1992b). In essence, this meant that Yugoslavia would have two core domestic policy principles and one foreign policy principle. In the case of domestic policies, these were self-management embodied in workers' councils, brotherhood and unity (i.e., the doctrine of ethnic harmony through one-party rule), and a unique path to development, as with economic and social reforms initiated soon after the break with Moscow in 1948. On the foreign policy front, the principle of nonalignment became the cornerstone of Yugoslavia's orientation to the East and West. One of the key purposes of nonalignment derived from domestic concerns, namely, to prevent foreign sponsorship of national conflicts in Yugoslavia. This foreign policy implicitly assumed that ethnic groups would serve as links with their kin across borders and thus help to improve relations with bordering states (Stavrou 1976).

Tito's version of liberalized communism addressed ethnic relations on both domestic and international fronts. The main political structure resembled a federalist, balance-of-power system, characterized by a shifting pattern of flexible coalitions (Ramet 1992a). Under Tito, "the Federal government in Yugoslavia often functioned as *primus inter pares* in a nine-actor universe" (Ramet 1992a: 277). This meant in theory that participation of all ethnic groups in decision making at the federal level had been provided for, with unanimous approval required through interrepublican committees.

At the end of the 1960s and the beginning of the 1970s, decision making shifted from the federation to the republics. A key feature of the federal system in its early years (i.e., 1962–66) had been mobilization of all federal units into the system, previously dominated by Croatia and Serbia (Midlarsky 1997). With the constitution of 1974, Yugoslavia turned into a de facto semiconfederation of semisovereign republics when the federal government became a joint committee of the six republics and two autonomous republics (Slovenia, Croatia, Serbia, Bosnia-Herzegovina, Montenegro, Macedonia, Kosovo, and Vojvodina). Vojvodina and Kosovo, the autonomous provinces within Serbia after the Second World War, acquired a dual status with this constitution, not only as parts of the federation but also as constituents of Serbia. (This technically means that they had equal status with other republics.) According to Ramet (1992a: 277), "Tito hoped to hold together a 'liberal system' not by force but by a common ideology, the ideology of 'conservatism.'" A unified party and dependable instruments of coercion became the two pillars of Tito's nationalities policy (Stavrou 1976).

Until this time, the political landscape had been dominated by Serb-Croat rivalries. Afterward, all of the republics began to engage in a pattern of shifting coalitions. Usually the underdeveloped republics allied with Croatia and Slovenia against Serbia on political issues. This system of shifting coalitions held together largely because of Tito's astute courting of both liberal and conservative contingents within the central apparatus. All component units, regardless of population, territory, or economic power, had equal representation not only in both chambers of the Federal Assembly, but in all federal decision-making bodies including the presidency of the state; this turned out to be an important feature of federalism in practice (Stanovcic 1992).

After Yugoslavia's independence, the central government in Belgrade faced the difficult task of addressing regional economic disparities among six republics and two regions. These disparities broke down along the main ethnic lines in the 1980s, which made the task even more difficult.

Yugoslav federalism's main deficiency was not the distribution of power between the federation and the constituent republics. The real limitation came from actual participation of republics in framing policy (Stanovcic 1992). The federation's multiethnic configuration and disparate levels of modernization, which presented successive Yugoslavian regimes with a narrow field of policy options, proved to be a key deficiency (Ramet 1992a).

Nationalist leaders who tried to advance the interests of their specific ethnic group began to emerge on the political scene. According to Ramet (1992a, 1992b), Croatia and Serbia often allied on economic issues but consistently opposed each other on political issues. In turn, the underdeveloped republics allied with each other on economic issues, and Slovenia and Croatia did so on political issues. For its part, the federal government, interested perhaps more than anything else in stability, tended to side with the preponderant bloc (Ramet 1992a).

While the central government remained the legitimate arbiter of Yugoslavian political and economic issues, the system worked. When the Yugoslav economy faltered after Tito's death in 1980, reform-minded middle-level bureaucrats waged a policy-based war against nationalist conservatives. Serbian nationalists and conservatives, including Slobodan Milosevic, an executive of an energy firm, came to the forefront of this struggle. However, economic decline and social unrest were not the only factors that led to the collapse of the Yugoslav political and constitutional system. Stability could not be achieved in spite of federal government efforts; the rise of nationalism and increasing ethnic polarization threatened the balance of power among national elites (Pavkovic 2000). One specific incident, as will become apparent, stands out as a precipitant to later conflicts.

When Albanian inhabitants of Kosovo province protested the failure of the Belgrade government to establish an effective and coherent economic policy in 1981, Serb leaders used this confrontation as a pretext for seizing land from ethnic Albanians. Conservative communist factions within the Serbian party organization stage-managed an internal coup in December 1987, which brought to power Milosevic and ousted most reform-minded politicians from the Serbian party leadership. It did not take long for significant changes to occur; Milosevic saw the opportunity here. He used the Kosovo situation in order to control the Serbian communist party in September 1987, and later he limited the autonomy of Kosovo and Vojvodina. Even more interesting is that while seizing the opportunity, he also issued a manifesto framing the Serbs as an oppressed and endangered people (Ramet 1992b). Prepared by members of the Serbia Academy of Sciences, the manifesto portrayed Serbia as an imperiled victim of an "anti-Serbian coalition" (Ramet 1992a). Since the late 1960s, Serbs were scared by the possibility that they would lose control in Kosovo. After these events, Serbian nationalism continued to rise and the fear of the non-Serbian population reached its peak (Rogel 1998).

As noted earlier, in 1988 and 1989 the Serbian communist party had succeeded in gaining power in Kosovo, Vojvodina, and Montenegro. In the wake of failure by the Communist Party's elders to assert firm control over Serbian conservatives, other regional nationalist leaders jumped to take advantage of the new confederalism. This process became highly visible when the Yugoslav economy collapsed in 1988 and vitriolic nationalism increasingly dictated the federal government's choices. In this context of political weakness, new agendas began to emerge along ethnic lines from the non-Serb republics as well.

In brief, the Yugoslav federation ultimately failed to frame coherent domestic and foreign policies because of Serb dominance in the decision-making process (Gagnon 1994). The internal balance of power, which had brought stability to Yugoslavia, collapsed under the weight of ethnic opportunism. In 1989, the Yugoslav Communist Party began to fracture along ethnic lines. Enmeshed within these processes was the monopolization of certain institutions by specific ethnic groups (Gagnon 1992, 1994/95). Subsequent inability of the leaders of the republics to develop a national consensus on policy can be traced to the rise to power of Serb nationalist leaders and failure of the other republics to pursue balancing policies (Ramet 1992a, 1992b). The emergence of nationalist leaders, chiefly concerned with advancing the interests of their ethnic group, followed the failure of Tito's heir to find a way out of the country's serious economic and political problems.[6]

Yugoslavia by the early 1990s had shifted from a society based on balancing, engendered by decentralized constitutional arrangements, to one in which ethnic control and coercion became central. Slovenian and Croatian leaders quickly took advantage of the formally decentralized structure of both the Yugoslav Communist Party and the state to develop their own strategies for crisis management and reform.

In response, the Belgrade regime shifted toward more coercive measures in an effort to neutralize and marginalize the main threat to Serbian domination: democratic and reformist appeals to greater representation of minorities. Subsequent efforts to create an enlarged Serbia ensured a greater majority of Serbs (who are distributed throughout the republics), and that secured both the continuing existence of the conservative ruling party's hold on power and preservation of the existing power structure (Gagnon 1994, 1994/95)

Reformers, in the waning days of Yugoslavia's life, held fast to the view that the constitution and economy could be restructured along existing political arrangements.[7] The failure of reformist policies to take hold discredited them and their followers. These leaders could match neither the populism of ethnic elites nor their political visions. When power derives from ethnic sensibilities, there is an inherent problem: a high potential for intransigence among leaders. At some point, the benefits from weakening the decentralized structure exceed those of maintaining it (Saideman 1997, 1998b). Domestic ambition then transforms into international conflict.

3. Precrisis: The Road to Secession, April 1990 to 25 June 1991

Multiparty elections occurred throughout the country from April to December 1990 (*Globe and Mail,* 11 December 1990). By the fall of 1990, Slovenia, Croatia, and Bosnia-Herzegovina came under noncommunist rule and Macedonia, under a coalition government with a communist minority. Only in Serbia and Montenegro did the communists continue to hold on to power, and those in Serbia already had distanced themselves from Tito by undertaking a strategy that embraced all ethnic Serbs under the Socialist Party of Serbia (SPS). In Serbia the SPS managed to win 62 percent of the seats and then set its sights on Serbian interests elsewhere, especially in Croatia and Slovenia (Gagnon 1994).

Nationalist political mobilization in Yugoslav politics ended up bringing many new faces to power. In the past, all political elites had the same kind of interest and shared Yugoslav ideology, which held the country together. However, new communist national elites had very different political interests, and this facilitated fragmentation. The newly elected governments led by Kucan in Slovenia and Tudjman in Croatia wanted to achieve a "confederation of sovereign states" and insisted on the right to secede (Kaufmann 2001; Pavkovic 2000). In this sense, elections can be seen as the end of the period of political fragmentation—under way since the 1960s—and the beginning of the political impasse (Pavkovic 2000).

Two points of contention emerged between the new leaders of the republics. First, who would control the army? (Midlarsky 1997). More specifically, for Serb leaders with an interest in Slovenia, the question referred to control over the Territorial Defense Forces (established by Tito)—the Slovenian Government versus the Yugoslavian National Army (JNA), then under Serbian control (Saideman 1998b). The second point of contention, in Croatia, concerned finding a response to the Serbian question. The Serbian minority already had begun to protest against Croatian political dominance. In response, Belgrade engineered the takeover of Croatia's Serbian party (SDS) by hard-line forces, known as the Krajina, in the Croatian region of Dalmatia. Any Serbs willing to negotiate with Zagreb over their status within Croatia became discredited by the words of the SDS and SPS (Croatia's Serbian party) (Saideman 1998b).

After the elections, the idea of unilateral declaration gained popularity in Slovenia and Croatia. Such a declaration, however, not only would breach the territorial unity of Yugoslavia, but also stimulate a military confrontation with the Yugoslavian National Army (JNA). At the same time, Serbs in the Krajina Region in Croatia would be expected to resist the idea of independence and try to keep their ties with Yugoslavia and Serbia (Pavkovic 2000).

By May 1990, neither the Slovenian nor Croatian governments were ready militarily to fight (or in case of Croatia, with Serb rebels supported by Serbs [Pavkovic 2000]). Therefore, instead of announcing independence right away, both governments tried to negotiate "with other republican leaders the transformation of Yugoslavia into a confederation of sovereign states while, at the same time, building up their own military forces for any future showdown with their opponents" (Pavkovic 2000: 125).

Armed by the JNA, the SDS-led Croatian Serb minority established numerous enclaves, blocked roads, and seized control of the local facilities by April 1991. In Kosovo, a harsh crackdown by the Serbian government stimulated further Albanian riots. Serb intransigence signaled a decisive shift in Serbian crisis management strategy. Belgrade characterized events in Kosovo and Krajina as "inter-ethnic fighting," thereby necessitating the immediate intervention of the army. In reality, the SPS wanted to bring all Serbs under one state and used these conflicts as a pretext for intervention. To recentralize the system, one that worked to the advantage of the Serbs, Milosevic suggested that force might be necessary. Croatia and Slovenia, by contrast, still held to the now-crumbling dream that the system could be fully decentralized, with retention of only an economic union and coordination in foreign policy and military matters (Ramet 1992b).

When the Slovenian and Croatian governments declared that they wanted to assert sovereignty for their republics and have a confederation of sovereign states, the president's response was clear. Assigning any special rights to nations would not be acceptable under any circumstances (Pavkovic 2000; Cohen 1992, 1993). After that reply, on 23 December, Slovenians voted for independence. The Slovenian president made it public that Slovenia no longer wanted to be a part of a confederal Yugoslavia that could not safeguard its independence (Kaufman 2001).

According to Pavkovic (2000: 128), at the time of independence, Serbs constituted an absolute majority in eleven municipalities of the Krajina region and substantial minorities in fourteen municipalities in Western and Eastern Slavonia. Therefore, in January 1991, the Serb Autonomous Region of Krajina became established in four Serb-controlled areas. In May 1991, the Krajina area of Western Croatia proclaimed unification with Serbia, but the Serbian parliament refused to accept this assertion. Serbs in that region got support and aid from Milosevic and his government in different forms. This support came in the first of many attacks on Croatian populations as well as uncooperative Serbs and signaled the beginning of "ethnic cleansing."[8]

On 25 June 1991, Croatia and then Slovenia declared independence from Yugoslavia. With Yugoslavia's territorial integrity threatened, Belgrade issued a warning statement to the Slovenian and Croatian governments. It called the republics' actions illegal and ordered the national army (JNA) and police units to seize control posts along Slovenia's borders (Ramet 1992b).

4. The Yugoslav Crisis

4.1 The Slovenian Crisis Theater—26 June to 6 July 1991

Leaders of Yugoslavia's six republics held a series of meetings on 26 June 1991 designed to avert a crisis.[9] The two chief antagonists, Slovenia and Serbia at this time, showed no sign of compromise. Slovenia and Croatia announced that unless some interrepublican agreement could be reached on a new political formula for Yugoslavia, they would terminate their association with the federation. These statements claimed to be not unilateral acts of secession but declarations of sovereignty in which the authority of the federal organs, including the army, would continue to be recognized.[10] Milosevic opposed outright secessionism but not the idea of a confederation. The large Serbian contingent in the country's military establishment shared this view. However, Milosevic maintained the idea that Serbia needed to continue its support for the unity of Serbs and particularly the large Serb communities in Croatia and Bosnia. If self-determination for other ethnic groups did not infringe on the same right of Serbs, Milosevic could be supportive. If necessary, Milosevic would transform the borders of Croatia and Bosnia-Herzegovina to protect Serb minorities (Gagnon 1994/1995; Saideman 1998b). Leaders of Bosnia and Macedonia, who sensed the importance of international support in case Milosevic implemented his plans for a greater Serbia, made overtures to the European Community in spite of their preferences also to declare independence (Ramet 1992b).

Under instructions from Milosevic, Yugoslavia's prime minister, Markovic, called for the JNA to take control of all international borders.[11] By that time, however, the federal army was in the process of weakening significantly. Slovenia, starting from autumn 1990, declared its national guards separate from the JNA and began to increase its arms supply. Similarly, Croatia was busy buying special weapons for its forces. As discussed earlier, Serbia had great influence on the JNA throughout the dissolution period (Rogel 1998).

Under a 1990 mutual defense pact, Tudjman and Slovenian leaders had agreed to coordinate defense and security policies. When the JNA entered into a ten-day war with Slovenian forces, however, the Croats did not heed the agreement and remained neutral. They feared that involvement would provoke escalation of the conflict.[12] At this stage, international engagement in the Slovenian crisis remained restricted to attempts at mediation in several cease-fires and imposition of sanctions on what then still existed as the state of Yugoslavia.[13]

By mid-July the JNA had moved to Croatia, where intermittent fighting in Serbian-held enclaves—Krajina and Slavonia—already had been underway (Ramet 1992b). Even without the assistance of Croatia, Slovenian forces managed to defeat units of the JNA in a short time period. Additionally, the JNA faced a major international protest. Thus, the Yugoslav president ordered termination of military action and initiated negotiations with the Slovenian government to reach a cease-fire. However, until EC intervention, all attempts at cease-fire failed (Pavkovic 2000). In early July 1991 the European Community (EC) successfully negotiated a cease-fire and an agreement that provided for a three-month moratorium on further moves toward independence by Croatia and Slovenia. The agreement also included EC-sponsored negotiations among the republics about their future. As for crisis abatement, the war in Slovenia effectively ended and JNA forces agreed to withdraw from Slovenia on 18 July 1991. With the withdrawal process completed on 26 October 1991, Slovenia reiterated its declaration of independence.

The Serb decision to withdraw from Slovenia had two important effects. First came spillover of the conflict into Croatia and Bosnia-Herzegovina, triggered by the JNA's decision to step up operations in Serb-dominated areas in the two republics. The second effect consisted of the impact that escalation had on Serbian opposition in Serbia. The war had polarized Serbian society, and a civil war appeared imminent (*Economist*, 5–11 June 1993). With the JNA firmly behind him, Milosevic's political position remained solid, partly because organization among Serb moderates continued to be in shambles and any hopes of a confederal Yugoslavia dissolved with it. Criticism of Milosevic or the army was portrayed as treason or as an attempt to "split the Serbian nation" (Ramet 1992b).

In sum, Slovenia's road to independence, with fewer than seventy Slovenians killed, was relatively short, easy, and less bloody as compared to the efforts of other republics in Yugoslavia. When the military conflict shifted to Croatia, Yugoslavia's civil war—a foreign policy crisis characterized by internal threats to its integrity—had become a full interstate ethnic conflict (Sciolino 1993).

4.2 The Croatian Crisis Theater—20 May 1991 to August 1995

Like the Yugoslav-Slovene war, which set the stage for the Croat-Serbian war, this conflict can be characterized as the event that set the stage for violence in Bosnia. The Croat-Serbian war started with secession of Krajina from Croatia in 1991 and ended with the Croatian army's recapture of these areas in 1995.

Croatia received diplomatic recognition from Austria and Germany on 14 January 1992. Yugoslavia, therefore, no longer existed de facto.[14] Only a rump state, consisting of Serbia and Montenegro, remained.[15] Sporadic fighting, led by Serbian irregulars determined to secede from Croatia, spread rapidly. The Serb-dominated JNA laid siege to and bombarded key Croatian cities. Vukovar was hit hardest, while Zagreb escaped relatively unscathed.

On 25 August, 1991, Tudjman, president of Croatia, responded to the JNA offensive by saying that, if the JNA did not stop helping Serb rebels in Croatia and withdraw by the end of August, he would declare the army an occupying force (*Globe and Mail*, 26 August 1991: A1). This statement signaled a shift among Croatian leaders; they showed willingness to escalate the crisis to a full-scale interstate war.

By September 1991, Croatia had lost control of large chunks of its terri-
tory either through slow advances made by the Federal Army or by loss of
Serb-held territory that seceded from Croatia as enthusiasm for quitting
Yugoslavia grew. In a radio interview, Milosevic reinforced the point that
Croatian independence would not be accepted "unless the Serbs who live in
the republic are permitted to secede" (*Globe and Mail*, 24 September 1991:
A1). He continued to hold to the argument that the JNA was being used sole-
ly to pull the two sides apart.

At this juncture, the government in Zagreb pleaded for international intervention. In response, the EC remained divided. Germany and Austria advocated both immediate recognition of Croatia and Slovenia and expanded EC
involvement, while Britain and France urged a more cautious approach.
NATO first declared the crisis to be an out-of-conflict area and would not
take action at that time (Cohen 1992, 1993). NATO eventually altered its
constitution so that it could provide military assistance to nonmilitary multilateral organizations, which led to the July 1992 deployment of naval forces
in the Adriatic Sea to assist in sanctions against Serbia. Throughout the fall,
the EC, which appointed Lord Carrington as its crisis representative,
attempted a series of unsuccessful cease-fires. In reality, both sides used the
cease-fires to reinforce their existing positions (*Globe and Mail*, 18
September 1991: A1).

On 5 October, both Croatia and Slovenia proceeded to full independence.
Implementation of their previous independence declarations had been placed
on hold for three months as quid pro quo in the peace negotiations
(*Economist*, 5 October 1991: 12). At the same time, federal army barracks
came under siege in Croatian cities (*Globe and Mail*, 24 September 1991:
A1). By November, Serb-dominated forces controlled almost 35 percent of
Croatia. Ethnically mixed regions became the preserves of either Serbs or
Croatians. The embattled cities of Dubrovnik and Vukovar fell under Serbian
control. The enfeebled and barely operating Yugoslavian presidency, under
Stipe Mesic, requested that UN peacekeeping troops be sent to Croatia and
ordered the army to return to barracks. Both pleas were ignored.

Finally, after four months of brokered mediation efforts and at least fifteen
failed cease-fires, the EC turned its mission over to the United Nations. The
UN, which previously remained on the sidelines because of its own divisions
about the propriety of intervening in a seemingly domestic conflict, successfully negotiated a truce between the leaders of Croatia and Serbia in late
November. Under pressure from Belgrade, Serb-led forces in Croatia reluc-
tantly had to agree to the plan. Croatian leaders expressed concern about UN
involvement; they wanted a six-month deployment of UN forces and argued

that any long-term deployment would allow Serbian irregulars to reinforce control of their territory. It was decided that the UN peacekeeping mission in Croatia would end on 21 February 1993. The cease-fire called for UN peacekeepers to patrol the one-third of Croatia held by Serbs, called for restoration of those areas to Croatian control, and endorsed the right of an estimated 200,000 Croats, who fled during the fighting in 1991, to return home (*Globe and Mail*, 29 January 1993: A1). By the time of the last UN cease-fire, 10,000 people had been killed, 30,000 soldiers and civilians had been wounded, and 730,000 (230,000 Serbs and 500,000 Croats) had become refugees.

Established in early 1992 as an interim measure to create the conditions of peace and security required for the EC-initiated negotiation of an overall settlement to the Croatian crisis, the United Nations Protection Force (UNPROFOR) responded to the disintegrating situation in Yugoslavia. It evolved into a traditional disengagement mission in Croatia, a humanitarian support mission in Bosnia and Herzegovina, and a small observation mission in Macedonia (*New York Times*, 14, 15, 18 1992: A1).

In Croatia, UNPROFOR initially separated the two opposing groups. Rogel (1998: 26) interpreted this as follows: "In a way, the UN safeguarded Serb military gains, allowing Milosevic to attend to other matters." Simultaneously, Croats hoped to get these Serb-held areas back, which eventually would occur in August 1995.

After a Croatian cease-fire was in place and peace talks had started at a permanent conference in Geneva, Milosevic's stance regarding union with Serbians in Croatia softened substantially. He cited the UN intervention as "the beginning of a peaceful solution to the Yugoslav crisis" (*New York Times*, 29 February 1992: A1). On 27 February 1992, Milosevic declared the war to be over. The Croat leader, Tudjman, ordered the demobilization of twenty thousand reservists, which signaled a decisive deescalation in tensions in the crisis. This transformation can be attributed to two factors.

First, Serbia had undergone catastrophic economic difficulties during the war. Prices in May 1992 rose 1,915.7 percent higher than in May 1991, and the inflation rate stood at 80.5 percent (Ramet 1992b). Faced with increased domestic pressure from hard-line political opponents, the cease-fire provided Milosevic the opportunity to address both Serbia's economic woes and his opponents.[16]

Second, international involvement, including recognition of Slovenian and Croatian independence, indicated that Serbia ultimately would be portrayed as the aggressor in the Balkan War.[17] World opinion already had shifted against Serbia, and Milosevic proved quite willing to leave Croatia's Serbs hanging in the balance to bolster his world image.

Both Tudjman and Milosevic purveyed the image that extremists in all camps constituted the greatest threat to the peaceful management of the conflict. This was true especially in Croatia, where the Serbs of Krajina repeatedly failed to comply with the UN agreement. How Milosevic and Tudjman responded to these extreme pressures can be understood best in events that followed the collapse of the UN peace plan twelve months later. These events are discussed below.

On 2 August 1992, President Franjo Tudjman returned to power in Croatia's first elections since declaring its independence a year earlier.[18] Centralization gave the leader increased freedom to pursue his twin strategies of reclaiming Serb-held Croatian territory and obtaining Croat-dominated territory in Bosnia. More specifically, Tudjman wanted to press Croatian Serbs to accept the creation of an autonomous Serb region under Croatian control. The Serbs, for their part, wanted to be part of a greater Serbia, which was not adjacent to all of the areas of Croatia that they controlled.

Faced with upper-house elections in January 1993, Tudjman intentionally took a risk that at once would bolster his support at home and take advantage of a supportive international community. Tudjman's adroit playing of the Serbian card served as an important part of this calculus. Realizing that Milosevic's greatest international interest was to portray himself as a "peacemaker," Tudjman calculated—correctly—that attacks on Serb-held enclaves would not be matched by military reinforcements from Serbia. Thus, on 22 January 1993, Croatia's army launched an offensive to retake territory held by Serbs in southern Croatia (*Globe and Mail,* 13 February 1993: A1). The important strategic role played by the Krajinas came to the fore as the crucial overland link between the capital Zagreb and Dalmatia along Croatia's Adriatic coast.

Justification for the offensive into the Krajina, shielded by UNPROFOR troops, derived from the belief that the UN had failed to oversee the return of Serb-held areas of Croatia to the Croatian government. Tudjman's calculation of the outcome proved to be astute. Milosevic and the international community reacted weakly; furthermore, the UN did not match condemnation of the attack with any punitive action. A second attack on the remaining parts of the Krajina, this time forcing ethnic Serbs to flee their homeland, occurred in August 1995. The mission succeeded dramatically; all of the Krajinas were retaken, save Brcko, which remained a neutral city under the watchful eye of NATO and the OSCE (Organization for Security and Cooperation in Europe) until such time it could be determined to whom the city should be returned.[19]

The Croatian offensive against Serb-held territory was matched by an effort to stake a claim to territory in Bosnia. As Croatian forces in Croatia held fast, their counterparts in Bosnia-Herzegovina had entered a three-way fight for control. The crisis in Croatia had not ended, but merely shifted venues to the most destructive of the three war zones.

Throughout the spring of 1992, Serb forces already had managed to carve out a substantial portion of territory in Bosnia, including Sarajevo, by ignoring a series of cease-fires (*New York Times,* 19 April 1992: A1). Now the Croats prepared for a third confrontation with Serb forces, this time with Bosnian Muslims (i.e., Bosniacs) as their nominal allies.

There is no doubt that Croatia's war was much longer and harder than Slovenia's. The case of Croatia included two wars. The first was for liberation of Croatia from the Yugoslavian army and the second was in the Krajina region. In both wars the removal of the JNA was the highest priority (Pavkovic 2000). Neither Slovenian nor Croat forces had enough power to remove the JNA. Since the Yugoslav federal army did not threaten any state beyond Yugoslavia, "the Slovenian and Croatian governments could not hope for outside military intervention which would force the Yugoslav army to withdraw from the two republics" (Pavkovic 2000: 155). Therefore, they "played it safe" and neutralized the army by restricting its movements through international monitoring and pressure. For the Croatian war in particular, this tactic worked very well and brought about withdrawal of the JNA (Pavkovic 2000).

4.3 The Bosnian Crisis Theater, 2 March 1992–21 November 1995: Crisis Spillover

Two key factors must be recognized from the beginning. First, the war was different than in Slovenia and Croatia; in Bosnia and Herzegovina, conflict focused on the constitutional setup of the state itself. Second, out of six Yugoslav republics, Bosnia and Herzegovina were most diverse, with no majority national group. The three major parties were organized along ethnic lines: The Party of Democratic Union-Muslim (SDA), the Croat Democratic Union (HDZ), and the Serb Democratic Party (SDS). Each had different perceptions about the country's future. These parties continuously formed coalitions and ruled the country after 1990 (Pavkovic 2000).

When an overwhelming number of Bosnians chose independence in the referendum on 2 March 1992, the act had the simultaneous effect of triggering foreign policy crises for both Croatia and Serbia.[20] In the referendum, Muslims, Croats, and Serbs outside of Serb-controlled areas voted overwhelmingly for a "democratic" and independent Bosnia. On 6 April 1992 the

EC extended diplomatic recognition to Bosnia-Herzegovina. Due to recognition by the EC and later the United States, Serb officials decided to withdraw from the government. This was the harbinger of the crisis.

Among the three crisis theaters, Bosnia-Herzegovina is the most complex. First, although the Bosniacs are a numerical plurality (somewhat more than 40 percent of the population), they did not possess the equivalent political clout and military power of their numerically smaller Serbian and Croatian counterparts. One party to that coalition, the Bosnian SDS, armed with JNA equipment, already had proved successful in stalling any political solution to the future of Bosnia. The fact that the majority of the JNA was stationed in Bosnia-Herzegovina prior to the conflict and that the republic was the site of most of the federal army's weapons factories aided this stalling tactic (Allcock 1988; *New York Times,* 3 March 1992: A1). The other two parties, the SDA and HDZ, established an alliance to balance the SDS.

As the conflict in Croatia diminished in January of 1992, the SDS declared an independent "Serbian Republic of Bosnia-Herzegovina" made up of regions that the SDS had taken over during the summer of 1991. This signaled the beginning of the armed conflict. Around the time of the referendum, Serb and Croat forces began fighting in key regions of Bosnia. Serbian guerrilla forces threw up roadblocks around Sarajevo and other cities and began a process of orchestrated terror against dissenters.

After all, in their view, the Serbs, led by Radovan Karadzic, head of the Serbian Democratic Party, had not agreed to independence according to the principle of three constituent nations. The real concern for Milosevic focused on controlling the unpredictable zealotry of the Bosnian-Serb leadership in order to reduce the possibility that their "ethnic cleansing" would stimulate outside military intervention.[21] This could be achieved best by maintaining a controlling interest in the Bosnian conflict and by staking claims to much of Bosnia.

Again, domestic interests became paramount in this calculation. By portraying itself as the sole arbiter of Serbian politics, in and outside of Serbia, the SPS could justify both its continuation and preservation of the existing power structure (Gagnon 1994). Since Serbia itself is only 65 percent Serbian, by bringing the approximately 30 percent of Bosnian Serbs into the political fold, the SPS would be able to increase the total Serbian proportion substantially. This strategy, combined with nullification of internal appeals for increased democratization, in effect would secure the SPS's hold on power for many years to come. In the event that democracy did come to Serbia, the elected leadership undoubtedly would be sympathetic to the Serbian cause. A key ingredient in Milosevic's ability to consolidate his power within Serbia was his ability to appeal to nationalist sensibilities and control the hypernationalism of his allies in Croatia and Bosnia (Saideman 1998b). Milosevic's Serbian Socialist Party supported the Serb's mobilizing efforts in Croatia and Bosnia, providing them with money, weapons, and strategic advice (Glenny 1993b).

By the summer of 1992, especially after the Bosnian proclamation of independence in April 1992, the number of Bosnians escaping from ethnic cleansing increased extensively. The Muslim population became the main target, and the Bosnian government was not ready for war at this time. Thus, Izetbegovic, the leader of Bosnia's collective presidency and leader of the Bosniacs, requested weapons for Bosnia's defense and a peacekeeping force for Bosnia in March 1992. The United States and other Western governments knew that, but chose not to become involved right away (Rogel 1998). After recognizing Bosnia-Herzegovina as separate independent state, the UN responded positively to this call and imposed sanctions on the Serbian side. As in Croatia, the request was met by foot dragging and a series of unsuccessful cease-fires that lasted throughout the year. In August the number of UN peacekeepers in Bosnia-Herzegovina rose to eight thousand, most of these concerned with ensuring the flow of humanitarian assistance (Lefebvre and Jakubow 1993).

On 8 August 1992 the warring factions agreed to a cease-fire to begin talks in Geneva on a constitutional settlement (*Globe and Mail,* 28 August 1992: A1). For his part, the leader of Bosnia's breakaway Serbs, Radovan Karadzic, vowed to end immediately the shelling of four besieged cities—Sarajevo, Bihac, Goražde, and Jajce. Both Karadzic and Mate Boban, the leader of the self-styled Croatian state of Herzeg-Bosnia, favored the canonization of the republic, with Muslims allocated patches of territory neither the Serbs nor Croats claimed. This agreement, known as the Cutilier Plan, had two weaknesses. First, the leaders of the main participants in the conflict would not be parties to the negotiation process. (Since his state remained internationally unrecognized, Karadzic was not present [*Globe and Mail,* 28 August 1992: A1].) Second, there remained no international military presence to enforce the pact, only the threat of tighter sanctions and increasing isolation for Serbia.

With no constitutional settlement in sight, international opinion about the conflict had shifted by December 1992. The apparent willingness of the Western powers to intervene in the conflict became notable. For example, President Clinton suggested that, unlike his predecessor, he would use force to aid the UN in its humanitarian assistance (*Globe and Mail,* 30 July 1993: A1). The problem had become even more complicated, as all three factions showed intensified hostility toward each other. The alliance that once suited Muslims and Croats against the Serbs crumbled. Clashes between them already had broken out in the central Bosnian towns of Vitez and Novi Travnik (*Globe and Mail,* 26 November 1992: A1). The U.S. administration had been considering all options except for sending ground troops to Bosnia. The United States rejected the latter plan as too provocative; it would endanger the peace talks and the lives of aid workers. In effect, the international community signaled the Serb leader, Milosevic, who held a tight reign on Karadzic, to either resolve the conflict through negotiations or face tighter sanctions.[22] Initially, this strategy worked.

UN-imposed sanctions that included a naval blockade and condemnation of Serb involvement clearly had only a partial effect. Oil continued to get to Serbia, and both sides still used heavy armaments. The international community had three options: (*a*) lifting of the arms embargo on the Bosnia government (designed to aid the Bosniacs); (*b*) selective air strikes against Bosnian Serb positions; or (*c*) both in some combination. Simultaneously, to ensure safe havens for civilians ensnared in the conflict, NATO began to implement plans for military enforcement of a no-fly zone. The actual enforcement could not take place, however, until the UN Security Council had approved it.

Bosnian-Serb leaders dropped their demands for a separate state and signed a short-lived peace plan, Vance-Owen, proposed by the international community, on 11 January 1993. The plan gave each of the three ethnic groups control of ten nominally equal "provinces" within Bosnia. Sarajevo would become an open city—effectively, a UN supervised province. The concession coincided with the arrival of Milosevic at the Geneva Peace Talks, and for a time at least, it appeared that the long-held dream of a greater Serbia would be achieved. The proposed map of the new Bosnian state showed that both the EC and the United States, now parties to the talks, would be willing to allow Bosnia to be redrawn along ethnic lines, with the Serbs controlling almost 70 percent of the former Yugoslav territory. In effect, territorial boundaries gained through military means became legitimate (*Globe and Mail,* 10 January 1993: A1).

On 6 May 1993 the Bosnian-Serb parliament met and rejected the Vance-Owen peace initiative, as they would the later Owen-Stoltenberg Plan (*International Herald Tribune,* 7 May 1993: A1). In response to the Vance-Owen Plan, the Serb parliament decided instead to put the issues to a May referendum that also failed to provide support. International reaction turned out to be mixed (Lewis 1993a, 1993b). The rump-Yugoslavia government, buckling under sanctions, cut off aid to Bosnian Serb forces in an attempt to force them to agree to peace. In Europe there remained no consensus on whether to lift the arms embargo against the former Yugoslavia or to allow the Muslims to defend themselves through access to weapons.

At the peace talks that began on 27 July 1993, a revised constitutional plan for the future "United Republics of Bosnia and Herzegovina" was unveiled. The proposal would create a union of three "constituent republics"—a confederation of three ethnic units—comprising "three constituent peoples" and "others" (*Globe and Mail*, 27 July 1993: A1). A key change in the plan was that at least 31 percent of Bosnian territory would be yielded to Bosnian Muslims, who controlled only 15 percent at the time. The Croats and Serbs would be allowed to retain 17 percent and 52 percent of Bosnia, respectively. The plan also called for a rotating presidency and a weak central government responsible only for conducting foreign affairs. Known as Owen-Stoltenberg, the plan required acceptance from Bosnia's ten-member collective presidency and the Bosnian parliament (Lewis 1993a, 1993b).

Izetbegovic remained unconvinced about dividing the country based on ethnic lines and insisted on keeping the state united but multinational (Rogel 1998). In August 1993 the Bosnian leader indicated that he would not ask the Bosnian parliament to approve the plan. It would be difficult, in his view, to wrest the necessary 15 percent of the territory from either the Serbs or the Croats. The leaders of the other two groups showed intransigence. The Bosnian Serb leader, Karadzic, said that "there will be no more negotiations" on further Serb concessions at the Geneva peace negotiations (*Globe and Mail*, 24 August 1993: A1). Thus, the peace talks of August 1993 had two purposes: (1) to convince all three Bosnian leaders and their supporting coalitions to recognize the separation of Bosnia into three distinct republics and (2) to prevent Serb and Croat forces from making gains on the territory they already held. On 24 August 1993 the Bosnian wing of Croatia's ruling party formally proclaimed the Croat state entity as "Herzeg-Bosnia." Later in 1993, Bosnian Croats wanted to expand their territory by military action at the Muslims' expense, which meant "ending a formal alliance with the Muslims and fighting against the Bosnian government" (Rogel 1998: 35). As a result, war and ethnic cleansing began on both sides.

Serb forces already had been requested to withdraw from areas surrounding Sarajevo. To assure they would comply by 30 August 1993, the deadline for the plan to take effect, U.S. President Clinton requested on 30 July that NATO make its strike aircraft operational. This effort ensured that the momentum that began with the Vance-Owen Plan would not be lost. The influence of ethnic allies—Milosevic and Croatian leader Franjo Tudjman in particular—became integral to the process. In combination with sanctions and an embargo, the Western powers proved reasonably effective in containing the conflict and directing its flow. In effect, NATO hoped to isolate the Bosnian-Serb militia in order to drive a political wedge between them and their main line of support in Serbia. In turn, it is unlikely that without diplomatic pressure on Milosevic and Tudjman as well, a mediated settlement would have been possible in so short a period.[23] To escape the constraints imposed on Serbia, Milosevic withdrew tangible support for the Serb breakaway leadership in Bosnia.

NATO air strikes had very important consequences for the war. The first set of strikes targeted the Bosnian Serb command and troop barracks as well as communication centers. The main purpose was to prevent Serbian attack. NATO continued bombing until 14 September 1995, although the alliance suspended it twice to let Serbian artillery withdraw and allow for negotiations (Pavkovic 2000).

Although the Vance-Owen and Owen-Stoltenberg Plans did not succeed, they provided the basis for the negotiated settlement that would take place almost three years later. The Dayton Accord, known also as the General Framework Agreement for Peace, signed in 1995, came at a price: exclusion of the Bosnian-Serb leaders from the negotiating table and substantial territorial gains for Bosnia-Croats in comparison to what had been offered to them under Vance-Owen and Owen-Stoltenberg. In essence, territorial boundaries gained through military means became legitimate through the agreement. While it confirmed the independence of Bosnia-Herzegovina as a two-part state, the Bosnian Serbs' territorial stranglehold would be reduced to 49 percent of Bosnian territory and the Bosnian Croat and Muslim federation would control the rest of the Bosnian land. By most standards, the accord merely reaffirmed what long had been recognized: Bosnia would be two effectively independent nations—the Republic of Srpska and the Bosnia Federation. The two territories would be separated by an interentity boundary line, and both sides would be monitored closely by NATO forces—first the Implementation Force, or IFOR, and its successor, the Stabilization Force (SFOR).[24]

Two and a half years after the Dayton Accord, immediate and ongoing sources of insecurity included the return of thousands of displaced ethnic minorities to their homes in areas dominated by other ethnic groups. These refugees, whether Serbian, Croat, or Bosniac, returned only to find their homes either completely demolished by the war, occupied, surrounded by minefields or booby traps, or destroyed by arson shortly thereafter.[25] Many, mostly the young and skilled, continue to stay away—preferring instead refuge in Germany or Italy, or in resort towns along the Adriatic coast with better employment opportunities. The Federal Republic of Yugoslavia (Serbia and Montenegro), for example, became the home to more than 200,000 Serbian refugees.

4.4 Postcrisis Period: December 1995–Present

Some observers claim that the Dayton agreement was accepted by the parties not because it was seen as the best solution to the problem but due to NATO actions and international pressure on all parties. According to this view, there is still a potential for renewed hostilities between and among Serbs, Croats, and Bosniacs (Pavkovic 2000).

The previously mentioned city of Brcko, a tiny island of neutrality in a sea of hostility, is a case in point. In March 1998, SFOR troops trained in anticipation that Brcko would be handed back to one of the warring factions. It was anticipated widely that any concrete decision, one way or the other, would precipitate renewed clashes. To prevent this from happening, SFOR troops performed daily armed patrols in villages and towns, monitored all significant movements of the three armed forces, and controlled access to heavy weapons by maintaining cantonment sites throughout the region. Eventually the issue was resolved peacefully and Brcko became a district of Bosnia-Herzegovina in 2000. Similarly, claims about the possibility of renewed hostilities came to be true with the developments in Kosovo after 1996.

In the postcrisis period, even starting from 1991, Slovenia seemed stable and peaceful. After its formal recognition by the EU and United States in 1992, Slovenia joined the UN, with Milan Kucan reelected as president. Based on the results of the referendum held in March 2003, 89.61 percent of the population voted for joining the EU and 66.02 percent supported NATO membership. Slovenia became a member of NATO in March 2004 and joined the EU along with nine other states on 1 May 2004. (In February 2005, Slovenia's parliament ratified the EU's constitution.) Slovenia seems past its most difficult days and is proceeding with caution along a new path to the future.

Croatia restored its diplomatic relations with Yugoslavia in 1996, and the parliamentary elections held in 2000 resulted in a coalition of social democrats and social liberals. In September 2001, Milosevic was charged for war crimes and crimes against humanity in the war against Croatia. Like Slovenia, Croatia seeks closer ties with the EU and formally applied for EU membership in 2003.

Bosnia-Herzegovina seems much more stable after the Dayton agreement.

In the 2000 elections, moderate parties won on the Muslim-Croat side but nationalists gained the upper hand in the Serb entity. A coalition government was formed and headed by moderate Prime Minister Mladen Ivanic. However, in the 2002 elections, nationalists regained power in presidential, parliamentary, and local elections.

Milosevic was elected president of Yugoslavia in July 1997 and in 1998. The Kosovo Liberation Army rebelled against Serbian rule. NATO launched air strikes against Yugoslavia in March 1999. These strikes ended on 10 June, with the withdrawal of Serbian troops from Kosovo. In the September 2000 elections, Milosevic lost and Vojislav Kostunica became the new president. In April 2001, Milosevic was detained and handed over to The Hague war crimes tribunal. His trial began at The Hague in February 2002 and continues at this time of writing. In May 2002 the accord ending the federation was ratified by the federal parliament, and this act cleared the way for the new constitution of Serbia and Montenegro. In February 2003, the Yugoslav parliament approved the constitution of the new union of Serbia and Montenegro.

What remains of Yugoslavia is a loose union between Serbia and Montenegro. Tensions between different ethnic groups still exist, as with Serbs and Albanians in the Presevo valley in late 2000 and in Macedonia in 2001. The worst clashes between Serbs and ethnic Albanians in Kosovo since 1999 took place in March 2004 in the town of Mitrovica. The future of the former Yugoslavia remains clouded but seems to be improving.

5. Analysis and Propositions

Three stages of interaction took place. At stage 1, an aggressive Serbian foreign policy emerges with respect to the newly created states of Bosnia and Croatia. Slovenia and Macedonia, in contrast, depart Yugoslavia with very little violence (Saideman 1998b). This difference reflects the varying ability of the Serb leader, Milosevic, to build a coalition of forces willing to restructure the neighboring states to create a Greater Serbia. At stage 2, Serb aggression is reinterpreted as an international security issue because of the perceived threat to Serbs living in Croatia and Bosnia. Serb leaders take advantage of the cleavages created by Serb-held enclaves in Croatia and Bosnia and escalate the crisis to war in stage 3.

Serbia used force to expand its influence and support brethren in Croatia and Bosnia. It proved less willing to do so in Slovenia. The security issue became problematic for the international community because each ethnic group had made its basis of security the discomfort of another ethnic group. Even if the extremists in Serb-held enclaves did not want violence, they knew that intransigence rather than compromise would be the best strategy to follow. Compromise by any of the leaders, but especially Milosevic (who had come to power on the basis of protecting Serb interests), would have meant a loss of both relevance and power (Harvey 1998).

Elements of both secessionism and irredentism appear throughout the conflict (Saideman 1998b). Over time, the enthusiasm for irredenta waned, while support for secession, especially among Bosnian Serbs, remained high. At stages 1 and 2, Milosevic's government supported extremist breakaway leaders in Bosnia and Croatia. The important implication is that the support entailed a narrowing of policy options for Milosevic. Once extremist leaders of an ethnic group gain credibility, as in the case of those in Bosnia, moderates may find it difficult to maintain control.

June 26, 1991 marked the onset of Yugoslavia's foreign policy crisis. At that time, Yugoslavia's already crumbling federal government faced two major internal threats, to territory and regime, as a result of political acts. The perception of crisis conditions came about because of Slovenian and Croatian claims to independence. The military conflict following onset of the crisis initially took the form of a civil war. After Germany and then the EC recognized Slovenian and Croatian claims to sovereignty, the crisis setting transformed because of the introduction of these two republics as independent states. (See Saideman 1997, 1998b for a discussion of the motivations of other actors in the conflict.) The claims to independence of these states *and* their subsequent international recognition therefore serve as the triggers to an international crisis and an interstate ethnic conflict. Conflict in Croatia had decisive spillover effects for the conflict in Bosnia-Herzegovina, not the least of which was the forcing of Bosnian (as well as Macedonian) leadership to choose independence or to be incorporated into a truncated Yugoslavia. The entire crisis period is marked by fluctuations in intensity, characteristic of a protracted conflict.

Initial deescalation of the interstate ethnic conflict in Slovenia during June 1991 signaled termination of a foreign policy crisis for Slovenian leaders. Croatia's leaders then experienced a foreign policy crisis in August 1991 when Croatian territory succumbed to Serbian attacks. The conflict appeared to be winding down until Croatian counteroffensives in February 1992 and again in 1995 regained most Serb-held territory in the Krajinas. Until this period, Serb forces continued to hold on to at least 10 percent of the Croatian territory that is geographically contiguous with Serbia. Sporadic fighting between Serb and Croatian forces through the fall of 1993 and 1994 made the division of Serb- and Croatian-held territory by lightly armed UNPRO-FOR troops difficult.

The decisive shift to the Bosnian crisis theater occurred in March 1992, as both Serbian and Croatian leaders staked claims to Bosnian territory. March 2, 1992 constitutes an escalation in the larger Yugoslavian interstate ethnic conflict, with the direct involvement of Bosnia-Herzegovina and several non-state actors (i.e., breakaway Bosnia-Croatian and Bosnia-Serbian self-styled governments). Bosnian declarations of independence at that time triggered foreign policy crises for both Croatia and Serbia.[26]

Cessation of hostilities between JNA forces and the breakaway republics marked the beginning of a slow but steady deescalation of the crisis through 1994 and 1995. The Bosnian crisis, in particular, is marked by sporadic attempts at peaceful negotiation, failed cease-fires, and international debate over various strategies of conflict management (ranging from sanctions to military intervention). The Bosnian crisis theater also is characterized by at least three failed peace plans: the Cutilier Plan in 1992, Vance-Owen in April 1993, and Owen-Stoltenberg in October 1993. The effects of the fourth, the Dayton Peace Accord, are inconclusive but encouraging.

Deescalation of the interstate ethnic conflict is marked by two sets of events. First came the compliance of two of the three Bosnian ethnic groups with the Vance-Owen Plan in 1993, which coincided with the decision by Serbia's leader Milosevic to desist from support for the Bosnian Serbs. The second set of events refers to acceptance by all three states' leaders of the Dayton Accords in 1995.

Politicization of ethnicity as the primary means of mobilization and sub-sequent polarization of political issues on the basis of Serb-Croat rivalries represented key factors in the initial escalation of the conflict. Milosevic, faced with an ethnically dominant society and limited institutional con-straints, acted in ways that are compatible with Proposition P_1 regarding strategies of commitment. While exploring limited variations in tactics, the overall strategy stayed consistent and highly coercive. Milosevic's responsive-ness to nationalist extremism correlated with signals issued by the Serbian elite, although he did soften (temporarily) in response to massive public demonstrations. Critics in the early 1990s would seize upon signs of weak-ness relative to ethnic adversaries, and that encouraged Milosevic to act very firmly toward rival ethnic groups. Thus, in comparison to the highly con-strained leaders, Milosevic could commit in advance to a more consistent and highly confrontational strategy.

Subsequent political maneuvering by Milosevic, which included initial intransigence, participation in peace talks, and eventually sanctions against

Bosnian Serbs, suggests that domestic and international factors conditioned his strategies on the Bosnian and Croatian fronts. Serb leadership had to convince Serb opposition (including hard-liners) that it had engaged in actions sufficient to protect Serb interests elsewhere, while also limiting the effects of international condemnation (including sanctions and continuing threats of armed intervention).

The most important characteristics of Milosevic's commitment problem stem from demography. Yugoslavia's ethno-religious groups, which included Croatians, Slovenians, Muslims, and Serbs, tend toward geographic concentration. The Serbs also constituted significant portions of the populations of other states, including Croatia and Bosnia. While not a majority of Yugoslavia's population, the Serbs always were its single largest ethnic group. Instrumental in shaping Serb domination is the fact that the Serb leaders controlled the army and political apparatus for at least ten years before the outbreak of war in Yugoslavia.

Transnational ethnic affinities, as in the cases from earlier chapters, created a security dilemma for Serbia, Bosnia, and Croatia (although less so for Slovenia) and had ramifications for the subsequent formation of Serb policy toward each of the seceding states. For example, in relative terms, far fewer Serbs are found in Slovenia and Macedonia as compared to Croatia and Bosnia. Thus, the primary concern in the conflict between Slovenia and Serbia was to prevent further decentralization within the Yugoslavian political structure. Efforts to protect, retrieve, or even use the small minority of Slovenian Serbs for organizational leverage stayed secondary in importance to the larger issue of maintaining Yugoslavian integrity (Gagnon 1994/95; Saideman 1997). This setting of priorities may explain, in part, why Serbia relinquished control of Slovenia so quickly as compared to the conflicts in Croatia and Bosnia. Perceived benefits to Serb leaders did not match the costs of attempting to retain Slovenia (Gagnon 1994/95; Saideman 1998b).

Affinities do not wholly explain the use of force in all three crisis theaters. Like Croatia, Slovenia had strong ties to the West and its own defense forces. According to Saideman (1998b), the ties to the West showed through when Germany sponsored Slovenia's transition to independence. Potential confrontation with the West, coupled with fewer domestic benefits to the Serb leadership, converged to create a situation of relatively peaceful political transition. Force could be used as long as the international community viewed the conflict as a civil war and an internal affair of the still-existing Yugoslavian regime, which it did.

Short-lived attempts at second-order secessionism by Serbs in Croatia and

Serbs *and* Croatians in Bosnia (i.e., minorities within minorities) characterized the Bosnian conflict. As a result, three processes of interstate ethnic conflict occurred simultaneously. The secessions of Yugoslavia's republics comprised the first process. The second, which consisted of retrieval by the Serb-dominated JNA and irregular forces, is the irredentist struggle. The third phase is made up of the simultaneous declarations of independence by the self-styled minority Serb and Croatian governments. A fourth and as yet undecided phase would include the absorption of parts of Bosnia into Croatia and Serbia.

For Serbia, the main source of cleavage was not interethnic rivalry but intraethnic discord. Milosevic faced the prospect of uniting a broad spectrum of Serbian opinion on the conflict, ranging from far right ultranationalist perspectives, which framed the conflict as a Croatian/Muslim conspiracy, to more moderate sensibilities, which had as their chief concern the effects of sanctions on the Serbian economy. The latter appear to have surfaced in the early stages of the conflict when mass protests against the Milosevic regime took place. However, as the conflict wore on and Milosevic's position softened, these protests diminished.

Proposition P_2, which focuses on pacific strategies in diverse settings, is supported by the way that Yugoslavia as an ethnically diverse state framed its foreign policy and then how the more homogenous units within it approached the problem of transition. The last ten years of Yugoslavia's existence witnessed the gradual turning away from an overarching arrangement of elite-based consensus in which all republics participated in framing policy. However, such an arrangement had not been designed to cope with rapid change, especially in economic terms, in which regional disparities increased dramatically over the short term. Consequently, Yugoslavia's political arrangements had three distinct dimensions that all led to reduced constraints on the leaders of each republic. At the national level, levels of repression and electoral competition appear to have been defined along interrepublic and ethnic lines. Party coalitions also followed those patterns. Finally, over time, policies were implemented to advance the interests of specific ethnic groups (Saideman 1998b).

Consequently, Yugoslavia's political structures, originally designed to be inclusive, became mechanisms for exclusion of specific groups and leaders. For example, Milosevic's national party (SPS) came to power through an internal coup. In Croatia and Serbia, political parties formed on the basis of ethnic allegiance and parliaments became the domains of demagogues and chauvinists. Despite apparent regulation of participation and constraints on executives, it is reasonable to assume that during the period of transition,

Yugoslavia's republics did not feature high levels of institutional constraint. Prewar Yugoslavia's political system was on its way to becoming an ethnically based, bureaucratic-authoritarian system—an exclusionary political arrangement led by Serb technocrats and the military in order to bring Yugoslavia more fully into an open market economy.[27]

With the outbreak of war, Serbian leaders began to pursue more "hawkish" policies, defying both international condemnation and those within the Serbian camp considered to be soft on secession. The positioning of Milosevic as a "hawk" meant that any response by either Croatian or Bosnian leaders to Serbian hostilities would be portrayed as unacceptable to the Serbian people. This observation implies, up to a point, greater autonomy for the Serbian elite. Serbia's leaders proved especially effective in building on nationalist claims by convincing their supporters that Serbs could be safe only if the state obtained the capability to attack and defeat rival states in which Serbs existed as a minority. An aggressive campaign against Croatia and Bosnia came as the final, logical step in this process. To escape the constraints imposed on Serbia (namely, sanctions and embargoes), Milosevic had to find an alternative strategy to building support at home, which eventually resulted in sanctions on the Serb breakaway leaders in Croatia and Bosnia.

Extremism among all ethnic groups that resulted from the breakup of Yugoslavia did not indicate an intraethnic consensus. For example, some Croatian leaders, including Tudjman, were willing to offer autonomy to Serb minorities (including local self-management), while those opposed preferred a hard line of no compromises. Illegal, private Croatian militia began to form in response, although Tudjman arrested the leaders of the Party of Rights in part because of its use of neofascist symbols. These and other opposition leaders were accused of having "considerably contributed to the difficult political and security situation in Croatia" (Ramet 1992a: 261).

Extreme views on both sides of the issue existed in Serbia as well; Milosevic took a position in the middle. Accusations of selling out the Serbian interest forced Milosevic to harden his position: "Questions of borders are essential questions of state. And borders, as you know, are always dictated by the strong, never by the weak. Accordingly, it is essential that we be strong" (Ramet 1992a: 264).

Proposition P_3 focuses on forceful intervention and concentration of costs and benefits. The proposition finds support from Serbian behavior (and that of Croatia, which also could be highlighted in much the same way as what follows). In particular, the decision to use force had low-cost implications for the Serbian regime. Internal opposition to the use of force was countered through manipulation of repression, while two processes nullified international condemnation: circumvention of embargoes and constant control of Serb secessionist leaders. When international pressures did appear to have some effect, the Serb regime reined in the Serb minority leaders.

Where political resistance is low or support is "general purpose" (as in the case of Serbia), more confrontational tactics are expected. For an authoritarian regime, payoffs from a successful ethnically based intervention are immense. A systematic connection between domestic political gain and initiation of interventionist strategies is clear in the Serbian case. Pursuit of domestic political benefits is obvious. However, the benefits accrued mainly to the Serbian political elite, as did the longer-term costs of overexpansion. Had the Serb regime pursued and lost a sustained, all-out war with either Slovenia or Croatia, there is little doubt that the regime would have been overthrown (Midlarsky 1997).

Within Serbia, opposition to using force was primarily elite generated and concentrated within the military. For example, Milosevic's plan to grant Slovenia and Croatia greater autonomy ran into considerable opposition. Many Yugoslav-oriented officers wanted to maintain the integrity of Yugoslavia and, consequently, Milosevic hardened his position on the question of deconfederation (Cohen 1992, 1993).

The main problem facing Milosevic was to manage the resistance that Serb policies engendered in the international arena. The primary constraint facing the Serb leaders was the array of international factors shaping the implementation of confrontational policies. In this instance, sanctions and the threat of intervention served as the primary constraints on Serb policy. Neither appears to have been fully successful in deterring Serbia's expansionist policies or from achieving most of its objectives. Failure by all members of the international community to comply with the agreement to enforce sanctions became fundamental to Serbia's ability to press its advantage (Midlarsky 1997).

The threat of international involvement, however, presented Serb leaders with a second-best solution. If Serbia could not maintain sovereignty over an integrated Yugoslavia, then it would at least control all that territory with significant Serb populations through proxy militias established in Serb-held enclaves. Of course, the organizational leverage that Serbia had at its disposal, namely, control of the JNA and well-armed and loyal Serb irregulars in Croatia and Bosnia, played key roles (Glenny 1992a, b, c).

Proposition P_4 focuses on the impact of affinities and cleavage on crisis escalation. Lack of control over ethnic insurgents in Bosnia and Croatia generated significant uncertainty for Serb leaders. In general terms, manipulation of foreign perceptions through the control of ethnic allies is a risky strategy, even for heads of authoritarian states. Serbia and leaders of the self-styled breakaway Serb republics of Bosnia and Croatia also had an uneasy relationship. This alliance was based on the Serb assumption that support would create a more predictable environment for undertaking and controlling activities beyond its borders. Unfortunately, despite their initial involvement in mediation (i.e., Vance-Owen Peace Plan), these breakaway leaders also turned out to be the most opposed to a final negotiated settlement as manifested in the Dayton Peace Accord.

Ethnic linkages provided Serb leaders with the leverage necessary to stake a claim to portions of Croatia and Bosnia (Saideman 1998b). These affinities also created negative reverberations by enhancing Serb perceptions of insecurity. The most important aspect in this regard is the behavior of Serbian leader Milosevic toward the Serb minorities in Croatia and Bosnia. Evidence indicates that under international pressure for compliance, Milosevic was willing to apply pressure on the Serb breakaway leaders in these republics (Saideman 1998b). This is because the extremist strategies of Serb minority leaders, including Karadzic, threatened to draw in extraregional powers and produce tighter sanctions on Serbia. Milosevic's response is notable because it suggests that the usefulness of transnational linkages is conditioned by a broader spectrum of foreign policy objectives and domestic concerns.[28]

Another possibility is that Milosevic recognized these leaders (including Karadzic) as potentially unstable adversaries in his plans to control territories outside Serbia. The evidence for this is based on the assumption that Milosevic eventually would seek the support of Serbians outside Serbia in his plans to restructure the Serbian economy. To do this, the Serb leader would require the compliance of a dependent Serb minority leadership in Croatia and Bosnia.[29]

Presumably, Milosevic would not have pursued involvement in Slovenia, Croatia, and Bosnia (and Kosovo) if he had believed that would threaten his power. Evidence indicates that Milosevic formulated policies that appealed to his ethnic constituency even at the expense of other ethnic groups. He did so in order to mobilize his followers and potentially increase his share of domestic power. Subsequent efforts toward territorial retrieval must be seen in the context of Milosevic's domestic political situation.

When interelite competition within a dominant ethnic group is high, elites in some instances will introduce novel issues that discredit their opponents and thereby create new avenues of securing power. In other instances, elites will rely on manipulation of mass sentiment (Kaufman 1996). Serb leaders appear to have utilized both processes while securing power within Serbia.

For example, political opponents considered "soft" on relations with Croatia were either discredited or jailed. Repression in Kosovo appears to have stemmed from similar concerns. Indeed, based on the evidence, Serbian nationalist rhetoric was so fundamental to policy formation that overwhelming mass sentiment and hard-line opposition may have been prevented Milosevic, initially at least, from pursuing conciliatory or accommodating strategies with the other ethnic groups (Harvey 1998).

Proposition P_5 pertains to the relative likelihood and character of intervention. Serbia, taken to represent the former Yugoslavia in the postcollapse period, would be classified as an ethnically dominant, low-constraint state or Type I_a within figure 2.1. A state of this type is expected to show belligerence, and that is confirmed strongly by Serbia's conduct in the years following the breakdown of Yugoslavia. From the outset of the conflict, the main interest of Serbia's elites was retention of Serbian minorities first in Croatia and then in Bosnia. Milosevic wanted to bring all Serbs under one state and used conflicts in Kosovo and Krajina to justify intervention by the army in order to restrain interethnic warfare. Irredentism took a belligerent, violent form, accompanied by ongoing anti-Croatian rhetoric that emphasized a connection with the fascist past.

Consistent also with Serbia's Type I_a status are the respective roles played by the leadership versus the elite. Belligerence took an elite-led form, with mobilization of followers and aggrandizement of Milosevic's position as a key by-product of the entire process. At the same time, manipulation of group symbols and repression countered potential internal opposition to the use of force. In sum, both the form and substance of Serbia's ethnic intervention offer support to P_5.

6. Conclusions

Evidence from this case makes it is clear that leaders of ethnically dominant and institutionally underdeveloped states face a different set of opportunities than their more constrained and diverse counterparts in pursuing foreign policy objectives. International policies implemented to deter these states at the domestic level, like sanctions or embargoes, may be less effective than anticipated. In these situations, elites can become adept at creating ethnic solidarity and manipulating mass opinion in order to bring it in line with their foreign policy objectives. More specifically, sanctions and international condemnation may be necessary but not sufficient conditions for management of conflicts involving low-constraint, ethnically dominant states.[30] Would forceful and early intervention have resulted in a shorter, less intense conflict for the former Yugoslavia? The implications of the framework are favorable to that conclusion.

The paradox of diversity indicates that ethnically divided states attempting to make the simultaneous transition to a more economically open and democratic system face certain dangers. If the political system is arranged along ethnic lines and one group is allowed to become dominant, it will succumb to the politics of intransigence, confrontation, hypernationalism, and conflict. Leaders of ethnically based political parties will lack, over the short term, the capacity to widen the policy agenda to encompass nonethnic issues. When other bases of mobilization are weak, ethnic elites depend on direct support from their constituency (Kaufman 1996; Saideman 1997).

These and other concerns are taken up in chapter 8, where the propositions are reviewed in terms of their performance across the case studies as a whole.

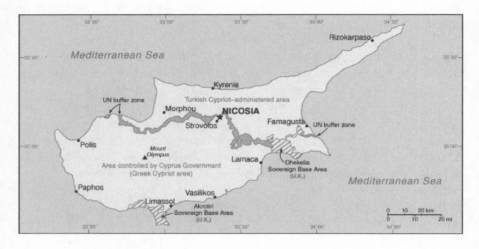

Cyprus, 2004. http://www.cia.gov/cia/publications/factbook/

CHAPTER SEVEN

The Cyprus Puzzle:
Two Nations, One Island

> The "suspicion syndrome" dominating Greek-Turkish relations and per-
> ceptions was also transplanted into Cyprus and eliminated any hope for
> constructive interaction between the rival ethnic groups. (Joseph 1997: 43)

1. A History of Conflict, Crisis, and War

With its long-lasting nature and international dimensions, Cyprus is a classic
example of protracted ethnic conflict.[1] Its history is complicated and features
numerous third-party interventions by ethnic brethren, superpowers, and
regional and global organizations. Although the matter is essentially internal,
external powers influence and dominate the Cyprus conflict. Therefore,
Cyprus provides scholars with a rich case study for understanding third-party
interventions and efforts toward conflict resolution. In virtually all aspects,
the Cyprus puzzle still is unsolved. It remains one of the most challenging and
potentially informative cases with respect to causal relations between ethnic
and other variables on the one hand and third parties and crisis outcomes on
the other.

Like the Thai Malay and Yugoslavia cases, Cyprus shows strains of both
secessionism and irredentism. In the past, while Greek nationalists demanded
union—*enosis*—of Cyprus with Greece, Turkish nationalists demanded partition—*taksim*—of the island. Especially after the 1974 intervention, discourse
on both sides has changed; Greek Cypriots supported the idea of a unitary
state, while Turkish Cypriots demanded a confederal system or secession.

Cyprus is home to a dispute that forms part of a complex and deep con-
flict between the homelands. The roots of the conflict between Turkey and
Greece go back to 1453, the time of the Ottoman conquest of Constantinople
(Istanbul). After a long war, Greece gained its independence from Ottoman
Rule in 1829. This lengthy association is what makes the case of Cyprus so
complex and hard to resolve.

What can be said of the case in the context of crises in world politics? The ICB Project's data set includes no fewer than nine crises under the heading of "Greece/Turkey protracted conflict" from 1920 to 1987. Many issues divide these old rivals and only three cases (Cyprus I [1963–64], Cyprus II [1967], and Cyprus III [1974–75]) are on the troublesome island of Cyprus itself.[2] In our conceptualization, the 1963 and 1967 cases constitute the background to the 1974 crisis, which featured intervention by Turkey. Our focus will be on the third crisis, which started with the military coup engineered in Cyprus by Greek officers and resulted in the overthrow of the government in Cyprus. This event triggered a crisis for Turkey, which sent troops to the island on 20 July 1974. Turkey's action subsequently served as the crisis trigger for Greece (Brecher and Wilkenfeld 1997b). Turkish intervention resulted in a de facto division of the island. Three decades later, the same situation holds.

To explain the patterns of Turkish and Greek interests and involvement in Cyprus, this chapter will examine issues and events within the larger protracted conflict. The primary focus is on the crisis surrounding Turkey's decision to intervene in Cyprus and its subsequent impact. Many outsiders refer to the Turkish intervention in 1974 as the beginning of the Cyprus "problem"; this designation, however, does not capture the full reality. Indeed, the origins of the problem go back to the establishment of the Cypriot republic. Communal fighting started on the island as a result of a constitutional crisis. Thus, analysis in this chapter will pay specific attention to these earlier developments.

This chapter unfolds in five additional parts. In the second part the historical and political background of the ethnic conflict is presented. Third, the precrisis period is analyzed and key developments that led to the 1974 intervention are explored. In the fourth part, the main focus is on the 1974 Turkish intervention on the island, with some attention to the Greek response and postcrisis developments as well. Fifth, propositions are tested. Sixth, and finally, implications for the framework are assessed.

2. The Origins of Ethnic Conflict on Cyprus: The Road to Independence

Located forty miles south of Turkey and five hundred miles southeast of Greece, Cyprus is the third largest island in the Mediterranean Sea. It has an area of 9,250 square kilometers, of which 3,355 square kilometers are in the Turkish Cypriot area. According to Freedom House country and related territory reports (2003), Greek Cypriots constitute 78 percent of the population, while Turkish Cypriots and others constitute 18 percent and 4 percent, respectively.[3]

Thanks to its geographic location and strategic importance—being at the crossroads of the continents—Cyprus has always been a strategic location. Cyprus has been ruled by Hittites, Egyptians, Assyrians, Persians, Romans, Byzantines, Lusignans, and Venetians. In 1571, the Ottoman Empire occupied the island, and it remained in their hands until the Congress of Berlin in 1878. During the Congress of Berlin, Cyprus was "rented" to the British with the condition that Britain would come to the Ottoman Empire's aid in case of a Russian attack. In 1914, when the Ottoman Empire established an alliance with Germany, Britain annexed Cyprus, and it became a British colony. On 24 July 1923, with the Lausanne treaty, Turkey officially recognized the British annexation. The island remained in British hands as a crown colony until 1959.

In 1910, Greece's Prime Minister Venizelos asserted his idea of reestablishing the Byzantine Empire or, the *megali idea*. The *megali idea* means unification of the Greeks in the whole region under one nation-state and liberation of Greek land from the Ottoman Empire. The following statement is important because it illustrates the idea that eventually Cyprus would join Greece, that is, *enosis*.[4]

> Our immediate needs come to mind when we consider Cyprus. There are various reasons for this project. The most important reason is that the Ionian Islands have permitted the expansion of the Greek Empire and strengthened it in the past. One of the first countries to help Greece in this matter is Britain, which will eventually give Cyprus to Greece. In brief, Greece wants Cyprus, Rhodes . . . and all islands along the Mediterranean. (Quoted from Ismail 2000: 7 in Bamanie 2002: 444)

As a result of the "divide and rule" politics of Britain throughout its reign, the two ethnic groups stayed distant from each other and held in reserve their primary attachments to Greece and Turkey.[5] Opposing worldviews of the two ethnic groups facilitated further polarization. While Greek Cypriots pursued the goal of *enosis* as a part of the *megali idea,* Turkish Cypriots supported either the idea of *taksim* (partition) or staying under British rule (Salih 1978).[6] Due to the island's strategic importance, Britain preferred to keep Cyprus under its rule. Thus the 1950s can be defined as a period of confrontation between Greek Cypriots and the British as well as of Turkish and Greek Cypriots over the issue of the island's future.

In 1950 the Orthodox Church conducted a plebiscite and 95.7 percent of

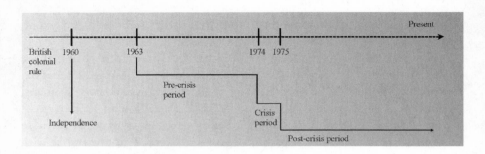

Figure 7.1. Cyprus Puzzle

the Greek Cypriot community over eighteen years of age voted for unification with Greece. A delegation from Cyprus submitted a demand to London
for *enosis*. The British, however, rejected their demand. Greece then decided
to bring the issue to the UN. The UN General Assembly's political committee preferred to shelve the issue, as Britain did earlier (Salih 1978). The failure of political attempts and a lack of resolution "left the Greek Cypriots
with no alternative but to resort to armed warfare," at least from their point
of view (Salih 1978: 8). At first the conflict focused on the armed struggle
with Greek Cypriot guerrilla organizations (EOKA).[7] Later on the conflict
enveloped the Turkish Resistance Organization (TMT) and EOKA.

During the mid-1950s, numerous attempts to achieve a peaceful resolution
occurred. Britain worked hard to find a plan acceptable to both parties, but
proposals never materialized. Efforts by the UN and NATO also failed. For
example, from 1955 to 1957, the Turkish government asserted that "if the
British rule were to end, then the island should be returned to its previous
owner—Turkey (as the inheritor of the Ottoman Empire)" (Sözen 1999: 14).
Adoption of such a policy ensured continuation of British rule on the island
that, for Turkish Cypriots, definitely looked like a better option than unification with Greece. However, when it became clear that the British would
withdraw from the island, the Turkish side changed its approach and began
to support the idea of *taksim* (Sözen 1999; Lumsden 1973).

Throughout this period, British requests and overtures from the Greek
government to the Soviet Union prompted the U.S. government to assume
responsibility to act as a primary mediator.

2.1 Establishment of the Republic of Cyprus

Figure 7.1 shows a time line for the conflict over Cyprus, beginning with independence in 1960 and continuing through to the present. With the failure of third-party attempts at finding a resolution, Britain asked for direct negotiations between Greece and Turkey. After a long period of confrontation, talks among Greece, Turkey, and Britain bore fruit, and an agreement on the future of the island was signed. The 1959 Zurich and London agreements led to the establishment of an independent, bicommunal Republic of Cyprus in 1960, and the Treaties of Establishment, Alliance, and Guarantee laid out the foundations of this new political structure.[8] According to these agreements, a republican form of government would secure the interests of both sides in Cyprus (Xydis 1967).[9] Each is described in turn.

The Treaty of Establishment, as its name suggests, established the republic and defined its territory, with the exception of two sovereign military bases—the Akrotiri and the Dhekelia base areas. It essentially secured British interests on the island. According to this treaty, Turkey, Greece, and Britain would consult and cooperate on the common defense of Cyprus.

The Treaty of Alliance originated from a common desire to maintain peace and safeguard security between and among Turkey, Greece, and Cyprus. It proposed the establishment of a tripartite headquarters on the territory of Cyprus, as well as stationing of contingents from Turkey and Greece to resist any aggression directed toward changing the status quo in Cyprus (Polyviou 1980).

In the Treaty of Guarantee, the main concern was recognition and maintenance of independence, territorial integrity, and security for the Republic of Cyprus. The Treaty of Guarantee prohibits "any activity likely to promote, directly or indirectly, either union with any other state or partition of the island" (Art.1). Article 4 states that in case of a breach of its provisions, Greece, Turkey, and the United Kingdom can take necessary measures to guarantee their observance: "Each of three guaranteeing powers reserves the right to take action with the sole aim of re-establishing the state of affairs created by the present treaty." Turkey used this very article to justify its intervention in 1974.

The constitution of the republic was based on dualism; in other words, the bicommunal state had the responsibility to regulate and protect its two ethnic communities. Almost all state branches were planned in a way that would have both communities contribute to their composition and functioning at least to some extent. The constitution allowed each side to keep its respective relationship with Greece and Turkey and exercise cultural, religious, and national traditions without any limitation (Joseph 1997; Polyviou 1980).

In terms of executive power, the new republic was presidential. Both the president (Greek Cypriot) and vice president (Turkish Cypriot) had the right of veto on issues regarding foreign affairs, defense, and security. Three Turkish Cypriot and seven Greek Cypriot ministers made up the Council of Ministers, with the condition that one of the three most important ministries—Ministry of Defense, Finance, or Foreign Affairs—would be given to a Turkish Cypriot. Decisions in the Council of Ministers were taken by absolute majority; however, the right of veto was given to the president and vice president in all circumstances (Sözen 1999).

According to the 1960 constitution, the House of Representatives, with thirty-five Greek Cypriot and fifteen Turkish Cypriot members elected by the two ethnic communities, would exercise legislative power (Republic of Cyprus 1960). The president of the house was to be a Greek Cypriot and the vice president a Turkish Cypriot. This simple division in the legislative branch provided an opportunity for each ethnic group effectively to run its own affairs. In other words, each community had autonomy in matters related to religion, education, culture, family affairs, and so on (Joseph 1997).

Likewise, under this system, the judiciary also reflected dualism. The Supreme Constitutional Court was composed of one Greek Cypriot, one Turkish Cypriot, and one "neutral" president. Public services allowed for 70 percent Greek and 30 percent Turkish Cypriot representation. The constitution also established a police force according to a ratio of seven to three and an army of two thousand men, based on a six-to-four ratio of Greeks to Turks (Polyviou 1980). Last, but not least, the constitution clearly stated that the territory of the republic was one and indivisible and the constitution "cannot, in any way, be amended."[10]

3. The Precrisis Period: 30 November 1963 to 15 July 1974

3.1 The Road to Intervention: Increasing Tensions

The establishment of the republic and the constitution led almost immediately to disagreements over provisions of the document and its application. The roots of the Cypriot conflict lay in the institutional foundations of the Cypriot state established in 1960 (Joseph 1997). All of the articles that supported inherent dualism clearly showed the complexity and rigidity of the constitution, and the relationship the two ethnic groups were expected to realize. Therefore, it is not difficult to conclude that while the constitution removed the ideas of *enosis* and partition, it facilitated further fragmentation of the two groups. By keeping the people separate and distinct from each other, the negotiated framework continued the "divide and rule" effect from the British era and set the stage for a series of crises over territory and ethnic identity. Constitutional rights and provisions granted with the establishment of the republic—especially exclusive power on religious, educational, cultural, and teaching issues—intensified and institutionalized ethnic differences. Mistrust and unwillingness to express loyalty to the new state grew (Trigeorgis and Trigeorgis 1993).

In many respects, the two sides perceived the constitution differently. "Instead of attempting to institutionalize bicommunual cooperation by workable provisions and living institutions based on the traditions and realities of the island, rigid and unworkable patterns and structures were set up" (Polyviou 1980: 23). Specifically, conflict arose over the veto powers of the vice president, application of the ratio of seven to three in the public service and the provision regarding municipalities and income tax legislation.

Greek Cypriots claimed that fundamental change was essential, since the constitution did not work properly. Turkish Cypriots, by contrast, rejected any attempts to bring significant changes to the constitution. They saw efforts toward change as a deliberate attempt by Greek Cypriots to eliminate at least some of their political rights. Factions in each community increasingly became suspicious of the intentions of the other group (Yesilada and Hewitt 1998). The result was increased ethnopolitical tension between the groups. A constitutional crisis marked the end of the newly established republic.

3.2 The Amendment Proposal: Initiation of Fighting and Violence

On November 30, 1963, President Makarios laid out his famous "13-point" amendments to then Vice President Küçük.[11] Perceptions of these amendments by both sides produced deadlock and violence on the island. Since amendments targeted the unalterable provisions of the Zurich treaty, Turkish Cypriots interpreted revision as an act against their equal partnership status because it sought to alter the consociational democratic system in which Turkish Cypriots would no longer have a veto power over decisions by the Greek majority. In the eyes of Turkish Cypriots, it represented a tactic or "a springboard for enosis" (Salih 1978: 16). The Turkish side also rejected the Greek argument that the agreement effectively had been imposed—signed only because no viable alternative existed at the time.

For Greek Cypriots, it was an imposed agreement, signed by Greek Cypriot leadership under coercion of guarantor powers. They therefore did not see it as a product of free will but, rather, necessity.[12] Additionally, the system created by the agreement was rigid and unworkable from the beginning.

The agreements "had put the Turkish minority, substantially, on the same level with regard to the exercise of political power with the Greek majority. This had been done despite its numerical strength (18 percent of the population) and its small proportion in land ownership and contribution to public expenditure," and therefore "it was contrary to every democratic principle" and "completely wrong" (Polyviou 1980: 36–37). Another element that created problems for the Greek side was the right of final veto accorded to the president and the vice president of the republic. The Greek Cypriots believed that the agreement did not serve their main purpose, namely, resolution of the basic communal problems on the island. Makarios, drawing on his thirteen-point proposal, unilaterally amended the constitution and treaties in 1964. On December 6, Turkey announced that it found the proposals to be unacceptable. Turkish Cypriot officials started to withdraw from their positions and stated that the government was no longer legitimate in their eyes (Sözen 1999).

The collapse of bicommunal government in such a short time destroyed internal coherence and increased minority fears; underground military groups emerged. Intercommunal clashes broke out on 21 December 1963, when a Greek police patrol insisted on searching a Turkish car. Fighting quickly spread to other parts of the island. Polarization increased quickly and intercommunal confrontation became violent. The Greek Cypriots gained control of almost the entire island, and a quarter of the Turkish community became refugees, formed enclaves, and isolated themselves from the Greek Cypriots. In this phase, Turkish Cypriots felt especially insecure and vulnerable due to the numerical superiority of Greek Cypriots. In turn, on 24 December, Turkish Cypriots appealed to Turkey for help. Turkey proposed that Britain, Greece, and the United States join her in restoring order on the island; none of them chose, however, to get directly involved (Kyriakides 1968; Volkan 1979; Trigeorgis and Trigeorgis 1993; Mirbagheri 1998; A. James 2002).

With the emergence of fighting, connections with Greece and Turkey became more visible. While the Greek Cypriot organization obtained financial and arms support from the military regime in Greece, the Turkish government supported the Turkish Cypriot side. Both sides, in the meantime, kept busy increasing their military buildup, in the expectation that the conflict would escalate. The Greek government supported not only the idea of revision of the treaties and the constitution but also the eventual aim, *enosis*. Turkey was heavily concerned about its own security, as well as the safety of Turkish Cypriots. Turkey blamed Greek Cypriots for destroying peace on the island and violating the constitutional rights of Turkish Cypriots.

From December 1963 onward, Turkey threatened that if violence continued, it might intervene according to the Treaty of Guarantee in order to protect Turkish Cypriots from the attacks (Salih 1978).

Late in December of that year, escalation of violence led Turkey to take a series of nonviolent, small-scale military acts. Turkey sent two jets over Cyprus to show concern as well as readiness to intervene, if it came to that. Greece and Greek Cypriots interpreted the action as a harbinger of Turkish military action. Not surprisingly, Greece stated that in case Turkey intervened on the island, Greece would do the same thing. Due to its broader security implications, this action alarmed both NATO and the United States. A letter from U.S. President Johnson, with its diplomatic yet firm tone, however, deterred a possible Turkish intervention.

From December 1963 onward and with the consent of all parties, Britain tried to play the mediator role in order to prevent a war between Greece and Turkey and safeguard its interests in the island. Similarly, Johnson attempted to mediate. These attempts at mediation turned out to be unsuccessful. As time passed, both sides became firmer about their opinions. The Greek Cypriot side insisted on the idea of revising the treaties. Turkish Cypriots decided not to insist on the 1960 constitution since recent events had made it obvious that the two groups could not live together peacefully even if the constitution had remained status quo. Therefore, they demanded partition or federation as well as geographical and physical separation between the two communities (Polyviou 1980).

3.3 Renewed Tensions between Turkish and Greek Cypriots

From 1963 to 1967, intercommunal violence continued and numerous mediation attempts took place to prevent war between Greece and Turkey. It appeared more like a complex game between Turkey and Greece than one strictly between the two communities on the island. When the interests and plans of the two homelands entered into the equation, the likelihood of peaceful resolution decreased. On 21 March 1964, the UN Security Council adopted Resolution 186, with the consent of the government of Cyprus, which authorized the dispatch of the UN Peacekeeping Force to Cyprus (UNFICYP) to preserve the security in the area, prevent recurrence of fighting, and supervise the cease-fire.

An attack by the Greek-Cypriot National Guard on two Turkish villages in November 1967 brought Greece and Turkey to the brink of full-scale military confrontation. In response, the Turkish government sent military aircraft to fly over Cyprus and ordered military forces to be ready in case of an intervention. These actions, according to Brecher and Wilkenfeld (1997b), constituted the crisis trigger for Cyprus and Greece. Turkey had indicated seriousness about her threat of intervention. U.S. diplomatic involvement and pressure led to a cease-fire, withdrawal of all Greek troops from Cyprus that exceeded the number specified in the London and Zurich agreements, and lifting of the blockade on enclaves (Dodd 1999; Polyviou 1980).

The events of 1967 demonstrated to the great powers and the rest of the world that even a small disturbance and subsequent fighting could spread easily all over the island and produce a war between Greece and Turkey. In the Cold War environment, however, a direct confrontation between Turkey and Greece stood out as too risky for the United States to permit.[13] The "Cyprus Syndrome" easily could have become part of the global "balance of power" game played by the superpowers. The United States preferred to be assertive only when the possibility of military escalation between Turkey and Greece heightened and did so in order to protect its own—and also NATO's—interests (Slengesol 2000). For example, after convincing the Turks not to launch a major naval attack, the head of the Supreme Allied Commander Europe (SACEUR) proposed a NATO peacekeeping force of ten thousand troops to maintain security in Cyprus for three months while a mediator less threatening to the respective parties could be found. This offer was rejected by Greece and prompted Soviet leaders to declare that NATO occupation of Cyprus represented a threat to global security. Upon the failure of this and subsequent U.S.-NATO initiatives, the UN Security Council moved to send its own peacekeeping force. Yet Turkey's continuing preparation for an invasion prompted U.S. President Johnson to threaten Turkey: NATO would not defend it should the Russians react to a Turkish offensive in Cyprus. This threat prompted Turkey to reassess its commitments to NATO, and it subsequently cooled relations with its Western allies.[14]

Similarly, for the USSR, Cyprus was important because it provided a good opportunity to balance the United States' influence. In this respect, both the presence of the Communist Party (AKEL) and a common religion—Orthodox Christianity—strengthened ties with the Greek Cypriots. Additionally, due to the multiethnic nature of the former Soviet Union and Russia, there was a tendency to support a solution based on unitary government on the island (Sözen 1999). Thus, the Soviet Union supported the Greek side morally, politically, and militarily.[15]

The mid-1960s witnessed a series of third-party attempts at conflict management. Although these attempts (especially those of the UN and United States, most notably the Johnson Letter) helped to prevent war and further loss of life, no permanent solution to the problem could be found by the parties involved (Bölükbasi 1993). In spite of a cease-fire established in August 1964—which definitely contributed to crisis abatement—actions by the United States and the UN provided no more than temporary relief to both sides. Tension continued and escalated into other crises in 1967 and 1974. From a broader perspective, despite their effectiveness in terminating individual crises, third-party attempts at intervention in this period cannot be designated as successful in solving the Cyprus puzzle. Since resolution of the conflict remained of secondary importance for the United States and the UN, underlying reasons for the tension were not eliminated and, in 1974, the whole scenario repeated itself with the same players (Theophanous 2000a, 2000b).

From 1968 to 1974, with the support of third parties, especially the UN, numerous intercommunal negotiations took place. However, the fact that neither community would cooperate to achieve a feasible settlement doomed all discussions to failure: "The objective of the Greek Cypriot leadership throughout the period was to arrive at a solution whereby the Turkish Cypriots were classed as a minority" (Mirbagheri 1998: 60). Turkish Cypriots staunchly rejected the Greek objective. After the events of 1963, they became even more convinced that it was impossible for the communities to live together. Thus, Turkish Cypriots tried to remain apart from Greek Cypriots and run their own affairs. On 28 December 1967, Turkish Cypriots created the Turkish Cypriot Provisional Administration to establish law and order within their community. However, effective isolation became unrealistic due to the economic embargo imposed by the Greek side, which in turn stimulated a considerable amount of support from Turkey. Turkish Cypriots came to believe deeply that the Greek side ultimately aimed to achieve unification with Greece. In short, not only reluctance to give concessions but also distrust between the two sides led to failure in talks (Mirbagheri 1998).

4. Beyond International Crisis

4.1 The Crisis Period—15 July 1974 to 24 February 1975

On 15 July 1974, the Greek Cypriot National Guard, led by Greek officers, overthrew the government of Cyprus with the intention of establishing a puppet government that would realize *enosis* (Necatigil 1989).[16] At that time Greece was controlled by the military. In terms of the future of Cyprus (i.e., the main question being how to achieve *enosis*), the views of the military in Greece and the president of the Republic of Cyprus, Makarios, differed completely. As a result of the coup, Makarios escaped to London, and Nikos Sampson became the president. In the meantime, heavy fighting went on between Greek and Turkish Cypriots.

Turkey, in response to the coup, asked for resignation of the new regime, withdrawal of Greek officers, and restoration of Makarios as president. When the Greek junta rejected this request, Turkey asked for support from Britain, but the British refused to conduct a joint intervention. As a result, Turkey intervened in the island on 20 January 1974 and claimed that was necessary to stop the bloodshed and human suffering as well as to prevent unification of Cyprus with Greece (Fouskas 2001; Bölükbasi 1993). Extensive fighting and violence resulted from the intervention. Turkey presented the Treaty of Guarantee, which gave Turkey, Greece, and Britain the right to intervene to restore constitutional order to the island as necessary, as the legal basis for its action.

Turkish leaders argued that the intervention took place due to circumstances that had been created by the Greek Cypriots and Greek government. Along those lines, Hale (2000: 181, quoted in Fouskas 2001: 99) argues that "[As opposed to the crises of 1964 and 1967] the crisis of 1974 was different, in that Turkey appeared to have a clearer mandate for intervention under the 1959 Treaty of Guarantee. If Turkey had not invaded, then Cyprus would probably have been united with Greece, the Turkish Cypriots massacred or expelled, and the Greek colonels' regime consolidated."

Greek Cypriots continued to interpret the Turkish action in 1974 as an invasion. Many Greek and Greek Cypriot authors, like Theophanous (2000a, 2000b), believe that for Turkey, the coup against Makarios on 15 July 1974 merely provided an opportunity to invade the island. Prior to 1974, Turkey threatened to invade the island on more than two occasions, so that the invasion and occupation of Northern Cyprus have served Turkish strategic interests over the protection of the Turkish Cypriots and that of Constitutional order in Cyprus. Along those same lines, Fouskas (2001: 100) argues that the second part of the intervention in August 1974 "was not an act of protection of the Turkish Minority. Rather it fulfilled a long-standing Ankara policy aimed at the division of the island along ethnic lines in order to pave the way for the strategic control of the whole of Cyprus and the exclusion of Greece from the Eastern Mediterranean basin." The size of the Turkish military, as well as the distance between

Cyprus and Greece, served to prevent Greece from responding militarily to the Turkish actions.

On 15 July the UN Security Council held an emergency meeting. The Security Council adopted Resolution 353, which called upon all parties to stop fighting, initiate talks to restore peace, and show full respect to the international status of the UN force. In addition, the UN took humanitarian action on the island and designated the UN High Commissioner for Refugees as Coordinator of UN Humanitarian Assistance for Cyprus. On 23 July 1974 civilian rule was restored on the island, and Glafkos Clerides became the acting president (Brecher and Wilkenfeld 1997b, 2000).

Two rounds of talks—the so-called Geneva talks—with the purpose of restoring peace on the island took place from 25 July to 14 August in that year, between the guarantor powers. These talks occurred in response to the request from the UN Security Council noted above. Due to failure of the talks, on 14 August 1974, Turkish forces carried out the second part of the military operation and gained control of almost one-third of the island's territory in the north. On 16 August 1974, Turkey called for a cease-fire. In February 1975, the Turkish Cypriot leadership declared establishment of the "Turkish Federated State of Cyprus" in the area controlled by the Turkish military forces. This event marked the end of the crisis (Brecher and Wilkenfeld 1997b).

Since 1974, the island has been divided—a de facto partition—by the so-called Green Line, and the two ethnically homogenous groups have lived totally isolated from each other.[17] After the intervention, the character of the conflict was transformed from internal fighting to international crisis and the role and importance of the respective homelands increased extensively.

4.2 Postcrisis: 25 February 1975 to the Present

On 15 November 1983, claiming the right of self-determination, Turkish Cypriots declared their own independent state, the Turkish Republic of Northern Cyprus (TRNC). Other than Turkey, no other state has officially recognized the TRNC. The Republic of Cyprus, the only recognized state on the island, exerted no control over the northern part of the island.

Under the auspices of the UN, intercommunal talks resumed again in 1975. The five rounds of talks, which took place from 28 April 1975 to 21 February 1976, ended in failure. Neither Turkish nor Greek Cypriots showed willingness to compromise. Greek Cypriots envisioned a unitary federal system; by contrast, Turkish Cypriots demanded a weak federal government or confederation with clear territorial boundaries in order to preserve their homogeneity and security (Trigeorgis and Trigeorgis 1993; Ertekun 1984).

On 27 January 1977, the Turkish Cypriot leader, Rauf Denktas, and his Greek counterpart, Archbishop Makarios, met in the presence of the Secretary-General's Special Representative in Cyprus. On 12 February 1977, they reached a four-point agreement as the basis for future negotiations.[18] After Makarios's unexpected death, another series of high-level negotiations took place on 19 May 1979 as an extension to the four-point agreement reached between Denktas and Kyprianou under the auspices of the UN. These negotiations produced a ten-point agreement (UN Doc. S/13369). The two agreements remain significant because they are the only criteria that the two sides agreed on formally and keep alive hopes for a solution (Sözen 1999; Mirbagheri 1998).

After the intervention, Turkey became a key actor in the complex game in Cyprus, especially due to a strong military presence in the northern part of the island. Turkey became more assertive, and its influence on the Cypriot government became more significant; any solution not supported by the Turkish government was unlikely to hold. Domestic politics and public opinion heavily influenced Turkey's approach to the Cyprus question. Between 1973 and 1979, seven governments ensued, and only four of them held a majority in the parliament. This made taking unpopular decisions extremely difficult. In addition, in September 1980 the military took power (Mirbagheri 1998), further affecting the future profile of Turkish policy in both general terms and in relation to Cyprus. With the intervention, Turkey had stopped the bloodshed, saved the lives of ethnic brethren, and secured its core interests in the island.

Greece, by contrast, remained dissatisfied with the status quo; lost was the *enosis,* and a significant portion of territory. However, like Turkey, Greece experienced major changes in its internal politics and did not pursue a path toward retribution, With the collapse of the military government on 22 July 1974 and the reestablishment of democracy, Greece's approach to the Cyprus problem was transformed. With removal of the military junta, which engineered the coup attempt in 1974, the Greek government lost its desire to dictate policy to Cyprus and did not perceive the problem as a main concern (Mirbagheri 1998). The newly established Karamanlis government took a conciliatory position toward Cyprus and consequently initiated backroom dialogue with Turkey.

Over the 1980s, various alternative formulae to resolve the Cyprus dispute were drawn up under the aegis of the UN Secretary-General. For example, following the unilateral Turkish Cypriot declaration of independence on 15

November 1983, the UN condemned it with Resolution 541. UN Secretary-General Perez de Cuellar made efforts toward a settlement. On 29 March 1985, Perez de Cuellar presented his draft framework agreement, which called for a bicommunal federal republic. This framework agreement differed from others in the sense that, for the first time, the UN abandoned "mini-package" approaches in favor of a presumably comprehensive solution. According to the agreement, the federal republic would include two provinces or federated states, a president, and a legislature composed of two chambers: a lower chamber with a seventy-thirty Greek Cypriot and Turkish Cypriot representation and an upper chamber with fifty-fifty representation (Necatigil 1989; Tamkoç 1998; Sözen 1999).

Both Denktas and Kyprianou, signed the agreement on 17 January 1985, but the Greek Cypriot leader encountered bitter criticism at home. After his consultation with Greece, Kyprianou altered his position and announced that the agreement would not be acceptable after all. UN Secretary-General Perez de Cuellar conducted extensive negotiations with both sides and presented the final draft framework agreement on 26 March 1986.[19] Turkish Cypriots accepted the revised draft, but Greek Cypriots then rejected the altered agreement after consultation with the Greek government. The UN Secretary-General asked Greek Cypriots to reconsider; further negotiations took place but eventually resulted in failure.

Between 1980 and 1986, both Greece and Turkey continued to play a role in the discussions and decisions regarding the future of the island. While the impact of Turkey's foreign policy on Cyprus stayed the same as in the postintervention period (1974–80), Greece's impact increased (Mirbagheri 1998). In early 1980, Turkey suffered from domestic violence and disorder and, in September, the military gained power and declared martial law. Important changes also occurred in Greece. In 1981, the Greek Socialist Party (PASOK), whose leader was more persistent than his predecessor, was elected. He strongly suggested that the Greek Cypriot president not sign any draft agreements. In general, the overall attitude of Greece to the peace process in Cyprus was unconstructive (Mirbagheri 1998).

In the last decade of the twentieth century, Boutros Ghali, the new UN Secretary-General, proposed a very long and comprehensive "set of ideals," which envisaged a Federal Cyprus (Bölükbasi 1995; Bahçeli and Rizopoulos 1996/97). To discuss the principles, the Greek and Turkish Cypriot leaders came together in New York in October 1992, but like previous efforts, the meeting was destined to fail. The two parties had irreconcilable views and differing perceptions of how a viable settlement would function. In 1995, the UN Security Council recommended a series of "Confidence Building

Measures" in order to eliminate the biggest problem on the way to achieving a peaceful resolution: deep mistrust between the two sides. Most significant among these measures were the opening of Varosha and the Nicosia international airport.

4.3 Involvement of the EC/EU*

Talks between the two sides changed extensively with entrance of the EU into the equation. Indeed, the EU turned out to be a most significant and influential third party.[20] The Association Agreement (1972) and the following protocol (1978) formalized the relationship between the EC and Cyprus. The Association Agreement suggested the establishment of a customs union between Cyprus and the EC over two stages over a ten-year period. In addition to the Association Agreement, from 1979 to 1998 Cyprus and the EC signed four financial protocols. On 4 July 1990, the Republic of Cyprus (i.e., the Greek Cypriot side) formally applied to the EC for membership on behalf of the whole island. Turkey, as one of the guarantors, claimed that the application violated the London-Zurich agreements and therefore asked for the process to be stopped or, otherwise, claimed that the political negotiations in the island would run into difficulties.

In its first opinion (1993), the EU concluded that Cyprus would be eligible for membership. The EU also emphasized, "among other things, the dynamism of the Cypriot economy and expressed the view that no major problems were anticipated in the process of harmonization with the *acquis communautaire.*" However, one provision also designated a solution to the Cyprus problem as a precondition for accession (Theophanous 2000b: 222–23).

The turning point in EU-Cyprus relations occurred in 1995, when the EU General Affairs Council reaffirmed the eligibility of Cyprus for membership and confirmed that it would be included in the next round of enlargement. So accession negotiations started on the basis of commission proposals six months after the Intergovernmental Conference (IGC) in 1996. At the Helsinki Summit of December 1999, the European Council announced that resolution of the Cyprus problem would not be a precondition for accession of Cyprus. This meant that although a peaceful solution to the political problems had not been obtained, the EU would go ahead and accept Cyprus without the participation of the TRNC (Papaneophytou 1994). Not surprisingly,

---

*The term EC, referring to the European Community, is used to describe the organization's involvement up to 1992, when it became the EU (European Union) under the Maastricht Treaty.

Turkey reacted harshly to the decision to give a firm date to Cyprus for beginning accession talks. Cyprus completed the *acquis* screening process in June 1999 (i.e., all thirty-one negotiation chapters were closed) and, in the meantime, substantive negotiations on certain chapters began. The accession negotiations were completed in December 2002. Cyprus signed the Accession Treaty on 16 April and joined the EU on 1 May 2004.

In 2002, UN Secretary-General Kofi Annan handed the leaders of the Greek and Turkish communities a peace plan that envisages a federation with two constituent parts, presided over by a rotating presidency. Due to deep resentment between the two sides, both Cypriot leader Denktas and Cypriot President Tassos Papadopoulos formally rejected the formula. "The Greek Cypriot side rejected the document on grounds that it failed to provide return of all Greek Cypriot refugees to the northern Turkish Cypriot part of the island, Denktas rejected the document on charges that it did not meet the fundamental demands of his people, headed by sovereignty, stipulated an unacceptable ratio of territorial concessions and fell contrary to the agreed principle of a bi-zonal settlement" (*Turkish Daily News,* 2 April 2003). The plan suggested a hybrid system of federation and confederation and gave each group a high level of autonomy. This rejection was important because the Annan Plan, 192 pages long even without the addenda, provided the only "comprehensive solution plan" in the history of Cyprus.[21]

Unlike the UN, the EU's presence as a party in the Cyprus conflict has a more measurable influence. The EU has had two effects on the disputants. First, the EU's influence changed the course of discussions. The EU never prepared its own peace plan. Instead, it always tried to back the UN's peace plan, through both political and economic means. Second, the political and economic benefits that come with EU membership encouraged the Turkish side to reconsider the possibility of unification with the Greek side. Another factor that forced Denktas to be softer and more conciliatory originates from Turkey's own aspiration to become a member of the EU (Kentmen 2003).

During initial private negotiations hosted by the UN in New York, Greek and Turkish Cypriot leaders reached an agreement regarding peace talks and committed themselves to simultaneous referenda on 21 April 2004. Unfortunately, the UN-brokered direct talks to reach an agreement to reunite the island also ended in collapse. While the Turkish side accepted the plan in the referendum, the Greek Cypriots overwhelmingly rejected the UN settlement plan. As a result, the Greek Cypriot–controlled Republic of Cyprus became a member of the EU on 1 May 2004, while the Turkish side remained isolated. In December 2004, Turkey agreed to recognize Cyprus as a member of the EU before the initiation of its own accession talks, scheduled for 2005.

5. Analysis and Propositions

As noted earlier, the Cyprus problem has gone through three main stages: (*a*) the establishment of the republic in 1960; (*b*) protracted conflict and crisis from 1960 to 1974; and (*c*) deescalation in tensions following Turkish military intervention in 1974. As the problem evolved through these periods, the scope and intensity of involvement for Greece and Turkey changed accordingly. More specifically, at stage 1, the two sides had different views about how the island should be governed after British rule. Greek Cypriots and Greece wanted unification, while Turkish Cypriots and Turkey preferred the idea of partition or of staying under British rule as a second choice. In these years, Greece and Turkey exerted little direct influence—mostly the result of diplomacy rather than actual military intervention.

At Stage 2, as the level of violence increased on the island, the influence of the homelands became more direct and extensive. The homelands backed their ethnic brethrens' point of view on both the constitution and the future of ethnic partnership. Eventually, both Greek and Turkish involvement took an aggressive, even violent form: Greece engineered a bloody coup to set up a puppet regime to achieve its ideal of unification, while Turkey responded with a full-scale military intervention.

De facto division of the island continued on into stage 3. This stage, characterized by continuous third-party attempts at conflict management and negotiations for peaceful resolution of the problem, represents a deescalation but also is protracted. The homelands became directly involved in the talks. The lurking presence of Greece and Turkey behind the discussions served as the main reason for ongoing complications and deadlock but also ensured that direct confrontation, already inhibited by membership in NATO and a strong U.S. presence, would be minimized.

This protracted conflict shows characteristics of both secessionism and irredentism. In this case, Greece stands out as the state that seeks to redeem Cyprus. Throughout history, Greeks have regarded Cyprus as a part of a cultural homeland, that is, the historic state. The claim to territory is based on transnational ethnic affinities and conditioned by the deep cleavage between Greek and Turkish Cypriots. The Greek nationalist concept of *megali idea* refers to Greek irredentism of the Byzantine Empire (Joseph 1997). As an extension of the nationalist movement, Greeks supported unification of Cyprus with Greece.

Irredentist conflicts are by definition interstate in scope and involve third-party support. Similarly, since irredentism pertains to another state's territory, which is a core value, there is a high potential for crisis and war. As expected, when the idea of unification with Greece rose to the surface, Turkish Cypriots and Turks felt threatened and sought out partition, that is, secession. In general, secessionist interstate ethnic crises refer to formal and informal aspects of political alienation in which one or more ethnic groups seek, through political means, reduced control by a central authority. In these kinds of ethnic conflicts, the group trying to secede seeks external support. This usually intensifies the level of internal cleavage and disruption and leads to interstate conflict and third-party intervention (Carment 1994b). Secession may not be formal or declared separation as in secession sensu stricto (Heraclides 1990, 1991). As a response to Greek demands for unification with Greece, Turkish Cypriots asked for partition. Turkish Cypriots appealed to Turkey for support, and the result was a military confrontation between two politically mobilized, organized, externally supported ethnic groups and de facto division of the island.

As mentioned in the first chapter, it is well known that affective and instrumental ties can play a decisive role in shaping the decisions of potential third parties (Suhrke and Noble 1977; Smith 1986a; cf. Heraclides 1990, 1991; Carment 1994b). Although some pragmatic concerns are involved, this case study is extremely useful in showing the importance of ethnic ties in third-party interventions. While Greek intervention mostly reflected ethnic ties, Turkish involvement originated from ethnic affinity as well as strategic concerns.

Starting in 1963, "ethnic ties served as the primary cause and vehicle for Greek and Turkish involvement in Cyprus" (Joseph 1997: 129). Eventually, these interventions damaged and even prevented communication and interaction—not only between Greek and Turkish Cypriots, but also between Turks and Greeks as a whole. External, ethnic intervention "sharpened and widened the conflict, thus shifting the focus of repeated crisis from the domestic Cypriot setting to the likelihood of an all-out confrontation across the Aegean" (129).

Testing of the framework's propositions focuses mainly on the Turkish military intervention of 1974. However, assuming that Turkish intervention responded to the coup staged by Greek officials, we also pay some attention to that event. Of course, until 1974, continuous non-military interventions and crises took place within the protracted conflict. The coup staged by Greek forces and the Greek National Guard on Cyprus in order to bring a pro-*enosis* government to power signaled the beginning of Cyprus's foreign policy crisis. The already crumbling internal balance totally collapsed with the overthrow of the government. Heavy fighting broke out between the two ethnic groups. Subsequent Turkish intervention triggered an international crisis and an interstate ethnic conflict.

Proposition P_1 asserts that constrained states will pursue multiple strategies when intervening in ethnic conflict. The Cyprus case supports this proposition. Although ethnic cleavage within Cyprus provided an occasion for Turkish leaders to maximize their domestic political fortunes, that did not occur. While it seemed that, due to the ethnic affinities, the public supported the idea of intervention most of the time, it still was a very hard step for Turkish leaders to take. The timing of the intervention—in the middle of the Cold War—made it especially risky. Being accountable to their people, leaders in Ankara did not accept the risks of intervention lightly. Despite the fact that Turkey is classified as ethnically dominant, for a long time, ethnic affinities alone proved to be an insufficient justification for direct interstate intervention. On two occasions, Turkey threatened Greek Cypriots that she would not hesitate to intervene if the situation on the island got any worse. These threats, however, did not result in intervention until 1974. For example, when Makarios demanded reduction of the powers of the Turkish minority in 1963, fighting broke out and violence quickly spread all over the island. As a response, Turkey basically used two tactics: threat of intervention and small-scale military acts. Turkish leaders, due especially to domestic pressure, believed that they had to defend Turkish Cypriots. The method used, however, remained limited to small-scale military acts due primarily to the letter from President Johnson, the high costs and risks of military intervention, and Prime Minister Ismet Inönü's predominant personality trait—cautiousness (Bölükbasi 1998).[22]

Up to 1974, Turkey applied several strategies—diplomatic, economic, and political—all less costly than military intervention. Turkey backed the Turkish insurgency groups, and especially TMT, politically, militarily, and financially. When a coup attempt with the purpose of unification with Greece took place, Turkish leaders became convinced that they had no choice other than a potentially costly military intervention. A greatly heightened sense of danger to ethnic brethren, along with domestic costs from not pursuing involvement in Cyprus's internal conflict, became too intense for the Turkish leaders to ignore. Public pressure in favor of intervention became extensive and sustained.

From 1967 to 1974, the regime lacked a base of popular support and stayed in power primarily if not exclusively through terror. In 1969, Greece withdrew from the EC and, since the military government did not have any other need to legitimize its actions, it became relatively attractive to stage a coup in Cyprus. The military junta was ready to go to war with Turkey at the time of Turkish intervention. Collapse of the military junta and its successor prevented further military action (Joseph 1997). As noted earlier, in a Type I_a

state, power is concentrated at the top, and therefore the elite is free from domestic pressures. In this kind of setting, an elite is unlikely to face criticism at home as a result of external confrontation. The people at the top have much greater room to adopt an interventionist, hawklike strategy without incurring high political costs. Right after Turkish military intervention in Cyprus, the military government ended, and Greece returned to democracy under the leadership of Konstantinos Karamanlis. A referendum in December 1974 abolished the monarchy. After 1974, Greece could be classified as a Type II_a state, with high institutional constraint and a dominant ethnic group.

Proposition P_2 focuses on the preference for nonviolent strategies by ethnically diverse states. The underlying assumption behind this proposition is that ethnic diversity in a society can limit or redirect actions by the COG. When constituencies have political influence, leaders face difficulty in mobilizing an optimal response to an international opportunity. The demographic characteristics of Greece and Turkey do not allow us to evaluate this proposition directly since both of them are ethnically dominant states. However the behavior of the homelands is basically consistent with the underlying assumptions of this proposition. Therefore, in an indirect way, P_2 gets some support.

When a society is ethnically diverse, leaders experience constraints as different groups demand varying strategies for handling of issues related to secessionism or irredentism. Elites depend on the support of more than one ethnic group, so domestic forces easily can limit the options available to leaders. This, in turn, leads to a reduced likelihood of violent methods of intervention. By contrast, when a society is ethnically dominant, as in the case of Greece and Turkey, elites may prefer policies that will appeal to their ethnic constituency at the expense of smaller groups. This is done, most of the time, to increase their popularity and share of power. Since elites in these kinds of societies neither depend on support from other groups nor see any significant threat to their power, the likelihood of pursuing more aggressive methods, such as initiating an intervention with violence, is higher than in ethnically diverse societies.

Although the level of institutionalization may have changed, basic demographic characteristics have stayed the same. Despite the ethnic dominance in their societies, both Greece and Turkey preferred nonviolent strategies until institutional change in 1974. Thus developments up to 1974 would seem to work against P_2, while the events of that year support it.

Proposition P_3 concerns forceful intervention as related to concentration of costs and benefits. According to this proposition, forceful intervention is more likely when institutional constraints are low, along with minimal political resistance among constituents or all-purpose support from members of the same ethnic group (i.e., ethnic group dominance) as with Type I_a states. This proposition finds support from the Cyprus case. Force ultimately became a central component of both Turkish and Greek foreign policy as related to Cyprus. Most notably, Greece sponsored a coup in 1974, and that ultimately produced Turkish military intervention.

When constraints are low or one ethnic group is dominant, these kinds of states can be expected to show belligerence or forceful intervention as third-party interveners. While the level of institutionalization differed between the two interveners, both of these ethnically dominant states ended up utilizing violent means in their policy toward Cyprus. Institutionalization did not play a restraining role. Apparently, even the existence of a high level of institutionalization did not prevent Turkey from conducting forceful intervention, which clearly suggests the importance of ethnic dominance and cross-boundary ethnic ties.

Since the Turkish experience with democracy is not a uniform one, it is useful to focus briefly on events from 1971 to 1973 in attempting to explain why the state might have acted toward Cyprus as it did in 1974. Turkey was democratic from 1961 till 1971 and from 1973 to 1979. The role of the military within those intervening years creates some "question marks" regarding the level of institutionalization in Turkey. Rather than taking over the government directly, on 12 March 1971, commanders of the Turkish armed forces presented a memorandum to the president. The memo demanded establishment of a credible government with real power, an end to socioeconomic unrest and violence prevailing in the country, and application of some economic and social reforms. The military commanders also made it clear that in case these demands were not met, they would overthrow the elected government—"a coup by memorandum" as labeled in the Turkish politics literature. The prime minister, Süleyman Demirel, resigned immediately, and chiefs of the armed forces asked Nihat Erim to form an above-party government. The military appointed a series of above-party cabinets that governed the country until the 14 October 1973 elections. The result was a coalition government set up by the Republican People's Party, National Salvation Party, and Republican Reliance Party. With these elections, Turkey returned to democracy (Hale 1994).

Bearing in mind the problems with Turkish democracy, the country still exhibited enough institutional limitations on elite power to be counted as a high-constraint state in 1974.[23] Thus domestic institutions, as well the Cold War environment, stand out as the main reasons why Turkey preferred a relatively mild strategy of nonviolent intervention until 1974. Ethnic affinities and cleavage did not prove powerful enough to produce forceful action from the Turkish side. However, when *enosis* became a real possibility and huge pressure emerged from the public, the dominant ethnic elite in Turkey moved forward and conducted a forceful intervention. At that point, ethnic dominance, along with ethnic affinity and cleavage, proved to be more powerful in determining the outcome (the nature of the intervention). Similarly, as expected, low levels of institutionalization increased the likelihood of noncooperative and even aggressive foreign policy in Greece. Therefore, the Greeks provided relatively strong support for autonomy of ethnic brethren in Cyprus.

Proposition P_4 concerns the role of high affinities and cleavage in exacerbating tensions between states. As noted, the presence of ethnic ties, as well as cleavages between groups, can increase the chances of a state initiating an ethnically oriented policy that leads to a crisis. Ethnic ties and cleavage can create opportunities to be exploited and therefore increase the likelihood of involvement in ethnic conflict. Along those lines, it is clear that the two ethnic groups in Cyprus are connected to their homelands in many respects. The two communal groups have regarded themselves as different from each other, based on origin, culture, language, and religion. Both sides have maintained ethnonationalist rhetoric for many years, and eventually, this behavior facilitated expansion of the conflict and interventions by the respective homelands. Historically, Greece and Turkey have strong relations with the island and continuously have expressed their interest in the issue of its permanent disposition regarding sovereignty. Even after the establishment of the republic in 1960, loyalties to Greece and Turkey continued to exist in the form of strong historical, educational, cultural, and religious ties. Granting the right to use the Greek and Turkish flags and celebration of national holidays that belong to the homelands are examples that show the lasting power of these ties (Joseph 1997).

In sum, "outside intervention along ethnic lines has been an important and influential factor in the society and politics of Cyprus since independence" (Joseph 1997: 39). Removal of colonial administration prepared suitable grounds for Greece and Turkey to establish close relations with the new state, increase their ties with, and voice in, Cyprus, with the idea of promoting national goals (Joseph 1997). Despite establishment of an independent state, Greek and Turkish Cypriots did not identify themselves with the new entity as much as they did with their homelands.

Even a cursory review of the establishment of a constitution, dualism and nonstop interventions of Turkish and Greek governments in the internal affairs of Cyprus (i.e., rejection of amendments from Makarios by Turkey and coup d'état attempts by the Greek junta) is sufficient to show how

(a) the two sides are inclined to intervene along ethnic lines;
(b) external interventions increase misperceptions;
(c) interventions deepened the antagonisms; and lastly
(d) third-party actions decreased the chances of a stable and peaceful resolution.[24]

Perhaps old ethnic animosities and external involvement are equally important in understanding the current impasse.[25] Political and social interactions between Cypriots have reflected "instruction on one level by 'ancient affections'—that is, lessons of history, past communal relations, stereotypes, prejudices, religious and other cultural and social factors—and on another level by external influences, both direct and indirect" (Sambanis 1994: 130). While interventions may have resulted from long-standing hatreds, mistrust between the two sides increased with respective actions by Greece and Turkey.

The 1959 treaties of Guarantee and Alliance, decided mainly by Britain, Greece, and Turkey, are examples of direct external influence (Sambanis 1994). These agreements are significant reasons for deadlock and aggravation of existing tensions between Turkish and Greek Cypriots. (An instance of indirect external influence is the educational system designed by the British, which emphasized the differences between the two communities [Sambanis 1994].) Efforts by Greece and Turkey throughout the history of the case stand out as mainly self-serving and unproductive. Most of the time, the actions of the homelands limited the options of the Cypriots and deepened divisions between the ethnic groups. Therefore, rather than bringing about a solution, Greece and Turkey have helped to perpetuate the conflict (Sambanis 1994).

Proposition P_5, which concerns the relative likelihood of ethnic intervention, also finds support from this case. In the typology presented in figure 2.1, Turkey and Greece would be classified as ethnically dominant, high-constraint (Type II_a) and ethnically dominant, low-constraint (Type I_a) states, respectively.[26]

According to our framework as presented in chapter 2, options for decision makers are affected mainly by the relative size of ethnic groups, affinity, and cleavage (the affective variables) and the level of institutionalization within the state (the political variable). The basic reason for expecting sporadic interventionism from a Type II_a state is its mixture of ethnic dominance and high institutional constraints. While institutions make third-party involvement harder, ethnic dominance makes it easier.

Why did forceful intervention occur despite a high level of institutionalization? Two competing arguments can be offered. One explanation focuses on the underlying nature of the conflict. Due to high costs—both domestic and international—Turkey for a long time refrained from utilizing military means. But when no other means worked, Turkish leaders ordered military intervention. Turkey's apparent attitude and nonviolent actions prior to 1974 support the claim that institutions mattered in the decision to intervene. The other argument, which emphasizes the importance of ethnic dominance, is in essence the contrary. Although a democracy since 1946, Turkish armed forces overthrew the elected government in three instances—1960, 1971, and 1980. Thus, it might be argued that at the time of intervention, Turkey was not a vibrant democracy in *practice* and unconstrained ethnic dominance led to intervention. Turkey's *attitude and behavior* are in line with expectations.

For Greece, a low-constraint, ethnically dominant state in 1974, the expectation is belligerence. Elites seized power and disregarded the results of popular elections. Between 1967 and 1974, the military dictatorship in power remained relatively immune from domestic pressure.

6. Conclusions

The goal of this chapter was to evaluate the interstate dimensions of ethnic conflict and the impact of institutions and ethnic constraints on intervention in a setting with both irredentist and secessionist characteristics. The results indicate that ethnic diversity and institutional constraints have the capacity to explain Turkish and Greek decisions to get involved in the Cyprus conflict. We also have looked at the role that linkage variables, ethnic affinity, and cleavage played in third-party interventions and found them to be important sources of elite involvement in an ethnic conflict.

In order to understand the patterns of Turkish and Greek interests and involvement in the Cyprus conflict, we started with an account of the events that led to crisis in 1974. Greek and Turkish interventions in 1974 have been examined in detail, and the five propositions developed in chapter 2 have been tested. Based on the historical evidence, we can claim that developments in Cyprus generally are in line with expectations. In evaluating the Greek-staged coup and Turkish military intervention, not only affective and political variables, but also enabling conditions, played a major role. The high level of ethnic ties with homelands and the deep cleavage between the groups in Cyprus increased the likelihood of Turkey and Greece applying ethnically oriented policies. Indeed, these are the two main reasons behind the protractedness of the conflict.

Another interesting finding is that, as seen in the Somalia and Indo-Sri Lankan cases, high-constraint states (both diverse and dominant) are not as immune to using force. Turkey, a high constraint–dominant state, preferred support for insurgency movements to direct military involvement for a long time. Elites used the threat of intervention as a means to achieve their goal in the short term. However, in 1974, the level of cleavage, hostility, and fighting reached a point that caused Turkey to intervene militarily. At that point the role of institutions seemed relatively less influential as compared to the impact of ethnic dominance, affinity, and cleavage.

Finally, in evaluating this case, it is essential to take into consideration the relationship between Greece and Turkey as parties to a protracted conflict while also members of a defensive alliance. Results of previous studies show that conflicts within that type of setting work differently from the ones outside that context (Colaresi and Thompson 2002). Crisis actors within protracted conflicts are more likely to experience violent triggers, to perceive a more basic threat, and to employ violence with high severity and prominence in crisis management. A prolonged history of conflict and violence between the same adversaries creates mistrust and expectation of further hostility. Moreover, the periodic resort to violence in the past reinforces the expectation of violence in the future (Brecher and Wilkenfeld 1997b). In this case, mutual distrust between the two ethnic groups and between Turkey and Greece played a decisive role in the evolution of the conflict. Similarly, the mistrust and the protracted conflict setting affected the calculations of the elites on both sides when they were thinking about intervention. Therefore, the context of this conflict needs to be taken into consideration in explaining the actions of Greece and Turkey in 1974. To this day, Cyprus continues to complicate the relationship between Greece and Turkey. However, like the Thai Malay case, it is important to note how countries facing a common security problem can be brought together. In this case NATO membership had a constraining effect on both states. Granted, immense U.S. pressure was brought to bear, especially on Turkey—which militarily had the upper hand. One can only imagine what kind of wars would have raged had neither country been a member of NATO or had the UN not become involved. NATO involvement reduced levels of conflict between ethnic groups and their alliance members.

In this case, there was a sense of collective responsibility to respond to regional conflicts based on the fear that such conflict would draw in the major powers or lead to regional instability. This may still be the case for some conflicts, but the absence of a "Cold War mentality" as an additional factor may influence and alter a state's decision's to act in harmony with others. This suggests a paradox; the Cold War provided elements of order whose dissipation has changed the context within which military intervention is possible and yet perhaps less desirable from the perspective of some states (Cooper and Berdal 1993). The Cyprus conflict holds one further lesson. The Cyprus case could be an instructive guide whose rules NATO should apply with respect to the inclusion of members from the former Warsaw Pact. Regional conflicts between these members have been and will prove to be as intractable as those between Greece and Turkey. Unless ongoing efforts are taken to resolve these differences, NATO will again be in a precarious position whereby its (in)action may divide the alliance.

CHAPTER EIGHT

Conclusions:
Taming the Untamable?

> If we consider international relations as a whole—as a body of thought over the centuries, as a collection of research findings, as a conventional wisdom, as a set of disciplined propositions about the world and the way it works—then we find that a message is waiting for us. It is a distinctive message about behavior in the world and ipso facto, about how to approach and analyze conflict. (Banks 1986)

1. Introduction: Taming the Untamable

Interstate ethnic conflicts comprise a significant but not well understood part of world politics. This inquiry contributed to an understanding of these conflicts through case studies of intervention. The cases span five regions—South Asia, Southeast Asia, Africa, Europe and the intersection of Europe, Asia, and the Middle East—and include states ranging from homogenous to diverse in ethnic composition, along with secessionist- and irredentist-based conflicts that extend from minor violence to full-scale war. Interstate conflicts encompassed by the case studies focus on major religious communities, such as Buddhist (Sri Lanka, Thailand), Christian Orthodox (Serbia, Croatia, Bosnia, Ethiopia, Greece), Hindu (India, Sri Lanka), and Muslim (Malaysia, Somalia, Bosnia, Turkey) and include states that range from highly institutionalized democracies to the extremes of unconstrained autocracy, with India and Somalia (after 1969) as polar instances. Given the range of actors and situations included, the present study seems in line with the epigraph to this chapter, which calls for a comprehensive approach to international relations. This study derives an overall message about ethnic conflict, interstate crisis, and intervention by considering all matters ranging from classic ideas to research findings. The message, in the end, is that ethnic intervention as associated with interstate crisis reflects demographics, institutional makeup, and more nuanced factors such as affinity and cleavage that impact upon the potential for conflict escalation.

This chapter unfolds in four additional sections, the first three of which correspond to the major goals of the study as set forth in chapter 1. The second section will review evidence about the framework and suggest priorities for its elaboration and improvement. Section 3 covers the propositions and results from testing, while section 4 derives implications for policy regarding ethnic conflict management and reduction. Section 5 provides a few final thoughts.

2. A Framework for Analysis of Intervention

The framework, which consists of three stages of interaction, appears consistent with the five case histories of ethnic intervention included in this book. Since these cases cover five world regions and a wide range of cultures and background conditions, confidence increases in the framework's general relevance. A few illustrations, corresponding to how respective stages of the framework have worked out in the case studies, will follow.

Stage 1's four ideal types of state, each with different preferences for involvement in ethnic strife, result from the interaction effects for ethnic composition and institutional constraints. On the one hand, chapter 3's analysis of India, a Type II_b state, reveals a slow and halting path ultimately leading to a relatively limited intervention in Sri Lanka. On the other hand, chapter 6 conveys a story in which Serbia, a Type I_a state, is well disposed from the outset toward violent intervention, most notably in Croatia and Bosnia, where only very heavy casualties and exceedingly poor prospects for victory eventually managed to bring highly destructive conflict to at least a temporary halt.

Stage 2, which assesses whether foreign policy will lead to interstate conflict and crisis through intervention, sees two additional variables, affinity and cleavage, come to the fore. Affinity and cleavage can combine to create a security dilemma for states, because the Chief of Government must decide on how to address them in the context of internal politics and even pressure from extremists. For states facing high domestic costs because of institutional constraints and ethnic diversity, the use of force is the least attractive option due to likely domestic repercussions and aggravation of the security dilemma. When cleavages and affinities are high, crisis escalation becomes more likely because elites of both states are disposed to initiate a conflict in an attempt to address perceived security weaknesses. Consider two examples: Somalia and Greece. Somalia's high affinity with Ogadeni and Darod clan members in the Ogaden, as compared to ethnic Somalis in other clans in

Kenya and Djibouti, explains crisis escalation between Somalia and Ethiopia. Described in chapter 7, the 1974 coup in Cyprus, backed by Greece, can be traced directly to very high ethnic cleavage on the troubled island, along with salient affinities between Greek Cypriots and their compatriots in Greece. Thus affinity and cleavage can create, in such cases, a second stage of effects beyond the mere disposition to act as derived from the first stage.

During stage 3, which corresponds to intervention itself, low-constraint, ethnically dominant states (Type I_a) should have a higher preference for the use of force than do high-constraint ethnically diverse states (Type II_b) because of low domestic costs. Types II_a and I_b fit between these two extremes. A state primarily interested in defending its security (i.e., Type II_b) is not necessarily an aggressor. This idea may be controversial because, as the Indo-Sri Lankan case shows in chapter 3, it often is difficult to identify the aggressor state in an interstate ethnic conflict. In this instance, neither state would be labeled as aggressive because each primarily defended its security. By contrast, as the Ethiopia-Somalia case shows in chapter 4, the aggressor sometimes is more clearly identified. In still other cases, such as Yugoslavia in chapter 6, culpability is diffuse because most participants, notably Serbia and Croatia, took aggressive actions to defend and reclaim territory and ethnic brethren.

Three areas stand out as priorities for further work on an elaborated and improved framework. Each will be addressed briefly in turn.

First, the relationship of an elite to its political constituency in shaping preferences for intervention is extremely important. Elites sometimes represent a dominant ethnic group, but that entity is highly divided between two or more constituencies. In turn, this relationship will affect the way the political process is played out, especially if institutional constraints are high and ethnicity is the basis for political mobilization. In some societies, crosscutting cleavages are an important way of counteracting the effects of internal divisions; ethnicity then may be less of a basis for political mobilization and an ethnically based foreign policy becomes less likely. It might be possible to evaluate, through surveys, for example, differences between elite and mass preferences to find out if these converge on certain foreign policy issues.

Second, affinity and cleavage appear to have important explanatory power in their own right. Further analysis could focus on, for example, the impact that diasporas have on the propensity for violent interstate ethnic conflict. These factors should be treated as structural preconditions that influence the magnitude and salience of a state's security dilemma.

Third, and finally, the framework should make explicit the role of extraregional actors in escalating, managing, and resolving conflict. This study has focused primarily on why the main antagonists become involved, but not the levels of support expected from extraregional actors. Two reasons make the latter subject a priority. First, many cases simultaneously involve multiple actors, most notably major powers, the United Nations, and regional organizations. Actions taken by extraregional entities like great powers or international organizations (whether governmental or otherwise) can be important elements in the promulgation and resolution of ethnic conflict. Second, it also would be useful to know more about how and why geographically distant but ethnically linked states provide support for an ethnic conflict.

3. Propositions and Testing

Proposition 1, which asserts that constrained states will pursue multiple strategies when intervening in ethnic conflict, finds support. In particular, ethnically diverse, constrained states must shape their strategies in response to those of other states. When faced with the decision to use force against a state with fewer visible political costs (e.g., an ethnically dominant and low-constraint state), that decision to escalate will depend primarily on the strategy of the latter state, which possesses substantially more leeway in deciding what to do.

For three reasons, elites in unconstrained situations are in a better bargaining position when faced with those who have dispersed power. First, they are less prone to involuntary defection because their low-constraint, ethnic homogeneity allows them to control more effectively domestic political outcomes. Second, a belligerent ethnic foreign policy can be expected to create fewer domestic ramifications. Among other things, the leaders of these states do not have to worry about reelection. Third, if cooperation tentatively does emerge, low-constraint ethnically dominant states might be more tempted to defect voluntarily because of low political costs associated with doing so. In brief, the decision to use force is contingent primarily on the degree of cooperation from the state with fewer anticipated costs.

Consider the multiple strategies pursued by the two most highly constrained states assessed in this book: India and Malaysia as described in chapters 3 and 5, respectively. Indian leaders over the years tried limited backing for the Tamil insurgents in Sri Lanka, mediation of ethnic strife on that island, military intervention, and combinations of strategies as well. Malaysian strategy converged over time toward a limited degree of support for the Thai Malay, with leaders of the Kelantan province sometimes pressing the issue harder than the central government. Furthermore, more favorable policies on the part of the Thai government toward the Thai Malay attenuated support for either union with Malaysia or a separate state. The diverse strategies of these states contrast, for example, with the relentless irredentism of Type I_a Somalia or undemocratic Greece.

Proposition 2, which asserts that ethnically diverse states are less likely to initiate crises with violence, is supported. India, Malaysia, and Yugoslavia (before 1990) provide direct evidence about diverse states in chapters 3, 5, and 6, respectively. India, an ethnically diverse and institutionally constrained state, did not initiate force directly against the Sri Lankan regime. India did, however, use force at a later point against the Tamil rebels. Evidence suggests that India was constrained in using force against Sri Lanka, but did everything short of that in trying to achieve its domestic and international objectives, which included imposing a solution of regional autonomy on the Sri Lankan government. India's elites could not allow Sri Lankan aggression against Tamil civilians in the north to go unchecked because of the impact on politics in South India. The solution of sending "peacekeeping" troops to Sri Lanka represented a compromise that would appease both the Sri Lankan government and South Indian Tamils.

Similarly, Malaysia's leaders remained averse to direct support and escalation of violence throughout the series of tense interactions with Thailand. Wariness about Islamic fundamentalism, along with the desire not to exacerbate internal divisions in a multiethnic society, inhibited the use of violent tactics. Furthermore, the right of hot pursuit granted by Thailand to Malaysia represented a major recognition of interest in the fate of the Patani province and also encouraged an evolutionary rather than revolutionary approach. Malaysia's restraint is echoed by that displayed by members of the Yugoslav federation prior to 1990. The components of that very diverse union knew that Belgrade would tolerate nothing beyond the occasional discussion of how the federation might evolve in its structures and processes.

Proposition 3, which asserts that crises are more likely to be severe when unconstrained, ethnically dominant states are involved, finds support. Somalia (after 1969), Serbia (after 1990), and Greece (ca. 1974), in chapters 4, 6, and 7, respectively, provide direct evidence.

When tracing interactions between Somalia and Ethiopia from Somali independence onward, changes in its decisions to use force can be linked to the latter's institutional developments. With Somalia's transition to autocracy in 1969, the Type I_a state moved steadily toward war with its neighbor over the Ogaden. Somalia made repeated violent attempts at retrieval, which culminated in full-scale war by the end of the decade.

Serbia's elite benefited from forceful interventions in Slovenia, Croatia, and Bosnia. Although elements in the military still loyal to the integrity of Yugoslavia objected, using force on behalf of ethnic brethren in these proto-states had wide and popular appeal. The JNA and well-armed coethnics in Croatia and Bosnia, in particular, increased the relative severity of crises that unfolded in the immediate aftermath of Yugoslavia's breakup.

Aided by Greek Cypriots, Greece initiated a coup in Cyprus. This dramatic action by the Type I_a Greek state produced an intense crisis that ultimately elicited Turkish military intervention on the fervently disputed island. Although Turkey would be classified as a Type II_a state at the time of its intervention, Ankara's use of force in 1974 fits the anticipated profile of sporadic interventionism. Turkey, which had not previously intervened directly in Cyprus, took limited military intervention to prevent *enosis*.

Proposition 4, which asserts that high cleavage and affinities increase the probability of intense interstate ethnic conflict, finds the strongest support. In general, ethnic cleavage and affinity influence foreign policy preferences significantly; they appear to be virtually necessary for interstate ethnic conflict and crisis. High levels for both increase fundamental and widespread insecurities, and elites will generally choose to act on them. Evidence suggests that when cleavages and affinity are high, there is a greater likelihood that the preferences of all states will shift toward policies that increase tension and sustain conflict.

For example, India's millions of Tamils had great affinity with ethnic brethren in Sri Lanka, and, as chapter 3 reveals, high cleavage on the island produced increasing levels of involvement in the conflict by the region's leading power. This process culminated in the Indian intervention of 1987, although countervailing factors, such as India's status as a Type II_b state, undoubtedly helped it to avoid taking actions that would lead to interstate warfare. Affinity and cleavage, by contrast, prove to be near sufficient conditions for war in chapter 4's account of Somali invasion of the Ogaden. Somali leaders used the issue of the Ogaden effectively in creating a vision of a Greater Somalia that could be manipulated to great political advantage.

For Malaysia as described in chapter 5, rogue elements in Kelantan constituted the greatest policy concern vis-à-vis potential crisis with Thailand. In spite of affinity and some degree of cleavage, the relatively small size and limited resources of the Thai Malay minority ultimately reduced the chances of escalation to an interstate ethnic crisis. In particular, there is no evidence that cleavage ever rose to the level seen in the case of Cyprus or even Sri Lanka. This contrasts with the situation in Yugoslavia as described in chapter 6, where ethnic affinities and cleavages permeated the shattered federation. The collaboration of Serbia with minorities in other emerging states is merely the most notorious part of the overall story of secessionism, irredentism, and ethnic cleansing. Perhaps the same could be said of chapter 7's account of Greek and Turkish efforts toward *enosis* and *taksim,* respectively—words steeped in the ideas of ethnic affinity and cleavage.

Proposition 5 asserts that ethnic intervention is most likely, in descending order, for Types I_a, II_a, I_b and II_b. The case studies collectively reflect this ordering and also the more specific expectations regarding style of intervention as conveyed by figure 2.1. The Type I_a states, Somalia (after 1969), Yugoslavia (after 1990), and Greece (1974), all intervened in ways that can be equated with belligerence. Perhaps the only remaining question here is, "Why did Greece wait until 1974?" although that is answered to some degree in chapter 7. Somewhat more restrained are the Type II_a states, Somalia (before 1969) and Turkey (1974), which indeed show sporadic interventionism as a reflection of both circumstances and intermittent ethnic outbidding. Neither intervened in its respective target area with any degree of consistency, but each showed the potential for more intense involvement—realized in the case of Turkey when it intervened in Cyprus in response to the Greek-inspired military coup on that island. Next in line is Yugoslavia (before 1990), the Type I_b state, where passive lobbying predominated within the federation. This activity picked up after the death of Tito, the founder of post–World War II Yugoslavia, but did not break out into civil war until after the transition of 1990, when an ethnically homogenous Serbian state took the lead in promoting irredentism and ultimately ethnic cleansing. Finally, the activities of the Type II_b states, India and Malaysia, follow the anticipated path of realpolitik. While India did intervene in Sri Lanka in 1987, even then it did so as part of a plan to stabilize the island's embattled government rather than promote irredentism across the Palk Straits.

Taken together, the five propositions perform rather well across the five cases. Further case studies may alter the conclusions reached in this exposition, but that is a subject for another time. The generally positive performance of the framework and its attendant propositions lead naturally into a discussion of policy implications.

4. Conclusions and Implications about Interstate Ethnic Conflict Management and Prevention

Evidence from the five case studies in this book suggests that when combined, internal ethnic diversity and institutional constraints are associated with lower levels of interstate ethnic conflict. These conditions lead to mutual vulnerability among states that, in turn, reduces the potential for aggression and violence. The presence of these two conditions may make a head of government think twice about involvement in secessionist and irredentist strife, if there is any choice in the matter. Two problems, however, arise as a by-product of this conclusion.

First, ethnic diversity does not mean that domestic strife involving such states will be resolved more easily; rather, conflict management and reduction are more practical goals. The crucial task is to find an internal balance of power among ethnic groups, such as Yugoslavia before Tito's death. The implication is that societies that attempt to address their diversity through redistributive policies that favor one ethnic group, while perhaps politically astute for some elites at the domestic level, stand a greater chance of triggering interstate ethnic conflict if and when one group becomes preponderant. All of the states examined in the case studies within this book pursued some kind of redistributive policy that favored one ethnic group over another, but only two of the conflicts (Ethiopia-Somalia and Yugoslavia) resulted in direct interstate violence. These cases are distinguished, as established already, by the presence of Type I_a states and high levels of ethnic affinity and cleavage.

The second problem is managing political transition. Evidence indicates that both new states and those undergoing political transition are most susceptible to involvement in interstate ethnic conflict. New states experience levels of domestic disorder that divide a state's elites, complicate decision making, prolong a crisis, or plunge a state into a protracted conflict with the consequence of inviting external intervention. This is true especially for newly democratized states, so it is essential to encourage alignments based on interests other than ethnicity and reduce disparities between groups so that dissatisfaction among minorities declines. For new states, their multiethnic character, compounded by internal cleavage and transnational affinities, may prove overwhelming for fragile institutions to manage. When political parties are aligned along ethnic interests, diverse and institutionally constrained developing states are prone to outbidding that can enhance the potential for interstate conflict.

Relevant in a practical way is the finding that external mechanisms, possibly formal regional alliances, may assist in reducing conflict among states. In this respect, it is important to distinguish security threats perceived by the regime and the general population from each other. The two do not always share the same security concerns; occasionally, the population itself constitutes the main internal threat to a regime and vice versa. The key point is to focus on issues of security that are shared by elites and masses within as well as between states. Shared security concerns may be the best way to prevent interstate ethnic conflict. To date, few security issues engender this kind of sharing between masses and elites, although environmental problems and economic development often are cited as sources of interstate and intrastate cooperation. Working in tandem with this kind of cooperation is the important international monitoring of human rights abuses that may help push elites further in a more humane direction.

Another policy-related implication, brought out most directly in chapter 5's analysis of the Thai Malay strife, is that voluntary defection by one or both states in an ethnic conflict can be reduced when there is awareness of mutual vulnerability. Involuntary defection, a problem for constrained, diverse states, can be reduced if elites perceive it to be in their long-term interests to cooperate. For example, the Kelantan region represented Malaysia's potential for involuntary defection because of its support for the Thai Malay. This could have caused Malaysia to renege on its reciprocal agreements with Thailand. Pressure (and possibly incentives) applied on Kelantan leaders, however, eventually resulted in their tacit withdrawal from the issue. Furthermore, cooperation can be maintained even after the original threat dissipates, as in the Thai Malay case. Efforts to reduce defection among states seeking to support ethnic groups elsewhere can be successful. In this case, an alliance structure, based on a threat shared between Thailand and Malaysia, enhanced the relative attractiveness of military and political cooperation. Since ethnically diverse, constrained states already are oriented toward finding cooperative solutions, the key issue is finding ways in which to restrain less diverse or institutionally unconstrained states.

Another policy-related finding is that ethnically divided states attempting to make the simultaneous transition to more economically open and democratic systems will succumb to the politics of intransigence, confrontation, and conflict if the political system is arranged along ethnic lines and one ethnic group is allowed to become dominant. Leaders of ethnically based political parties will lack, over the short term, the capacity to widen the policy agenda to encompass nonethnic issues. When other bases of mobilization are weak, ethnic elites depend on direct support from their ethnic constituency, and in turn, elites seek to control and influence these groups. Thus the key problem raised by the conflict in Yugoslavia, for example, is finding ways to ensure conflict reduction within the state rather than having secessionist minorities leave. Given the right international and domestic conditions, which may include democratization, more liberal trade, and incentives for interethnic cooperation, secessionist minorities may reduce their demands for autonomy. Unfortunately, in the Yugoslav case, there were too few incentives for Slovenia and Croatia to stay and too many for them to defect.

5. Some Final Thoughts

The absence of a revised overarching framework of policies on ethnic conflict management and resolution is linked intimately to changes in thinking about the nature of state sovereignty, which includes the conduct of states external to a conflict, and internal changes, including democratization, that states are experiencing. While the passing of the Cold War removed impediments to an examination of the preceding factors, the collapse of communism ushered in a volatile period of political experimentation in which, over the short term at least, domestic ethnic conflicts continued on toward the end of the twentieth century and beyond. The sudden overthrow of authoritarian regimes in the early 1990s was accompanied by a rapid escalation of ethnic tensions on a global scale. Intense, violent full-scale wars emerged. This was as true in Africa as in Eastern and Central Europe. In some cases the potential for inter-state ethnic conflict remains high; Azerbaijan, Georgia, Sudan, Angola, the Congo, and the Ukraine come to mind, while others have gradually dissipated with time. Only time will tell how many more Yugoslavias may be out there waiting to happen, but everything possible should be done to anticipate, prevent, or at least manage such crises. The framework developed and tested in this book is intended as a step in the direction of greater understanding, in order to establish the foundation for a more comprehensive analysis of ethnic conflict, interstate crises, and intervention.

NOTES

Chapter One

1. A classification of all major active conflicts, either internally or externally driven, appears in table 17.3 of M. Brown (1996: 582).

2. In the 1990s, international crises with an ethnic dimension included Yugoslavia, Mauritania, Rwanda-Burundi, Senegal, Togo, Nigeria, Kenya, Papua, New Guinea, Algeria, China, Bhutan, Brazil, Mexico, India, Kosovo, Albania, Greece, Bulgaria, East Timor, the Republic of Macedonia, Kashmir, Moldova, Cyprus, Burma, Sudan, Indonesia, Iraq, Azerbaijan, and Tadjikistan. Little doubt exists that ethnic conflicts cut across territorial boundaries and influence the interaction of states in the global arena; case studies (Suhrke and Noble 1977; Heraclides 1990, 1991, 1997; Midlarsky 1992; Zartman 1992; Van Evera 1994; M. Brown 1996; Kaufman 1996; Lake and Rothchild 1996, 1998; Midlarsky 1997; Saideman 1997, 1998a, b; Kriesberg 1997; Taras 1997; Taras and Ganguly 2002; Young 1997) and aggregate data analysis (Carment 1993, 1994a; Carment and James 1995, 1996; Davis, Jaggers, and Moore 1997; Brecher and Wilkenfeld 1997a; Marshall 1997; Maoz 1997a) already have identified a range of factors leading to the internationalization of ethnic conflict.

3. While Suhrke and Noble's (1977) seminal assessment of eight ethnic conflicts produced the conclusion that domestic ethnic conflicts did not constitute a significant source of interstate strife, political scientists have reassessed that result and found that ethnic alliances, to name but one linkage, are a significant source of interstate conflict (Davis, Jaggers, and Moore 1997; Saideman 1997; Lake and Rothchild 1998).

4. Taras and Ganguly (2002) define four alternative processes that can lead to the internationalization of ethnic conflict: international diplomatic activities, partisan intervention, international terrorism, and flow of refugees.

5. For a detailed discussion of diffusion and its conceptual history, see Marshall 1997. There is some divergence in definitions among Starr (1990), Vasquez (1992), Marshall (1997) and the MAR Project (1998, http://www.cidcm.umd.edu/inscr/mar/). MAR, in particular, refers to diffusion as a demonstration effect of antiregime activity by a group in one country to kindred groups in other (usually adjoining) countries; see also Collins 1973 on conflict diffusion in Africa.

6. For more details on the effects of internal conflicts on regions as whole, and especially on neighboring countries, see M. Brown (1996).

7. For example, Crighton and MacIver (1991) argue that vertical escalation corresponds to at least three necessary and sufficient conditions: a threat to the identity or existence of the ethnic group, elites with the political skills and resources to play

on those fears, and third-party military, political, and economic support for the cause. Van Evera (1994) also addresses interdependence between states as a causal factor in his study of war and nationalism and measures the relative importance of structural (geographic and demographic), political/environmental (institutions), and perceptual (nationalist self-image) variables to determine when and under what conditions nationalist sentiments are more or less likely to lead to interstate confrontation.

8. Our interest is not exclusively with crises, which are understood to form part of more encompassing stories of conflict. The approach here will be inclusive with respect to the makeup of an interstate ethnic conflict.

9. It should be noted that ICB's concept formation includes both foreign policy and international crises. Conditions of finite time, threat to values, and high probability of military hostilities are necessary and sufficient for a foreign policy crisis to occur. An international crisis occurs, as noted in the text a moment ago, when a foreign policy crisis creates a disruption in process and the potential for a change in the international system. Accordingly, ICB data are bifurcated to recognize these related but separate forms of crisis. The actor-level data set on foreign policy crises focuses on decisionmaking and unit-level attributes, while the system-level data on international crises includes the collective experiences of the actors involved. The ICB data are available online at http://www.cidcm.umd.edu/icb.

10. Theoretically, ethnic linkages are not essential for irredenta; efforts toward reunification can be based exclusively on territory (Horowitz 1991; Vasquez 1992: 310–11; Sullivan 1996). In reality, however, many irredenta are associated with ethnic identity, and challenges usually involve mobilization of ethnic groups. For those reasons and because the focus of this investigation is on ethnic factors that encourage interstate conflict, irredentism is defined as territorial *and* ethnic in nature.

11. This type of definition appears to be accepted by Heraclides (1990, 1991), Horowitz (1981), and Suhrke and Noble (1977). Secessions sensu stricto are different from "incremental" secessions that involve political activity aimed at independence or some form of autonomy but that do not entail any formal declarations of independence. Both kinds of cases are included here (Heraclides 1991: 1). Entities that possess a territorial base for a collectivity, a sizable and distinct human grouping, and claim that there is an unequal relationship between the minority group and the center meet the defining elements for secessionism (Heraclides 1991: 13). A minority group's territory also may have international borders; see Zartman (1992) and Grant (1997) for examples drawn from Central Europe and Asia.

Chapter Two

1. The origins of contemporary research on linkage politics, which connects intrastate with interstate behavior, can be traced to Rosenau 1969.

2. The term "rational" denotes behavior that is appropriate to specified goals in the context of a given situation. *Substantive* rationality refers to behavior judged to be optimally adapted to a situation. *Procedural* or *bounded* rationality refers to behavior that is adaptive within the constraints imposed by the external situation and

the capacities of the decision maker. The differences just noted define the gap between advocates of political psychology and rational choice. The former accentuate the capacities of decision makers as sources of foreign policy, while the latter emphasize external environmental conditions as constraints. In this volume, rationality refers to selecting the best means available under a given set of circumstances to accomplish a specified set of objectives. The decision maker must be able to comprehend both the nature of the objective and characteristics of the environment in which it arises (Maoz 1990, 1997b; James 1993). For a summary and applications of rational choice theory, see Booth, James, and Meadwell (1993).

3. Specific ethnic groups within the military and the bureaucracy can dominate the state through different means, notably (a) skewed recruitment and (b) a situation when the ethnic composition of military and civilian leadership is congruent. The basic challenge to peace is that soldiers who remain on the sidelines will have difficulty putting ethnic affiliations aside, and leaders may use intervention as a means of shoring up domestic support. Consider in that context the place of the military within the states of Eastern and Central Europe. The military suffers from extremely poor social conditions, low morale, high levels of absenteeism, low conscription, corruption, inadequate funding, and a general loss of purpose. The inability of governments to resolve these problems may become a prime reason for the armed forces to support ethnic leaders who promise that their concerns will be addressed. Obvious political benefits accrue to ethnic leaders from such promises.

4. Of course, some of the classic studies raise the possibility of alternative means toward reaching a decision. Allison (1971), for example, suggests that each of his three models—unitary rational actor, organizational process, and bureaucratic politics—captures part of a complex decision-making reality. Stein and Tanter (1980) went further by integrating their three models—analytic, cybernetic, and cognitive—and five functions of the decision process—diagnosis, search estimation and revision, evaluation and choice—into overall multiple paths to choice (see also Brecher 1972).

5. The following summary of the research enterprise on two-level games is based primarily on Evans (1993).

6. This argument suggests a paradox in the behavior of groups in multiethnic societies—common interest in assisting ethnic brethren should lead to a concerted action, but in highly diverse societies this is unlikely to occur unless political entrepreneurs strive to organize relatively homogenous groups that in turn exert pressure on national leaders. Classic expositions on the problems facing collective action appear in Olson (1965) and Sandler (1992).

7. In a more general sense, the purpose of a case study is to investigate the plausibility of the framework and make explicit the relationships between and among the terms specified in the propositions. This has three advantages. First, it allows an evaluation of the underlying assumptions that are embedded in much of the essentially ad hoc and correlational studies on ethnic conflict. Second, it stimulates development of different propositions that later can be tested in different ways. Third, a case study is an illustrative tool to assist readers in understanding how the propositions work (King, Keohane, and Verba 1994: introduction). In sum, a case study provides a valuable means for pursuing critical questions of causality and model refinement. Such an

approach is often justified as a tool to evaluate the logical consistency of an argument, clarify the propositions, and examine critical questions of inference.

Chapter Three

1. Quoted in the *Straits Times,* 17 May 1993. McGowan is author of *Only Man Is Vile: The Tragedy of Sri Lanka* (1992).

2. Although addressing the problem of international protracted conflicts, Azar, Jureidini, and McLaurin's (1978: 41–60) definition is equally salient to Sri Lanka's domestic strife: "Protracted conflicts are hostile interactions which extend over long periods of time with sporadic outbreaks of open warfare fluctuating in frequency and intensity. These are conflict situations in which the stakes are very high—the conflicts involve whole societies and act as agents for defining the scope of national identity and social solidarity."

3. According to the Minorities at Risk Project, the Tamils of Sri Lankan citizenship are ethnonationalists: regionally concentrated peoples with a history of organized political autonomy with their own state, a traditional ruler, or regional government who have supported political movements for autonomy at some time since 1945. Sri Lanka Tamils of Indian citizenship are an ethnoclass—ethnically or culturally distinct peoples, usually descended from slaves or immigrants, most of whom occupy a distinct social and economic status or niche. If an ethnoclass is a politically organized contender for a share in state power, it is designated as a communal contender. See http://www.cidcm.umd.edu/inscr/mar/home.htm.

4. Thus the Federal Party's separatist demands from the beginning focused on the existence of a definite territorial claim along existing regional boundaries. Without a Tamil majority in any of the provinces, it is likely that opinions would have diverged on separation as a realistic option.

5. Taras and Ganguly (2002), for example, argue that due to strong linguistic identity, language was the most important and divisive issue in ethnic relations in Sri Lanka after independence.

6. The LTTE became the sole Tamil insurgency movement (effectively having removed other rival groups in bloody internecine fighting between 1986 and 1989); in contrast with the LTTE, the leaders of the EPRLF decided to participate in Provincial Council elections.

7. In response to these separatist demands, the Second Republican Constitution of 1978 contained some measures to win back the Tamils but others that clearly favored the Sinhalese: Art. 2—The Republic of Sri Lanka is a unitary state. Art. 3—The Republic of Sri Lanka shall give to Buddhism the foremost place and accordingly it shall be the duty of the state to protect and foster the *Buddha Sasana* while assuring to all religions the rights granted by Articles 10 and 14. Art. 18—The Official Language of Sri Lanka shall be Sinhala. Art. 19.—The National Language of Sri Lanka shall be Sinhala and Tamil. Art. 20 (1)—The Official Language shall be the language of Administration throughout Sri Lanka. Provided that Tamil is the language of Administration for the maintenance of public records and the transaction of all business in the Northern and Eastern Provinces (Colombo: Department of Census and Statistics 1977, 1981).

8. The claim for a separate state during the 1950s engendered hostility from the Indian government, which had taken legislative steps in its own country to placate the separatist Dravidanadu movement in Tamil Nadu. India also confronted other separatist groups and did not sympathize with the Tamil cause.

9. Between July 1983 and January 1985 the Sri Lankan government announced that 356 civilians had died as a result of clashes between Tamils and Sinhalese. Monthly totals of dead, including civilians and soldiers, numbered in the 300s from January to March and then jumped to 842 in June 1986. Furthermore, India could not ignore the thousands of refugees flowing into Indian territory as a result of the violence. By 1986, Tamil Nadu had become the home for 125,000 Tamil refugees (*Asiaweek*, 1 June 1986).

10. As described by the accord, the main principles of the Provincial Councils were as follows: to widen regional participation in government and devolve authority in matters of agriculture and industry, education and culture, internal law and order, and land settlement in each province. A three-tier system of authority would exist: national, provincial, and local. As expected, the national government would retain widespread powers in defense, foreign affairs, state monetary policy, judiciary posts, customs, foreign trade, ports and aviation, broadcasting, and citizenship. Parliament would continue to be elected by districts every six years on a basis of proportional representation. No change would occur in the office of an elected presidency every six years.

11. This description is based on interviews with and notes from Canada's representatives in Sri Lanka (Canadian International Development Agency, Ottawa, October 1989). The less publicized demands of the accord imposed upon Sri Lanka by India had implications that went beyond resolving the ethnic conflict. Jayewardene's military advisers saw these demands as a violation of Sri Lankan independence.

12. This year also brought presidential elections. On 19 December 1988 voters could choose between the SLFP, led by Sirima Bandaranaike (who opposed the implementation of Provincial Councils), the UNP, led by Ranasinghe Premadasa (who had distanced himself from Jayewardene's arrangements with India), and the Sri Lanka Mahajan Party (SLMP), led by Ossie Abeygoonasekera (supported by the TULF and favoring the accord). With 55 percent of the electorate voting, Premadasa polled 2.6 million votes (50.4 percent); Bandaranaike received 2.3 million votes (44.6 percent) and Abeygoonasekera, 0.23 million, 4.5 percent of the vote. The rise to power of Ranasinghe Premadasa, who succeeded Jayewardene as president, signaled an escalation in verbal hostilities between Sri Lanka and India.

13. Bharata Janata Party (BJP) is an Indian political party that advocates Hindu nationalism. The BJP resolved to pull India out of Sri Lanka. The BJP played a major role in India's political life in 1990s. After the 1996, 1998, and 1999 elections the BJP formed governments with Bihari Vajpayee as president.

Chapter Four

1. In August 1963, Mogadishu Radio broadcast a Somali poem calling for all Somalis to be reunited. This quotation is part of the translated text (Drysdale 1964: 16).

2. According to the Minorities at Risk (MAR) Project the Somalis of Ethiopia are

an indigenous people, defined as conquered descendants of earlier inhabitants of a region who live mainly in conformity with traditional social, economic, and cultural customs that are sharply distinct from those of dominant groups. Indigenous peoples who had durable states of their own prior to conquest or who have given sustained support to modern movements aimed at establishing their own state are classified instead as ethnonationalists. See the MAR Project Web site at http://www.cidcm. umd.edu/inscr/mar/home.htm (9 January 2004).

3. The crises are as follows: Ethiopia-Somalia Crisis (1960), Kenya-Somalia Crisis (1963–64), Ogaden I (1964), Ogaden II (1977–78), East Africa Confrontation (1980–81), Ogaden III (1982), and the Ethiopia-Somalia Crisis (1987). See Brecher and Wilkenfeld (1997b) and Brecher and Wilkenfeld et al. (1988) for case summaries and data pertaining to these crises.

4. For details on the MAR Project, see http://www.cidcm.umd.edu/inscr/mar/ home.htm.

5. Minorities at Risk Project, http://www.cidcm.umd.edu/inscr/mar/home.htm, 01/1010 January 2004.

6. Ratification of the Somali constitution serves as the best example of differences between the two former colonies at this time. In the south (formerly Italian Somaliland) a substantial majority approved the constitution. However, it received less than 50 percent support in the former British colony. In December 1961 an attempted military coup in the north, led by officers, tried to break up the union. The coup failed but revealed the fissures between the north and south (Laitin and Samatar 1987: 72).

7. The following description of events from the 1990s onward is based primarily on a combination of coverage from BBC News, CNN, the *New York Times,* and the UN Web site.

Chapter Five

1. This analysis concentrates on the Malay Muslims of the southern provinces of Thailand as distinct from the smaller population of non-Malay Thai Muslims centered around Bangkok and elsewhere. The four southernmost provinces are Yala, Narathiwat, Patani, and Satul. Satul, however, is different from the other three Muslim provinces since, unlike the others, it does not have a history of separatism and confrontation with the Thai government. There also is lower tension between the Buddhist majority of Thailand and inhabitants of Satul because of their long history of close administrative interactions with Bangkok. Furthermore, the majority of people in Satul speak Thai. The district of Satul, therefore, does not play a very active role in the Muslim separatist movement (Yegar 2002: 89–90). On a separate note, until 1939 Thailand's official name was Siam.

2. According to the MAR Project, the Thai Malay are a "National Minority" defined as: "segments of transitional people with a history of organized political autonomy whose kindred control an adjacent state, but who now constitute a minority in the state in which they reside." The project does not distinguish, however, between Thai Muslims and Thai Malay. For details see http://www.bsos.umd.edu/cidcm/mar/ grtype.htn http://www.cidcm.umd.edu/inscr/mar/data/thamuslchro.htm.

3. By the end of the 1980s, Thai Malay leaders obtained several important political and economic concessions from the Thai government. Violence in these provinces subsided but, by some accounts, conflict between the state-center and minority increased in the early 1990s and continues sporadically into the twenty-first century, this time taking on a revived religious and transnational dimension (Chaiwat 1993). Past research on Thai Malay separatism traces the roots of the conflict to poor cultural and political relations between the Malay community and nationalist Thai regimes (Pitsuwan 1985; Forbes 1989; Suhrke 1989; Chaiwat 1993).

4. Research on the Thai Malay issue usually locates the primary causes of the conflict at the domestic political level. Conventional wisdom holds that an overall decline in violence in the southern provinces is a function of improved relations between the state-center and its marginalized minorities, namely, a reduction of cleavages within Thailand. For example, in Carment and Joseph's (1999) data set, Thailand scores four out of a possible five for an index of cleavage, which corresponds to moderate-high cleavage where there are high levels of repression and ethnic consciousness against more than one minority and occasional societal unrest leading to interethnic violence. Malaysia scores a five on the index, which corresponds to high cleavage where mass violence is likely, repression is widespread, ethnicity is highly politicized, and interethnic struggle leading to the collapse of the state is imminent.

5. Despite limitations in available data, it is possible to estimate the ethnic composition of the minority sector of the Thai population in a sample year, namely, 1987. Chinese constituted about 11 percent of the population, Malay about 3.5 percent, and long-term resident (as opposed to refugee) Khmer less than 1 percent. The remaining minority groups ranged in number from a few hundred to more than 100,000 (MAR Web link, cited above). More than 85 percent speak a dialect of Thai and share a common culture. This core population includes the central Thai (36 percent of the population), Thai-Lao (32 percent), northern Thai (8 percent), and southern Thai (8 percent). The language of the central Thai population is the language taught in schools and used in government. Several other small Thai-speaking groups include the Shan, Lue, and Phutai. The largest minorities are the Chinese (about 12 percent of the population) and the Malay-speaking Muslims of the south (3 percent). Other groups include the Khmer, the Mon (who are substantially assimilated with the Thai), and the Vietnamese. Smaller, predominantly mountain-dwelling tribes, such as the Hmong, Karen, and Mein, number about 500,000.

6. The language, religion, and culture of this small minority are significantly different from the rest of Thailand. The Malay belong to the Shafi'it Sect of Sunni Islam, the predominant sect of Islamic Southeast Asia. A minority of Malay Muslim are Shi'ite. The Malay converted to Islam in the fourteenth and fifteenth centuries A.D. (Che Man 1990: 35).

7. For an informative analysis of Thailand's non-Malay Muslim groups, who are predominately South Asian in origin, see Forbes 1982.

8. The Patani region became incorporated formally into Thailand in 1901. Until 1906, the seven districts had comprised the sultanate of Patani. After this time they were reorganized into the districts of Patani, Narathiwat, and Yala. In 1909 the Thai-Malaysian border was formally fixed, and Malay Muslims became citizens of the new

Thai nation-state. The decline in organized violence in the southern provinces is viewed as a function of improved relations between the state-center and its marginalized minorities.

9. This includes Malay, Chinese, and immigrants of Indian descent. Current figures indicate that the Malay constitute 59 percent, the Chinese 32 percent, and Indians 9 percent of the population, respectively. The percentages for Malays stayed below the 50 percent threshold in the 1960s (*CIA Fact Book,* various years).

10. Based on the lack of reaction from the central government to his comments, it is unclear whether the minister had voiced official Malaysian policy on the issue. Bangkok, however, made a more direct general response (*Straits Times,* 18 June 1974). The government expressed concern over foreigners in the Middle East acting on behalf of separatists (Pitsuwan 1985).

11. This irredentist movement espoused unification of all of Malaya, including Singapore and portions of territory across the straits of Malacca. The leaders of the organization had been arrested in 1961 after staging a revolt, but some managed to flee to Malaya.

12. The organization maintains a website by which to generate support in its ongoing struggles See PULO web page www.pulo.org. In a press realease of 26 October 2004, The Pulo notes that

> unrest in the Patani has been going on for more than 10 months now. There are very strong indications that a tragic ending of it is not far away any more. So, on behalf of justice and the right to live—we have no choice than—once again to appeal to the United Nations Security Council and the UN Human Rights Commission to come and bring about peace. However, the legacy of the brutal more than 100-years long Thai occupation and the effect of the violent aftermath of the consultation will last for long time. We believe that to give the world's newest nation a good beginning is necessary for the international community to pressurize the Thai government to expedite this process.

13. When the Vietnam War culminated in a communist victory in 1975, Bangkok's fear of Vietnamese expansion grew, which ironically led to increased pressure from Thai nationalists to dissolve the border agreement with Malaysia. Bangkok ignored these pleas.

14. The term "near crisis" is used because these internal acts against the state did not generate a full foreign policy crisis. (For more on the idea of failed or near crisis see Brecher 1993 and Brecher and Wilkenfeld et al. 1988.) The internal threat is but one of many developments that accounted for the regime's replacement. The security of the Thai state neither came into question nor did the event to lead to a higher probability of military hostilities between Thailand and any external actor, including Malaysia.

15. A second and related clue is the rise to power in 1976 of a civil authoritarian government in Thailand. This regime ruled without popular participation, brushing aside many problems that had been the concern of the previously democratically elected government of Seni Pramoj (Pitsuwan 1985). The three-year democratic regime of

Pramoj, elected in 1973, had brought about a change in tactics in the Thai Malay struggle. Political protests based on notions of equality, freedom, and guaranteed rights became the rallying cries of the Thai Malay leaders. In 1974, Bangkok had installed troops in the area. Massive demonstrations, including riots in 1975, helped raise awareness among Malay masses and served as constant sources of friction between Bangkok and Kuala Lumpur.

16. According to Bodansky and Forrest (1998), Iran and Pakistan transformed Thailand into a safe haven for Islamist terrorists in the entire East Asia region, with dozens of networks operating in the Bangkok area alone, and including members from Saudi Arabia, Pakistan, Bangladesh, and Syria (U.S. Congress Task Force on Terrorism and Unconventional Warfare 1998).

17. See Rand web page, http://www.rand.org/publications/MR/MR1344/ MR1344.ch9.pdf/, 1October 2004

18. Government provision of health, education, and welfare services proved to be inadequate or nonexistent; schools were established only in the cities, for the benefit of children of Central Thai officials. In the 1980s, King Bhumibol and government leaders, especially those from the South, became involved deeply in rectifying those inequalities, but resentment and suspicion hampered development.

19. However, it also is significant that Malaysia's minority communities are willing to be included in political change. In essence, the fear of a potential left-right split in Malaysian politics during the 1960s led to an alliance between conservative factions within Malaysia's three major ethnic groups.

20. An implication is that both SAARC and the OAU (now the AU) had been designed to advance the interests of only some of the participating states. In this context, consider the overwhelming influence that Ethiopia exerted in structuring the OAU Charter in response to Somalia's claim on its territories. For Sri Lanka, in relation to its internal conflict, India is the only real security threat.

Chapter Six

1. According to the MAR Project, the three major ethnic minorities under discussion here vary in their goals, political formation, and identity. For example, Serbs and Croats residing in what now is the independent state of Bosnia-Herzegovina are national minorities. Muslims living in Bosnia are ethnonationalists. Those Muslims living in what now is the Montenegrin part of the Federal Republic of Yugoslavia (FRY) are referred to as religious sects. The Bosnian Muslims refer to themselves as "Bosniacs" and consider the term "Muslim" derogatory; more importantly, they want to distinguish themselves from Muslims living outside of Bosnia. The term Bosniac will be used to refer to Bosnian Muslims. For more information see http://www.cidcm.umd.edu/inscr/mar/ home.htm

2. Exceptions exist; in Slovenia the principal language is Slovene and in Macedonia the principal languages are Macedonian and Albanian.

3. The major exception is the exodus of Italian and German minorities after World War II from different regions in Yugoslavia (Flere 1991).

4. In the 1981 census, Croats, Slovenes, Macedonians, ethnic Muslims,

Albanians, and even smaller groups such as Hungarians and Bulgarians were located in all eight federal units (Ramet 1992b). Serbs also can be found in all of the other former federal units of Yugoslavia. For example, the Serbs constitute roughly 12 percent of the population of Croatia and 32 percent of the population of Bosnia (Gagnon 1994, 1994/95).

5. In 1993, Albanians comprised 20 percent of Serbia's population, with Hungarians being the remaining 4 percent. The decline of Serbs in Kosovo is due to their emigration from that entity—regarded as the birthplace of Serbian nationhood and statehood—a predominantly Albanian populated area. Percentages of the dominant ethnic groups within the other states are as follows: Croatia—Croats 77 percent, Serbs 12 percent; Bosnia and Herzegovina—Slav Muslims 44 percent, Serbs 31 percent, Croats 17 percent; Slovenia—Slovenian 90 percent; Montenegro—Montenegrin 68 percent, Muslims 13 percent, Albanian 6 percent; Macedonia—Macedonians, 60 percent, Albanians 18 percent, Turks 4 percent (*Globe and Mail*, "Yugoslavia: The Roots of the Conflict" 7 March 1992. The percentages for 1991 are as follows: Slovenia—Slovenes 90 percent, Croats 3 percent, Serbs 2 percent, others 5 percent; Croatia—Croats 75 percent, Serbs 12 percent, others 13 percent; Bosnia-Herzegovina—Muslims 40 percent, Serbs 33 percent, Croats 18 percent, others 9 percent; Montenegro—Montenegrins 68 percent, Muslims, 13 percent, Albanians 6 percent, Serbs 3 percent, others 10 percent; Vojvochna—Serbs 56 percent, Hungarians 21 percent, others 23 percent; Serbia—Serbs 65 percent, Albanians 20 percent, Croats 2 percent, others 15 percent; Macedonia—Macedonians 67 percent, Albanians 20 percent, Serbs 2 percent, others 11 percent; Kosovo—Albanians 90 percent, Serbs and Montenegrins 5 percent, others 5 percent (Pavkovic 2000: 49).

6. Under Tito, the constitution invested sovereignty not only in the federal republics but in the nations of Yugoslavia as well. During the 1980s, this dual sovereignty came to mean that should one of the republics want to secede, it first had to secure the agreement of the sovereign nations that made it up. In effect, this mechanism had been designed to prevent the breaking off of Croatia and Bosnia, in which the Serbs are in a minority position. According to the notion of dual sovereignty, the original declarations of independence were illegal because these votes did not have the consensus of all the ethnic nations (Glenny 1993a, b). In contrast, the European Community demands only a simple majority of constituents to vote for independence. Thus, for the EC, all three acts of independence—Bosnia, Croatia, and Slovenia—were legal, although not by Yugoslavia's standards.

7. A weak and ineffective effort to unify Yugoslavia took place, with a Croatian reformist, Ante Markovic, selected as federal prime minister. He applied some economic reforms to control the inflation and massive labor unrest, believing incorrectly that such measures could save the country from dissolution.

8. Massive demonstrations in Belgrade that condemned Milosevic's policies led to a softening of his hard-line position in April 1991. He accepted the principle of confederal arrangement and later agreed to the principles upon which such a compromise would be based (Gagnon 1994/95). At the same time, however, the Serb regime and SDS had stepped up anti-Croatian rhetoric, which relied on sensationalist media reports that portrayed the Croatians as fascists. Milosevic blamed Germany and Austria as coconspirators in the Croatian fight for independence.

9. Designation of crisis onset and termination at the system level and the foreign policy level have no impact on the interpretation of events or their causal factors. It should be noted that Croatia already had adopted a new constitution in 1990, one that referred to Croatia as the sovereign state of the Croats (and other nations living in Croatia) but did not explicitly recognize the Serbian community (Cohen 1992).

10. Various countries, including the United States, the Soviet Union, China, Britain, France, Sweden, Denmark, Italy, Greece, Romania, Poland, and Hungary, initially rejected the new republics' declaration of independence; see Saideman 1998b for details.

11. Both the EC and the United States issued statements on 25 June 1991 that they would not recognize the republics if the latter voted for secession (*New York Times*, 25 June 1991). When the external allies of Slovenia and Croatia—as well as Macedonia and Bosnia, which later declared independence—threatened intervention, the crisis became fully internationalized. Only then did internal disruptions threaten regional stability (Ramet 1992a: 267).

12. At this time Slovenia had yet to gain recognition as an independent state. In November 1992, Germany and Austria became the first external actors to recognize Slovenia (*Globe and Mail*, 11 November 1992).

13. The United States halted trade with all six republics under a generalized system of preferences. Sanctions imposed by the European Community applied only to Serbia and its ally Montenegro (*Globe and Mail*, 7 December 1991). None of these sanctions prevented the illegal shipment of arms. For example, the JNA captured a Canadian, Anton Kikas, a Croatian by birth, on 1 September 1991. His chartered aircraft was found to be carrying eighteen tonnes of Singapore-made SAR-80 rifles.

14. The United States recognized the independence of Croatia and Slovenia, along with that of Bosnia-Herzegovina, in April. Toward the end of the war in Bosnia, Serbia proper became known as the Federal Republic of Yugoslavia (FRY). For purposes of consistency, "Serbia" will be used throughout.

15. Macedonians already had voted for a looser association with Yugoslavia. Full independence followed shortly thereafter.

16. Serbian general elections took place on 21 December 1992. Amid accusations of fraud, Milosevic returned to power, defeating his chief opponent, Prime Minister Milan Panic, by a margin of 57 percent to 33 percent (*Globe and Mail*, 22 December 1992: A1).

17. In August 1992 the UN formally expelled rump-Yugoslavia from the General Assembly (Cohen 1992).

18. Tudjman's governing Croatian Democratic Union won 57 percent of the vote in the 120-seat parliament; 3.5 million Croatians in and outside of Croatia were eligible to vote (*Globe and Mail*, 4 August 1992: A1).

19. Brcko is a strategically important town located in the northeastern part of Bosnia and Herzegovina. It was the only territorial issue left unresolved in the 1995 Dayton agreement. The International Arbitration Commission declared Brcko to be a district of Bosnia-Herzegovina on 8 March 2000. Before the war the population in Brcko was around 88,000—44 percent Bosniac, 25 percent Croat, 21 percent Serb, and 10 percent others. For more details see the official Web site of the government of Brcko district of Bosnia Herzegovina (www.brcko.ba) and NATO Web page (www.nato.int, 1 October 2004).

20. Tito elevated the Bosniacs in 1971 to the status of a Yugoslav "nation." In Bosnia-Herzegovina, three constituent "nations" were said to coexist. Before any constitutional changes regarding secession could be made, all three communities in Bosnia would have to agree, which they did not.

21. Russia's Yeltsin already had made it clear that Serbia no longer would receive arms from Russia; on 27 April 1993 this decision was announced formally (Glenny 1993a, b).

22. Achieving consensus among the NATO member states was a painfully slow process; see *Globe and Mail*, 6 December 1992: A1.

23. As before, the Bosnian Croatian leader Mate Boban and Muslim leader Izetbegovic proved receptive to the idea of the plan, which included a cease-fire, a political agreement, and a map reorganizing the former Yugoslav republic into ten separate regions under a central government. Karadzic's willingness to sign the agreement came only after immense pressure from Milosevic (*Globe and Mail*, 10 January 1993: A1).

24. After it had been negotiated in Dayton, Ohio, the General Framework Agreement for peace in Bosnia-Herzegovina was signed in Paris on 14 December 1995. On 16 December 1995 the North Atlantic Council (NAC) authorized SACEUR to deploy Enabling Forces into Croatia and Bosnia-Herzegovina in order to implement military aspects of this agreement. IFOR, a NATO-led multinational force, started its functions on 20 December 1995 with a one-year mandate. Its main duties were to supervise (a) selective marking of boundaries and (b) establishment of interentity boundary lines between the Republic of Srpska (RS) on the one hand and the Federation (Bosnian Croat and Bosniac forces) on the other. After the September 1996 elections, IFOR completed its mission, although a need to stabilize the region and keep the peace was very clear. SFOR was authorized by the UN Security Council and started its mission on 12 December 1996 as a successor of IFOR. Among other things, SFOR provided a secure and stable environment for the national elections in October 1998. For details see the official Web page of NATO at www.nato.int.

25. Portions of this chapter are based on interviews of IFOR/NATO personnel by David Carment while in Croatia, Bosnia, and the Federal Republic of Yugoslavia, 14–24 March 1998.

26. Debate continues as to whether states external to the conflict—Germany, the United States, Turkey, Greece, Hungary, and Albania—were crisis actors. Although in some instances these states place the military on higher than normal alert, only one of the three conditions necessary for a foreign policy crisis is present in all cases: threat to values (i.e., not finite time or heightened probability of military hostilities). Insufficient evidence exists to conclude that perceptions of these actors included a sense of limited time or probability of violence involving direct threats to themselves (Saideman 1998b).

27. Different phases of change among the republics, as mentioned above, led to varying perceptions of economic payoffs to each ethnic group within this structure. For Slovenia and Croatia the payoffs were low. The leaders of these republics, having activated the popular sector through carefully orchestrated elections and referendums, faced the prospect of further unrest among their minorities. To convince potential

external support that internal unrest was not so divisive as to scare off capital, the leaders of these new states had to present an image of unity and democracy, one that could be achieved most easily through appeals to nationalist identities. In Slovenia, perhaps due to its relative homogeneity, this strategy appears to have been successful. For Croatia under Tudjman, however, even greater repression followed internal unrest.

28. These affinities may have been vague from the outset, a view that finds support from a Belgrade political scientist, who comments, "[O]ur concept of Serbian ethnicity is linked with orthodoxy, but not with any cultural and historical totality which is much broader and which is generally accepted [elsewhere] in Europe" (Ramet 1992a: 264).

29. A second aspect of the positive and negative reverberations engendered by ethnic affinities in this conflict is the set of linkages between each ethnic group within Yugoslavia and the various regional actors. Most notable in this regard is the Serb-Russian linkage, which ensured Serbia a flow of oil and arms despite embargoes. Greece also has exhibited a perceptible pro-Serbian tilt throughout the crisis, a result both of Greek-Serbian economic interdependence and of long-standing Greek animosity toward Macedonia. Despite a substantial Serbian domestic arms industry and significant stockpiles, arms flowed from Greece and Romania to Serbia during this time (Saideman 1998b).

30. This does not mean that force is the only means to prevent states from escalating a conflict. In the Yugoslavian case, for example, failure by many outside states to comply with the sanctions on Serbia and Croatia also must be considered.

Chapter Seven

1. "Cyprus is a case study of ethnic conflict" (Kissinger 1999: 193, quoted from Fouskas 2001).

2. Cyprus, Smyrna, and the Aegean Sea are indicated as the main issues in the ICB data set. While the Aegean Sea disputes (case numbers 272, 349, 376) focus on the islands, most notably their continental shelf and territorial waters, the Smyrna dispute (case numbers 16, 18, 25) is about territory in Anatolia.

3. http://www.freedomhouse.org/research/freeworld/2003/countryratings/cyprusgreek.htm, 24 February 2003.

4. *Enosis* refers to the idea of unification of Cyprus with Greece. Turkish Cypriots fear this idea because, in the case of unification, they would become an ethnic minority in a Greek state. For more details on the historical evolution of the *enosis*, see Fouskas 2001.

5. The main reason behind politicizing communal differences between Greeks and Turks was to serve British interests in the Middle East. For more information on the impact of British rule, see Pollis 1973.

6. Turkish Cypriots initially preferred continuation of British rule to *enosis*. Starting from 1957, however, Turkish Cypriots began to support the idea of partition as the exact opposite of *enosis*. *Taksim*, the Turkish reply to the idea of *enosis*, refers to division of the island between Greece and Turkey (Lumsden 1973).

7. EOKA (the national organization of Cypriot fighters) was a guerrilla organization established under the military leadership of Colonel Grivas. The main purpose of this organization was to end colonial rule on the island and implement the idea of *enosis* (Holland 1998). On 1 April 1955, EOKA began an armed struggle (http://www.pio.gov.cy/cyprus/history/modern.htm, 25 November 2003).

8. The London and Zurich Agreements are the treaties that led to the creation of the Republic of Cyprus. For the texts of the Treaties of Establishment, Alliance, and Guarantee, see http://www.mfa.gov.tr/grupa/ad/add/f612.htm, 24 November 2003.

9. According to the census conducted by the Department of Statistics and Research in 1960 the island's population was 573,566, with 442,138 (77.1 percent) Greek and 104,320 (18.2 percent) Turkish. Figures from the Turkish-Cypriot administration are slightly different; they include the British sovereign bases. The total population of the island is said to be 577,615 inhabitants—448,857 (77.7 percent) Greek and 104,350 (18.1 percent) Turkish. For more demographic information, see the Republic of Cyprus Web page (http://www.pio.gov.cy/docs/euro/council_of_europe/parl_assembly/cuco/memorandum/demographic_data_upto_1997.htm, 24 November 2003).

10. *Art 182*: The Articles or parts of Articles of this Constitution set out in Annex III hereto which have been incorporated from the Zurich Agreement dated 11th February, 1959, are the basic Articles of this Constitution and cannot, in any way, be amended, whether by way of variation, addition or repeal. Subject to paragraph 1 of this Article any provision of this Constitution may be amended, whether by way of variation, addition or repeal, as provided in paragraph 3 of this Article. Such amendment shall be made by a law passed by a majority vote comprising at least two-thirds of the total number of the Representatives belonging to the Greek Community and at least two-thirds of the total number of the Representatives belonging to the Turkish Community. *Art 185*: The territory of the Republic is one and indivisible. The integral or partial union of Cyprus with any other State or the separatist independence is excluded; see http://www.pio.gov.cy/cygov/constitution/appendix_d_part13.htm, 25 November 2003.

11. The amendment proposed by Makarios to change the constitution of Cyprus included the following aspects: abandonment of the right of veto of the president and the vice president, establishment of unified municipalities, unification of the administration of Cyprus, abolition of the separate majority votes in the parliament, and participation of the two communities in the public service in proportion to their population. The Republic of Cyprus Web page lists the thirteen points (http://www.pio.gov.cy/docs/proposals/13points/index.htm, 22 November 2003); for further details about the amendment, see Necatigil 1977.

12. For the arguments of Greek Cypriots regarding the reasons for amendment, see http://www.pio.gov.cy/docs/proposals/13points/intro.htm, 23 November 2003.

13. Joseph (1997) and Sambanis (1994) argue that due to the transformation of the ethnic conflict into a case study in East-West polarization, the ability of the superpowers to settle the problems remained very limited. They could offer only superficial, blanket, Cold War–oriented approaches to the conflict.

14. For the purposes of this investigation, the significance of the Cyprus conflict is twofold. First, the Cyprus conflict is not resolved, but it has been successfully con-

tained and managed. Yet, according to critics of NATO, the incapacity of collective efforts to resolve ethnic conflict, whether it be Cyprus or Yugoslavia, indicate a crisis of authority in the alliance, characterized by a decline in regime effectiveness. This interpretation holds that the dynamics of these internal conflicts far outpace the rules and norms that the international community has in its possession to resolve them. Other, more conventional positions submit that NATO is an appropriate tool for managing ethnic strife. NATO was never created for the purpose of resolving ethnic strife insofar as it impinges on the interests and security of the alliance. Evidence from the conflict over Cyprus supports the view that NATO and other international instruments remain important elements in the management of ethnic strife.

15. Sözen (1999) interprets the behavior of the USSR/Russia as contradictory because as a member of the UN Security Council, it should have supported demilitarization, nonviolent resolution of the conflict, and the necessity of refraining from actions that could increase tension on the island. The decision to sell S-300 missiles to the Greek Cypriot side, despite condemnation from the international community, reflects the above-mentioned contradiction.

16. The Department of Statistics and Research of the Republic of Cyprus estimates the total population in 1974 at 641,000, with 506,000 (78.9 percent) Greek and 118,000 (18.4 percent) Turkish. The figure for the Greek-Cypriot population includes Maronite, Armenian, and Latin Christian minorities; they designated themselves as members of that community as permitted under the constitution. The Turkish-Cypriot administration provides a marginally different figure for the population of this community for that year, 115,758, but does not offer any figure for the island's total population. (The Republic of Cyprus Web page, http://www.pio.gov.cy/docs/euro/coucil_of_europe/parl_assembly/cuco/memorandum/demographic_data_upto_1997.htm, 24 November 2003).

17. Like the Berlin Wall of the past, the Green Line divides Nicosia/Lefkosa into two parts. Major differences separate the two parts in ways beyond mere location; for example, per capita GDP income (2002) is $14,466 in the Greek Cypriot and $4,610 in Turkish Cypriot areas, respectively (U.S. Department of State, background note on Cyprus, http://www.state.gov/r/pa/ei/bgn/5376.htm, 25 November 2003). For detailed analysis of the differences between the two sides of the Green Line, in terms of culture, religion, economy, infrastructure, banking, entrepreneurship, and tourism, see Dana and Dana (2000).

18. The Denktas-Makarios summit in 1977 produced four principles that are accepted as the basis of future mediation attempts (UN Doc S/12723): (1) An independent, nonaligned bicommunal federal republic; (2) the territory under the administration of each community should be discussed in the light of economic viability and productivity and land ownership; (3) questions of principles like freedom of movement, freedom of settlement, the right of property, and other specific matters are open for discussion, taking into consideration the fundamental basis for a bicommunal federal system and certain practical difficulties that may arise for the Turkish community; and (4) the powers and functions of the central federal government will be such as to safeguard the unity of the country, having regard to the bicommunal character of the state. See Russinow 1981 for more details on mediation attempts after 1974.

19. According to this agreement, Turkish Cypriots would have at least 29 percent of the island, the new state would be bizonal and bicommunal, the president would be Greek Cypriot and vice president Turkish Cypriot, the cabinet would have seven Greek Cypriot ministers and three Turkish Cypriots, and each community would have its own police force.

20. According to Yesilada and Hewitt (1998), "the decision of the ECJ and TRNC exports to UK and the decision of the European Council to include Cyprus among the first group of countries for next expansion of membership," which is against the treaties of 1959 and the constitution, worked against attempts made by the UN and United States in 1993 to bring the sides back to the negotiation table within the framework of confidence-building measures. For detailed information about discussions on settlement that emerged as a result of EU pressure, see Bahçeli 2000; Bahçeli and Rizopaulos 1996/97; Theophanaous 2000a, b; Brewin 2000; Vassiliou 2002; and Yesilada and Sözen 2002.

21. CNN "Cyprus Peace Talks End in Failure," Tuesday, 11 March 200

22. Bölükbasi (1998) regards Prime Minister Inönü's cautiousness as the most important factor in determining Turkey's decision not to intervene in 1964. By no means a risk taker, and aware of the fact that intervention could result with a war with Greece, Inönü exhibited great caution in making his decision.

23. The authoritative Polity data set codes Turkey at 9 out of 10 in terms of institutional democracy and 0 out of 10 for institutional autocracy for 1974.

24. For details about the impact of cross-boundary ethnic ties on polarization and widening of the conflict, see Joseph 1997.

25. See Kaufman 2001 for an exegesis of the idea of "modern hatreds" that come about through elite manipulation of the way in which mass populations "remember" history.

26. CIA World Fact Book (2003). The Greek nationalist right-wing military junta came to power in April 1967; however, the country returned to democracy two days after the Turkish intervention in Cyprus.

WORKS CITED

Ake, Claude, and Julius Ihonvbere, eds. 1989. *The Political Economy of Crisis and Underdevelopment in Africa*. Lagos, Nigeria: Jad Publishers.

Allcock, John. 1988. "Yugoslavia's Defense Preparedness in the Context of Yugoslav Society." In Marka Milivojevic et al., eds., *Yugoslavia's Security Dilemmas*. Oxford: Berg Press.

Allison, Graham T. 1971. *Essence of Decision: Explaining the Cuban Missile Crisis*. Boston: Little, Brown and Co.

Alpern, I. Stephen. 1974. "The Thai Muslims." *Asian Affairs: An American Review* 4: 246–54.

Anurugsa, Panomporn. 1984. "Political Integration Policy in Thailand: The Case of the Malay Muslim Minority." Ph.D. dissertation. Austin: University of Texas.

Arasarathnam, Sinappah. 1986. *Sri Lanka after Independence: Nationalism, Communalism, and Nation Building*. Monograph, University of Madras, Centre for South and Southeast Asian Studies.

Axelrod, Robert. 1977. "Argumentation in Foreign Policy Settings." *Journal of Conflict Resolution* 24, 1: 3–25.

———. 1984. *The Evolution of Cooperation*. New York: Basic Books.

Azar, Edward E. 1990. *The Management of Protracted Social Conflict*. Aldershot, England: Dartmouth.

Azar, Edward E., and John Burton, eds. 1986. *International Conflict Resolution*. Boulder, Colo.: Lynne Rienner.

Azar, Edward E., P. Jureidini, and P. McLaurin. 1978. "Protracted Social Conflict: Theory and Practice in the Middle East." *Journal of Palestine Studies* 29: 41–60.

Bahçeli, Tözün. 2000. "Searching for a Cyprus Settlement: Considering Options for Creating a Federation, a Confederation, or Two Independent States." *Publius: The Journal of Federalism* 30, 1–2 (Winter–Spring): 203–16.

Bahçeli, Tözün, and Nicholas X. Rizopoulos. 1996/97. "The Cyprus Impasse." *World Policy Journal* 13: 27–39.

Bamanie, Nuray. 2002. "Cyprus' Forgotten Turks." *Journal of Muslim Minority Affairs* 22: 443–49.

Banac, Ivo. 1984. *The National Question in Yugoslavia: Origins, History, Politics*. Ithaca, N.Y.: Cornell University Press.

Banks, Michael. 1986. "The International Relations Discipline: Asset or Liability for Conflict Resolution?" In Edward E. Azar and John W. Burton, eds., *International Conflict Resolution*, 5–27. Boulder, Colo.: Lynne Rienner.

Barth, Frederik. ed. 1969. *Ethnic Groups and Boundaries: The Social Organization of Cultural Differences*. Boston: Little, Brown and Co.

Baxter, Craig, and Syedur Rahman. 1991. "Bangladesh Military: Political,

Institutional, and Economic Development." *Journal of Asian and African Studies* 26: 43–60.

Bercovitch, Jacob, Paul F. Diehl, and Gary Goertz. 1997. "The Management and Termination of Protracted Interstate Conflicts: Conceptual and Empirical Considerations." *Millennium: Journal of International Studies* 26, 3: 751–70.

Bhardwaj, Raman G. 1979. *The Dilemma of the Horn of Africa*. New Delhi: Sterling Press.

Bienen, Henry. 1989. *Armed Forces, Conflict, and Change in Africa*. Boulder, Colo.: Westview Press.

Birch, Anthony Harold. 1989. *Nationalism and National Integration*. London: Unwin-Hyman.

Bodansky, Yossef, and Vaughn S. Forrest. 1998. *United States Congress Task Force on Terrorism and Unconventional Warfare*. Washington, D.C.: U.S. Government Printing Office.

Bölükbasi, Süha. 1993. "The Johnson Letter Revisited." *Middle Eastern Studies* 29: 505–26.

_____. 1995. "Boutros-Ghali's Cyprus Initiative in 1992: Why Did It Fail." *Middle Eastern Studies* 31: 460–83.

_____. 1998. *The Superpowers and the Third World: Turkish-American Relations and Cyprus*. Lanham, Md.: University Press of America.

Booth, William J., Patrick James, and Hudson Meadwell, eds. 1993. *Politics and Rationality*. Cambridge: Cambridge University Press.

Bowden, Mark. 1999. *Black Hawk Down: A Story of Modern War*. New York: Atlantic Monthly Press.

Brass, Paul. 1974. *Language, Religion and Politics in North India*. London: Cambridge University Press.

_____. 1990. *The Politics of India since Independence*. New York: Cambridge University Press.

———. 1991. *Ethnicity and Nationalism: Theory and Comparison*. Newbury Park, Calif.: Sage Publications.

Brecher, Michael. 1959. *Nehru: A Political Biography*. London: Oxford University Press.

_____. 1972. *The Foreign Policy System of Israel: Setting, Images, Process*. London: Cambridge University Press.

_____. 1993. *Crises in World Politics*. Oxford: Pergamon Press.

Brecher, Michael, and Patrick James. 1986. *Crisis and Change in World Politics*. Boulder, Colo.: Westview Press.

Brecher, Michael, and Jonathan Wilkenfeld. 1997a. "The Ethnic Dimension of International Crises." In David Carment and Patrick James, eds., *Wars in the Midst of Peace: The International Politics of Ethnic Conflict*, 164–94. Pittsburgh: University of Pittsburgh Press.

_____. 1997b . *A Study of Crisis*. Ann Arbor: University of Michigan Press.

Brecher, Michael, et al. 1988. *Crises in the Twentieth Century*. Vols. 1–2. Oxford: Pergamon Press.

Brecher, Michael, Blema Steinberg, and Janice Stein. 1969. "A Framework for Research on Foreign Policy Behavior." *Journal of Conflict Resolution* 13: 75–101.

Bremmer, Ian. 1995. "Understanding Nationalism in the Post–Communist States." Working Paper Series in International Studies. Stanford, Calif.: Hoover Institution.

Brewin, Christopher. 2000. "EU Perspectives on Cyprus Accession." *Middle Eastern Studies* 36: 21–34.

Brown, David. 1988. "From Peripheral Communities to Ethnic Nations: Separatism in Southeast Asia." *Pacific Affairs* 61, 1: 51–77.

Brown, Michael E., ed. 1996. *The International Dimensions of Internal Conflict.* Cambridge: MIT Press.

Bueno de Mesquita, Bruce. 2000. *Principles of International Politics: People's Power, Preferences, and Perceptions.* Washington, D.C.: CQ Press.

Bueno de Mesquita, Bruce, and David Lalman. 1992. *War and Reason: Domestic and International Imperatives.* New Haven, Conn.: Yale University Press.

Bueno de Mesquita, Bruce, Randy Siverson, and Gary Woller. 1992. "War and the Fate of Regimes: A Comparative Analysis." *American Political Science Review* 86: 638–46.

Bueno de Mesquita, Bruce, Alastair Smith, Randolph M. Siverson, and James D. Morrow. 2003. *The Logic of Political Survival.* Cambridge: MIT Press.

Burg, Steven L. 1993. "Nationalism Redux: Through the Glass of the Post–Communist States Darkly." *Current History* 92 (April): 162–68.

Burton, John W. 1986. "The History of International Conflict Resolution." In Edward E. Azar and John W. Burton, eds., *International Conflict Resolution,* 40–55. Boulder, Colo.: Lynne Rienner.

_____. 1987. "The International Conflict Resolution Priorities." *Forum: Peace Institute Reporter* (June): 5–12.

Carment, David B. 1987. "The Disintegration of a Model Colony: A Case Study of Sri Lankan Ethnic Mobilization from a Developmental Perspective." Unpublished research essay, Carleton University.

_____. 1991. "Profile of Ethnic Conflict in Sri Lanka." Paper prepared for the Canadian International Development Agency, Ottawa, Ontario.

_____. 1993. "The International Dimensions of Ethnic Conflict: Concepts: Indicators and Theory." *Journal of Peace Research* 30, 2: 137–50.

_____. 1994a. "The Ethnic Dimension in World Politics: Theory, Policy, and Early Warning." *Third World Quarterly* 15, 4: 551–82.

_____. 1994b. "The International Politics of Ethnic Conflict: The Interstate Dimensions of Secession and Irredenta in the Twentieth Century, a Crisis-based Approach." Unpublished manuscript.

Carment, David B., and Patrick James. 1995. "Internal Constraints and Interstate Ethnic Conflict: Toward a Crisis-Based Assessment of Irredentism." *Journal of Conflict Resolution* 39: 82–109.

———. 1996. "Two-level Games and Third-Party Intervention: Evidence from Ethnic Conflict in the Balkans and South Asia." *Canadian Journal of Political Science* 29:521–54.

_____, eds. 1997a. *Wars in the Midst of Peace: The International Politics of Ethnic Conflict.* Pittsburgh, Penn.: University of Pittsburgh Press.

_____. 1997b. "Secession and Irredenta in World Politics: The Neglected Interstate Dimension." In David Carment and Patrick James, eds., *Wars in the Midst of*

Peace: The International Politics of Ethnic Conflict, 194–231. Pittsburgh, Penn.: University of Pittsburgh Press.

———, eds. 1998. *Peace in the Midst of Wars: The International Politics of Ethnic Conflict.* Columbia: University of South Carolina Press.

———. 2000. "Explaining Third-Party Intervention in Ethnic Conflict: Theory and Evidence." *Nations and Nationalism* 6: 173–202.

———. 2003. "Third-Party States in Ethnic Conflict: Identifying the Domestic Determinants of Intervention." In Steven E. Lobell and Philip Mauceri, eds., *Ethnic Conflict and International Politics: Explaining Diffusion and Escalation*, 11–34. New York: Palgrave.

Carment, David B., Patrick James, and Dane Rowlands. 1997. "Ethnic Conflict and Third Party Intervention: Riskiness, Rationality, and. Commitment." In Gerald Schneider and Patricia A. Weitsman, eds., *Enforcing Cooperation: Risky States and Intergovernmental Management of Conflict*, 104–31. London: Macmillan.

Carment, David B., and Troy Joseph. 1999. "On the Relationship between Irredenta and Secession: A Quantitative Assessment." Paper presented at the Annual Meeting of the International Studies Association, Washington, D.C. .

Chaiwat, Satha-anand. 1987. *Islam and Violence: A Case Study of Violent Events in the Four Southern Provinces, Thailand, 1976–1981.* Tampa: University of South Florida Monographs in Religions and Public Policy.

———. 1991. "The Internationalization of Ethnic Conflict: The World According to the Thai Muslims." In K. M. de Silva and Ronald, J. May, eds., *Internationalization of Ethnic Conflict*, 148–57. London: Pinter Publishers.

———. 1993. "Kru-ze: A Theatre for Renegotiating Muslim Identity." *Sojourn* 8, 1: 195–218.

Chandra, Kanchan. 2004. *Why Ethnic Parties Succeed: Patronage and Ethnic Head Counts in India.* Cambridge: Cambridge University Press.

Chazan, Naomi., ed. 1991. *Irredentism and International Politics.* Boulder, Colo.: Lynne Rienner.

Che Man, W. K. 1990. *Muslim Separatism: The Moros of the Southern Philippines and the Malays of Southern Thailand.* Singapore: Oxford University Press.

Cioffi-Revilla, C., and Harvey Starr. 1995. "Opportunity, Willingness, and Political Uncertainty: Theoretical Foundations of Politics." *Journal of Theoretical Politics* 7: 447–76.

Cohen, Leonard. 1990. *The Indian Army: Its Contribution to the Development of a Nation.* New York: Oxford University Press.

———. 1992. "The Disintegration of Yugoslavia." *Current History* 91 (November): 369–75.

———. 1993. *Broken Bonds: Yugoslavia's Disintegration and Balkan Politics in Transition.* Boulder, Colo.: Westview Press.

Colaresi, Michael, and William R. Thompson. 2002. "Strategic Rivalries, Protracted Conflict, and Crisis Escalation." *Journal of Peace Research* 39: 263–87.

Collier, David. 1995. "Translating Quantitative Methods for Qualitative Researchers: The Case of Selction Bias." *American Political Science Review* 89, 2: 461–66.

———, and James Mahoney. 1996. "Insights and Pitfalls: Selection Bias in Qualitative Research." *World Politics* 49, 1: 56–91.

_____, James Mahoney, and Jason Seawright. 2004. "Claiming Too Much: Warnings about Selection." In Henry E. Brady and David Collier, eds., *Rethinking Social Inquiry: Diverse Tools Shared Standards*, 85–105. Lanham, Md.: Rowman & Littlefield.

Collins, John N. 1973. "Foreign Conflict Behavior and Domestic Disorder in Africa." In Jonathan Wilkenfeld, ed., *Conflict Behavior and Linkage Politics*, 251–93. New York: David McKay.

Connor, Walker. 1978. "A Nation is a Nation, Is a State, Is an Ethnic Group, Is a . . ." *Ethnic and Racial Studies* 1, 4: 377–400.

_____. 1987. "Ethnonationalism." In Myron Weiner and Samuel P. Huntington, eds., *Understanding Political Development*, 196–220. Boston: Little, Brown and Co.

Cooper, Robert, and Robert Berdal. 1993. "Outside Intervention in Ethnic Conflict." *Survival* 35, 1: 118–42.

Coser, Louis. 1956. *The Functions of Social Conflict*. New York: Glencoe Free Press.

Crighton, Edward, and M. A. MacIver. 1991. "The Evolution of Protracted Ethnic Conflict—Group Dominance and Political Development in Northern Ireland and Lebanon." *Comparative Politics* 23, 2: 127–42.

Dahl, Robert. 1982. *Dilemmas of Pluralist Democracy: Autonomy versus Control*. New Haven, Conn.: Yale University Press.

Dana, Leo P., and Terese Elizabeth Dana. 2000. "Taking Sides on the Island of Cyprus." *Journal of Small Business Management* 38: 80–87.

Davis, David, Keith Jaggers, and Will Moore. 1997. "Ethnicity, Minorities, and International Conflict Patterns." In David Carment and Patrick James, eds., *Wars in the Midst of Peace: The International Politics of Ethnic Conflict*, 148–63. Pittsburgh, Penn.: University of Pittsburgh Press.

Davis, David, and Will Moore. 1997. "Ethnicity Matters: Transnational Ethnic Alliances and Foreign Policy Behavior." *International Studies Quarterly* 41, 1: 171–84.

De Conde, Alexander. 1992. *Ethnicity, Race, and American Foreign Policy*. Boston: Northeastern University Press.

de Silva, C. R. 1978. "The Impact of Nationalism on Education: The School Takeover and the University Admission Crisis, 1970–1975." In M. Roberts, ed., *Collective Identities, Nationalisms, and Protest in Modern Sri Lanka*, 474–99. Colombo: Marga Institute.

_____. 1982. "The Sinhalese-Tamil Rift in Sri Lanka." In A. J. Wilson and Dennis Dalton, eds. *South Asia: Problems of National Integration*, 155–74. London: C. Hurst Company.

de Silva, K. M. 1981. *A History of Sri Lanka*. Berkeley: University of California Press, 1981.

_____. 1982. "The Model Colony: Reflections of the Transfer of Power in Sri Lanka." In A. J. Wilson and Dennis Dalton, eds., *South Asia: Problems of National Integration*, 77–88. London: C. Hurst Company.

_____. 1985. "Sri Lanka: Ethnic Conflict in a Third World Democracy." Paper prepared by the International Centre for Ethnic Studies, Sri Lanka for the United Nations University, Tokyo. May.

_____. 1993. "The Making of the Indo-Sri Lanka Accord: The Final Phase,

June–July 1987." In K. M. de Silva and S. W. R. de A. Samarasinghe, eds., *Peace Accords and Ethnic Conflict*, 112–55. New York: Pinter.

_____, ed. 1993. *Peace Accords and Ethnic Conflict*. New York: Pinter.

_____. 1997. "Sri Lanka: Surviving Ethnic Strife." *Journal of Democracy* 8: 97–111.

de Silva, K. M., Pensri Duke, Ellen S. Goldberg, and Nathan Katz, eds. 1988. *Ethnic Conflict in Buddhist Societies*. London: Pinter Publishers.

de Silva, K. M., and Ronald, J. May, eds. 1991. *Internationalization of Ethnic Conflict*. London: Pinter Publishers.

de Silva, K. M., and S. W. R. de A. Samarasinghe, eds. 1993. *Peace Accords and Ethnic Conflict*. New York: Pinter.

DeVotta, Neil. 2002. "Illiberalism and Ethnic Conflict in Sri Lanka." *Journal of Democracy* 13: 84–98

Diamond, Larry J. 1988. *Class, Ethnicity, and Democracy in Nigeria: The Failure of the First Republic*. Basingstoke: Macmillan.

The Dipavamsa. 1959. Translated by B. C. Law. Maharagam, Ceylon: Saman Press.

Dixon, William J. 1989. "Political Democracy and War." Paper presented at the Annual Meeting of the International Studies Association, London.

Dodd, Clement. 1999. "Historical Overview." In *Cyprus: The Need for New Perspectives*, ed. Clement Dodd. Huntington, UK: The Eothen Press.

Dower, J. 1986. *War without Mercy: Race and Power in the Pacific War*. New York: Pantheon.

Downs, Anthony. 1957. *An Economic Theory of Democracy*. New York: HarperCollins Press.

Drysdale, John. 1964. *The Somali Dispute*. New York: Praeger Press.

Duchacek, Ivo D. 1987. *Comparative Federalism: The Territorial Dimensions of Politics within, among, and across Nations*. Lanham, Md.: University Press of America.

Dumont, Louis. 1980. *Homo Hierarchicus: The Caste System and Its Implications*. Chicago: University of Chicago Press.

Eisenstadt, Shlomo N. 1980. *Ethnic Soldiers*. Harmondsworth, England: Penguin.

Ellingsen, Tanja. 1996. "Colorful Community or Ethnic Witches Brew? Political Regime and Armed Conflict during and after the Cold War." Paper presented at the Annual Convention of the International Studies Association, San Diego, Calif.

Enloe, Cynthia. 1980. *Ethnic Soldiers: State Security in Divided Societies*. Athens: University of Georgia Press.

Ertekun, Necati. 1984. *The Cyprus Dispute and the Birth of the Turkish Republic of Northern Cyprus*. Oxford: Oxford University Press.

Evans, Peter B. 1993. "Building an Integrative Approach to International and Domestic Politics." In Peter B. Evans, Harold K. Jacobson, and Robert D. Putnam, eds., *Double-Edged Diplomacy: International Bargaining and Domestic Politics*, 397–430. Berkeley and Los Angeles: University of California Press.

Farer, Tom S. 1976. *War Clouds in the Horn of Africa: A Crisis for Detente*. New York: Carnegie Endowment for International Peace.

Farouk, Omar. 1984. "The Historical and Transnational Dimensions of Malay-Muslim Separatism in Southern Thailand. In Lim Joo-Jock and S. Vani, eds., *Armed Separatism in Southeast Asia*, 234–57. Singapore: Institute for South East Asian Studies.

Fearon, James D. 1998. "Commitment Problems and the Spread of Ethnic Conflict." In David A. Lake and Donald Rothchild, eds., *The International Spread of Ethnic Conflict: Fear, Diffusion, and Escalation,* 107–26. Princeton: Princeton University Press.

Finer, Samuel E. 1962. *The Man on Horseback: The Role of the Military in Politics.* New York: Praeger.

Flere, Sergej. 1991. "Explaining Ethnic Antagonisms in Yugoslavia." *European Sociological Review* 7, 3: 183–93.

Forbes, Andrew D. W. 1982. "Thailand's Muslim Minorities: Assimilation, Secession, or Coexistence?" *Asian Survey* 22, 11: 1056–73.

_____, ed. 1989. *The Muslims of Thailand: Politics of the Malay-Speaking South.* Vol. 2. Gaya: Centre for South East Asian Studies.

Fouskas, Vassilis K. 2001. "Reflections on the Cyprus Issue and the Turkish Invasions of 1974." *Mediterranean Quarterly* 12, 3: 98–127.

Fox, Jonathan. 2001. "Religious Causes of International Intervention in Ethnic Conflicts." *International Politics* 38: 515–31.

Gagnon, Valere P. 1992. "Nationalism, Rationality and Foreign Policy: The Case of Serbia." Paper presented at the annual meeting of the American Political Science Association, Chicago, Ill.

_____. 1994. "Serbia's Road to War." In Larry Diamond and Marc F. Plattner, eds., *Nationalism, Ethnic Conflict, and Democracy,* 117–31. London: Johns Hopkins University Press.

———. 1994/95. "Ethnic Nationalism and International Conflict: The Case of Serbia." *International Security* 19, 3: 167–202.

Ganguly, Sumit. 1991. "From the Defense of the Nation to the Aid to the Civil: The Army in Contemporary India." *Journal of Asian and African Studies* 26, 1–2:11–26.

Geddes, Barbara. 1990. "How the Cases You Choose Affect the Answers You Get: Selection Bias in Comparative Politics." *Political Analysis* 2: 131–50.

Gellner, Ernest. 1983. *Nations and Nationalism.* Ithaca, N.Y.: Cornell University Press.

Glenny, Misha. 1992a. "The Massacre of Yugoslavia." *New York Review of Books.* 30 January.

_____. 1992b. "The Revenger's Tragedy." *New York Review of Books.* 13 August.

_____. 1992c. *The Fall of Yugoslavia: The Third Balkan War.* New York: Penguin Books.

_____. 1993a. "Is Macedonia Next?" *New York Times.* 30 July: A7.

_____. 1993b. "What Is to be Done?" *New York Review of Books.* 27 May: 14–17.

_____. 1994. *Encounters with Nationalism.* Oxford: Blackwell.

Goertz, Gary, and Paul F. Diehl. 1997. "Linking Risky Dyads: An Evaluation of the Relations between Enduring Rivalries." In Gerald Schneider and Patricia A. Weitsman, eds., *Enforcing Cooperation: Risky States and Intergovernmental Management of Conflict,* 132–60. London: Macmillan.

Goldstein, Joshua, and John R. Freeman. 1990. *Three-Way Street: Strategic Reciprocity in World Politics.* Chicago: University of Chicago Press.

Gopinath, Aruna. 1991. "International Aspects of the Thai Muslim and Philippine

Moro Issues: A Comparative Study." In K. M. de Silva and Ronald J. May, eds., *Internationalization of Ethnic Conflict,* 125–47. London: Pinter Publishers.

Gorman, Robert F. 1981. *Political Conflict in the Horn of Africa.* New York: Praeger Press.

Grant, Alison. 1997. "Ethnic Conflict in the Former Soviet Union: Explaining Ethnic Minority Intransigence." MA research essay, Carleton University.

Grieco, Joseph M. 1990. *Cooperation among Nations.* Ithaca, N.Y.: Cornell University Press.

Gurr, Ted Robert. 1974. "Persistence and Change in Political Systems, 1800–1971." *American Political Science Review* 68: 1482–1504.

_____, ed. 1980. *Handbook of Political Conflict: Theory and Research.* New York: Free Press.

_____. 1990. "Ethnic Warfare and the Changing Priorities of Global Security." *Mediterranean Quarterly* 1: 82–98.

_____. 1991. "Minorities at Risk: The Dynamics of Ethnopolitical Mobilization and Conflict, 1945–1990." Paper presented at the International Studies Association Annual Meeting, Vancouver, BC.

_____. 1992. "The Internationalization of Protracted Communal Conflicts since 1945: Which Groups, Where, and How." In Manus I. Midlarsky, ed., *The Internationalization of Communal Strife,* 4–24. London: Routledge.

_____. 1993. "Resolving Ethnopolitical Conflicts: Exit, Autonomy, or Access." In Ted Robert Gurr et al. *Minorities at Risk: A Global View of Ethnopolitical Conflicts.* Washington, D.C.: United States Institute of Peace Press.

_____. 1994a. "The Bluff that Failed." *New York Times.* 19 April: A1.

_____. 1994b. "Peoples against States: Ethnopolitical Conflict and the Changing World System." *International Studies Quarterly* 38: 347–77.

_____. 1996. "A Risk Assessment Model of Ethnopolitical Rebellion." Paper presented at a Conference and Workshop on Risk Assessment and Crisis Early Warning Systems at the University of Maryland, College Park, 14–16 November.

_____. 1997. "Minorities' Rights at Risk: A Global Survey of Political, Economic, and Cultural Discrimination in the 1990s." Paper prepared for the Panel on Human Rights and Minority Rights, International Political Science Association's XVII World Congress, 17–21 August, Seoul, Korea.

Gurr, Ted Robert, Barbara Harff, and Anne M. Speca. 1996. "Dynamic Data for Early Warning of Ethnopolitical Conflict." Paper presented at a conference and workshop on Risk Assessment and Crisis Early Warning Systems at the University of Maryland, College Park, 14–16 November.

Gurr, Ted Robert, Monty G. Marshall, and Deepa Khosla. 2001. *Peace and Conflict 2001: A Global Survey of Armed Conflicts, Self-Determination Movements, and Democracy.* College Park, Md.: Center for International Development and Conflict Management.

Hale, William. 1994. *Turkish Politics and the Military.* London: Routledge.

_____. 2000. *Turkish Foreign Policy, 1774–2000.* London: Frank Cass.

Hardin, Russell. 1995. *One for All: The Logic of Group Conflict.* Princeton: Princeton University Press.

Harff, Barbara, and Ted Robert Gurr. 1988. "Toward Empirical Theory of Genocides and Politicides: Identification and Measurement of Cases since 1945." *International Studies Quarterly* 32: 359–71.

Harvey, Frank. 1998. "Deterrence Failure and Ethnic Conflict: The Case of Bosnia." In David Carment and Patrick James, eds., *Peace in the Midst of Wars: Preventing and Managing International Ethnic Conflicts*, 230–64. Columbia: University of South Carolina Press.

Hechter, Michael. 1975. *Internal Colonialism: The Celtic Fringe in British Naval Development, 1536–1966*. Berkeley and Los Angeles: University of California Press.

———. 1987. *Principles of Group Solidarity*. Berkeley and Los Angeles: University of California Press.

Henze, Paul B. 1991. *The Horn of Africa: From War to Peace*. Hong Kong: Macmillan Press.

Heraclides, Alexis. 1990. "Secessionist Minorities and External Involvement." *International Organization* 44, 3: 341–78.

———. 1991. *The Self-Determination of Minorities in International Politics*. Portland, Ore.: Frank Cass.

———. 1997. "The Ending of Unending Conflicts: Separatist Wars." *Millennium: Journal of International Studies* 26, 3: 679–703.

Hill, Stuart, and Donald Rothchild. 1992. "The Impact of Regime on the Diffusion of Political Conflict." In Manus I. Midlarsky, ed., *The Internationalization of Communal Strife*, 189–203. London: Routledge.

Hislope, Robert Lee, Jr. 1995. "Nationalism, Ethnic Politics, and Democratic Consolidation: A Comparative Study of Croatia, Serbia, and Bosnia-Herzegovina." Ph.D. Dissertation, Ohio State University.

Holland, Robert. 1998. *Britain and the Revolt in Cyprus, 1954–1959*. Oxford: Clarendon.

Horowitz, Donald. 1981. "Patterns of Ethnic Separatism." *Comparative Studies in Society and History* 23, 2: 165–95.

———. 1985. *Ethnic Groups in Conflict*. Berkeley and Los Angeles: University of California Press.

———. 1991. "Irredentas and Secessions: Adjacent Phenomena, Neglected Connections." In Naomi Chazan, ed., *Irredentism and International Politics*. Boulder, Colo.: Lynne Rienner.

———. 1994. "Democracy in Divided Societies." In Larry Diamond and Marc F. Plattner, eds., *Nationalism, Ethnic Conflict, and Democracy*, 35–55. London: Johns Hopkins University Press.

Huntington, Samuel, P. 1957. *The Soldier and the State: The Theory and Politics of Civil-Military Relations*. Cambridge, Mass.: Belkhap Press of Harvard University Press.

Hyden, Goran. 1980. *Beyond Ujamaa in Tanzania: Underdevelopment and an Uncaptured Peasantry*. Berkeley and Los Angeles: University of California Press.

Ismail, Sabahattin. 2000. *Kibris'ta Yunan Sorunu, 1821–2000* (The Greek question in Cyprus). Istanbul: Akdeniz Publications.

Jackson, Robert H. 1990. *Quasi-States: Sovereignty, International Relations, and the Third World*. Cambridge: Cambridge University Press.

Jackson, Robert H. , and Carl G. Rosberg. 1982. "Why Africa's Weak States Persist: The Empirical and the Juridical in Statehood." *World Politics* 35, 1: 1–24.

Jaggers, Keith, and Ted R. Gurr. 1995. "Tracking Democracy's Third Wave with the Polity III Data." *Journal of Peace Research* 32: 469–82.

Jalal, Ayesh. 1990. *The State of Martial Rule: The Origins of Pakistan's Political Economy of Defence*. Cambridge: Cambridge University Press.

James, Alan. 2002. *Keeping the Peace in the Cyprus Crisis of 1963–1964*. New York: Palgrave.

James, Patrick. 1987. "Conflict and Cohesion: A Review of the Literature and Recommendations for Future Research." *Cooperation and Conflict* 22, 1: 21–33.

______. 1988. *Crisis and War.* Montreal and Kingston: McGill-Queen's University Press.

______. 1990. "The Causes of War: How Does Structure Affect International Conflict?" In David G. Haglund and Michael Hawes, eds., *World Politics: Power, Interdependence, and Dependence*, 38–55. Toronto: Harcourt Brace Jovanovich.

______. 1993. "Structural Realism as a Research Enterprise: Toward Elaborated Structural Realism." *International Political Science Review* 14: 123–48.

James, Patrick, and John R. Oneal. 1991. "The Influence of Domestic and International Politics on the President's Use of Force." *Journal of Conflict Resolution* 35: 307–32.

Jenkins, Craig J., and Augustine Kposowa. 1992. "The Political Origins of African Military Coups: Ethnic Competition and the Struggle over the Postcolonial State." *International Studies Quarterly* 36: 271–92.

Johnson, Thomas H., Robert O. Slater, and Pat McGowan. 1984. "Explaining African Military Coups d'état, 1960–1982." *American Political Science Review* 28, 3: 622–37.

Jones, Barbara. 1948. "Patani Appeals to UNO." *Eastern World.* April: 4–5.

Joseph, Joseph S. 1997. *Cyprus: Ethnic Conflict and International Politics: From Interdependence to the Threshold of the European Union.* New York: St. Martin's Press.

Kasfir, Nelson. 1976. *The Shrinking Political Arena: Participation and Ethnicity in African Politics, with a Case Study of Uganda.* Berkeley and Los Angeles: University of California Press.

Kaufman, Stuart. 1996. "Spiraling to Ethnic War: Elites, Masses and Moscow in Moldova's Civil War." *International Security* 21, 2: 108–38.

______. 2001. *Modern Hatreds: The Symbolic Politics of Ethnic War.* Ithaca: Cornell University Press.

Kearney, Robert. 1985. "Ethnic Conflict and the Tamil Separatist Movement in Sri Lanka." *Asian Survey.* 25, 9 (September): 1100–16.

Kennedy, Charles H., and David J. Louscher. 1991. "Civil-Military Interaction: Data in Search of a Theory." *Journal of Asian and African Studies* 26, 1–2: 1–10.

Kentmen, Cigdem. 2003. "Resolution of Cyprus Dispute through a Mixed Strategy." Unpublished manuscript.

Khory, Kavita R. 1991. "Separatism in South Asia: The Politics of Ethnic Conflict and Regional Security." Ph.D. dissertation, University of Illinois at Urbana-Champaign.

————. 1992. "Separatism in South Asia: The Politics of Ethnic Conflict and Regional Security." Paper presented at the annual meeting of the American Political Science Association, Chicago, Ill.

Kibble, Steve. 2001. "Somaliland: Surviving without Recognition; Somalia: Recognised but Failing?" *International Relations* 15: 5–25.

King, Gary, Robert O. Keohane, and Sidney Verba. 1994. *Designing Social Inquiry: Scientific Inference in Qualitative Research*. Princeton: Princeton University Press.

Kissinger, Henry. 1999. *Years of Renewal*. New York: Simon Schuster.

Knight, David B. 1982. "Identity and Territory: Geographical Perspectives on Nationalism and Regionalism." *Annals of the Association of American Geographers* 72, 4: 514–31.

Kodikara, Shelton U. 1982. *Foreign Policy of Sri Lanka*. Delhi: Chanakya Publications.

————. 1985. *The Separatist Eelam Movement in Sri Lanka: An Overview*. Colombo: University of Colombo Press.

————. 1987. "International Dimensions of Ethnic Conflict in Sri Lanka: Involvement of India and Non-state Actors." *Bulletin of Peace Proposals* 18, 4: 637–48.

————. 1989. "The Continuing Crisis in Sri Lanka: The JVP, the Indian Troops, and Tamil Politics." *Asian Survey* 29, 4: 716–24.

————, ed. 1990. *South Asian Strategic Issues: Sri Lankan Perspectives*. New Delhi: Sage.

————, ed. 1993. *External Compulsions of South Asian Politics*. Newbury Park, Calif.: Sage Publications.

Kohli, Atul. 1990. *Democracy and Discontent: India's Growing Crisis of Governability*. Cambridge: Cambridge University Press.

Kolsto, Pal. 1993. "The New Russian Diaspora: Minority Protection in the Soviet Successor States." *Journal of Peace Research* 30, 2: 197–217.

Kriesberg, Louis. 1997. "Preventing and Resolving Destructive Communal Conflicts." In David Carment and Patrick James, eds., *Wars in the Midst of Peace: The International Politics of Ethnic Conflict*, 232–51. Pittsburgh: University of Pittsburgh Press.

Kyriakides, Stanley. 1968. *Cyprus: Constitutionalism and Crisis Government*. Philadelphia: University of Pennsylvania Press.

Lake, David A., and Donald Rothchild. 1996. "Containing Fear: The Origins and Management of Ethnic Conflict." *International Security* 21, 2: 41–75.

————. 1998. *The International Spread of Ethnic Conflict: Fear, Diffusion, and Escalation*. Princeton: Princeton University Press.

Laitin, David, and Said S. Samatar. 1987. *Somalia: A Nation in Search of a State*. London: Gower Press.

Lefebvre, Stéphane, and Roman Jakubow. 1993. "War Termination Prospects in the Former Yugoslavia." Ottawa: Department of National Defence, ORAE Project Report 629: 3–5.

Legum, Colin, and Bill Lee. 1979. *The Horn of Africa in Continued Crisis*. New York: African Publishing Co.

Leng, Russell J. 1993. *Interstate Crisis Behavior, 1816–1980: Realism versus Reciprocity.* Cambridge: Cambridge University Press.

Lenin, Vladimir I. 1951. *Critical Remarks on the National Question.* Moscow: Progress.

Levy, Jack S. 1989. "The Diversionary Theory of War: A Critique." In Manus I. Midlarsky, ed. *Handbook of War Studies,* 259–88. Boston: Unwin Hyman.

Lewis, Paul. 1993a. "Top Bosnian Serb Facing U.S. Action, Signs a Peace Plan." *New York Times.* 3 May: A1, A10.

_____. 1993b. "Reluctant Warriors: UN Member States Retreat from Peacekeeping Roles." *New York Times,* International Edition. 12 December.

Lijphart, Arend. 1979. "Consociation and Federation: Conceptual and Empirical Links." *Canadian Journal of Political Science* 22, 3: 499–522.

Lijphart, Arend, and Carlos H. Waisman, eds. 1996. *Institutional Design in New Democracies: Eastern Europe and Latin America.* Boulder, Colo.: Westview Press.

Lumsden, Malvern. 1973. "Intergroup Conflict and British Colonial Policy: The Case of Cyprus." *Comparative Politics* 5: 575–99.

Lustick, Ian S. 1986. "Stability in Deeply Divided Societies: Consociationalism versus Control." *World Politics* 31, 3: 325–44.

Makinda, Samuel B. 1992. *Security in the Horn of Africa.* Adelphi Papers 269. London: International Institute for Strategic Studies.

Manor, James, and George Segal. 1985. "Causes of Conflict: Sri Lanka and Indian Ocean Strategy." *Asian Survey* 25, 12: 1165–85.

Maoz, Zeev. 1990. *National Choices and International Processes.* New York: Cambridge University Press.

_____. 1997a. "Domestic Political Change and Strategic Responses: The Impact of Internal Conflict on State Behavior." In David Carment and Patrick James, eds., *Wars in the Midst of Peace: The International Politics of Ethnic Conflict,* 116–47. Pittsburgh: University of Pittsburgh Press.

_____. 1997b. "Decisional Stress, Individual Choice, and Policy Outcomes: The Arab Israeli Conflict." In Nehemia Geva and Alex Mintz, eds., *Decision Making on War and Peace: The Cognitive-Rational Debate,* 163–81. Boulder, Colo.: Lynne Rienner.

Marshall, Monty G. 1997. "Systems at Risk: Violence, Diffusion, and Disintegration in the Middle East." In David Carment and Patrick James, eds., *Wars in the Midst of Peace: The International Politics of Ethnic Conflict,* 82–115. Pittsburgh: University of Pittsburgh Press.

Mastanduno, Michael, David Lake, and John Ikenberry. 1989. "Toward a Realist Theory of State Action." *International Studies Quarterly* 33: 457–74.

May, Ronald, J. 1990. "Ethnic Separatism in Southeast Asia." *Pacific Viewpoint* 31, 2: 28–59.

Mayall, James. 1990. *Nationalism and International Society.* New York: Cambridge University Press.

McGowan, William. 1992. *Only Man Is Vile: The Tragedy of Sri Lanka.* London: Farrar, Strauss and Giroux.

McVey, Ruth. 1984. "Separatism and the Paradoxes of the Nation-State in

Perspective." In Lim Joo-Jock and S. Vani, eds., *Armed Separatism in Southeast Asia*. Singapore: Institute for South East Asian Studies.

Meadwell, Hudson. 1991. "A Rational Choice Approach to Political Regionalism." *Comparative Politics* 23: 401–23.

——. 1992. "Transitions to Independence and Ethnic Nationalist Mobilization." Paper presented at the Meeting of International Conference of Europeanists, Chicago, Ill.

Midlarsky, Manus I., ed. 1992. *The Internationalization of Communal Strife*. London: Routledge.

——. 1997. "Systemic War in the Former Yugoslavia." In David Carment and Patrick James, eds., *Wars in the Midst of Peace: The International Politics of Ethnic Conflict*, 61–81. Pittsburgh: University of Pittsburgh Press.

Mintz, Alex, and Nehemia Geva. 1997. "The Poliheuristic Theory of Foreign Policy Decision-making." In N. Geva and A. Mintz, eds., *Decisionmaking on War and Peace: The Cognitive-Rational Debate*, 81–103. Boulder, Colo.: Lynne Rienner.

Mirbagheri, Farid. 1998. *Cyprus and International Peacekeeping*. New York: Routledge.

Mohan, V. 1985. "Sri Lanka Newsletter." *New Delhi* 3 (August 1983).

——. "The Ethnic Tangle." *Asian Profile* (December) 13, 6: 290–301.

Morgan, T. Clifton, and Sally H. Campbell. 1991. "Domestic Structure, Decisional Constraints, and War." *Journal of Conflict Resolution* 35: 187–211.

Morgenthau, Hans J. 1957. "The Paradoxes of Nationalism." *Yale Review* 46, 4: 781–97.

Most, Benjamin A., and Harvey Starr. 1976. "The Substance and Study of Borders in International Relations Research." *International Studies Quarterly* 20: 581–620.

——. 1978. "A Return Journey: Richardson, 'Frontiers' and War in the 1946–1965 Era." *Journal of Conflict Resolution* 22: 323–56.

——. 1980. "Diffusion, Reinforcement, Geopolitics, and the Spread of War." *American Political Science Review* 74: 932–46.

——. 1989. *Inquiry, Logic, and International Politics*. Columbia: University of South Carolina Press.

——, and Randy Siverson. 1989. "The Logic and Study of the Diffusion of International Conflict." In Manus Midlarsky, ed., *Handbook of War Studies*, 111–39. Boston: Unwin Allen.

Moynihan, Daniel Patrick. 1993. *Pandaemonium: Ethnicity in International Politics*. Toronto: Oxford University Press.

Muller, Edward N., and Erich Weede. 1990. "Cross-National Variation in Political Violence: A Rational Action Approach." *Journal of Conflict Resolution* 34: 624–51.

Myrdal, Gunnar. 1970. *An Approach to the Asian Drama*. New York: Vintage Books.

Nairn, Thomas. 1977. *The Breakup of Britain: Crisis and Neo-nationalism*. London: NLB.

Nayar, Baldev R. 1966. *Minority Politics in the Punjab*. Princeton: Princeton University Press.

Necatigil, Zaim M. 1977. *Cyprus Constitutional Proposals and Developments*. Nicosia: TFSC Press.

_____. 1989. *The Cyprus Question and the Turkish Position in International Law*. Oxford: Oxford University Press.

Neilsson, Gunnar P. 1985. "States and Nation Groups: A Global Taxonomy." In Edward A. Tiryakian and Ronald Rogowski, eds., *New Nationalisms of the Developed West*, 27–56. Boston: Allen and Unwin.

Nordlinger, Eric. 1972. *Conflict Regulation in Deeply Divided Societies*. Cambridge: Cambridge University Press.

_____. 1977. *Soldiers in Politics: Military Coups and Governments*. Englewood Cliffs, N.J.: Prentice-Hall.

_____. 1981. *On the Autonomy of the Democratic State*. Cambridge, Mass.: Harvard University Press.

Olorunsola, Victor A., ed. 1972. *The Politics of Cultural Sub-nationalism in Africa*. Garden City, N.Y.: Anchor Books.

Olson, Mancur. 1965. *The Logic of Collective Action*. Cambridge, Mass.: Harvard University Press.

_____. 1993. "Dictatorship, Democracy, and Development." *American Political Science Review* 87, 3: 567–76.

Olzak, Susan, and Joanne Nagel, eds. 1986. *Competitive Ethnic Relations*. Orlando, Fla.: Academic.

Opalski, Magda, B. Tsilevich, and Piotr Dutkiewicz. 1994. *Ethnic Conflict in the Baltic States: The Case of Latvia*. Distinguished Speaker Series in Political Geography, Royal Military College of Canada.

Ostrom, Charles W., and Brian Job. 1986. "The President and the Political Use of Force." *American Political Science Review* 80: 541–66.

Papaneophytou, Neophytos. 1994. "Cyprus: The Way to Full EU Membership." *Cyprus Review* 6: 83–96.

Pavkovic, Alexandar. 2000. *The Fragmentation of Yugoslavia: Nationalism and War in the Balkans*. New York: St. Martin's Press.

Pfaff, William. 1993. "Invitation to War." *Foreign Affairs* 72: 101–3.

Pfaffenberger, Bryan. 1988. "Sri Lanka in 1987: Indian Intervention and Resurgence of the JVP." *Asian Survey* 28, 2: 137–47.

Pitsuwan, Surin. 1985. *Islam and Malay Nationalism: A Case Study of the Malay-Muslims of Southern Thailand*. Bangkok: Thai Kadai Research Institute, Thammasat University.

_____. 1988a. "The Lotus and the Crescent: Clashes of Religious Symbolisms in Southern Thailand." In K. M de Silva, Pensri Duke, Ellen S. Goldberg, and Nathan Katz, eds., *Ethnic Conflict in Buddhist Societies: Sri Lanka, Thailand, and Burma*, 187–201. London: Pinter Publishers.

_____. 1988b. "The Ethnic Background of Issues Affecting Bilateral Relations between Malaysia and Thailand." In Guidieri Remo, Francesco Pelizzi, and Stanley J. Tambiah, eds., *Ethnicities and Nations*, 320–40. Houston: University of Texas Press.

Pollis, Adamantia. 1973. "Intergroup Conflict and British Colonial Policy: The Case of Cyprus." *Comparative Politics* 5: 575–99.

Polvyiou, Polyvios G. 1980. *Cyprus: Conflict and Negotiation, 1960–1980*. New York: Holmes and Meier Publishers.

Posen, Barry. 1993. "The Security Dilemma and Ethnic Conflict." *Survival* 35, 1: 27–47.

Provencher, Ronald. 1975. *Mainland Southeast Asia: An Anthropological Perspective.* Pacific Palisades, Calif.: Goodyear Pub. Co.

Putnam, Robert. D. 1988. "Diplomacy and Domestic Politics: The Logic of Two-Level Games." *International Organization* 42: 426–60.

Ramet, Sabrina P. 1991a. "The Breakup of Yugoslavia." *Global Affairs* 6: 93–110.

_____. 1991b. *Social Currents in Eastern Europe.* Durham, N.C.: Duke University Press.

_____. 1992a. *Nationalism and Federalism in Yugoslavia, 1962–1991.* Bloomington: University of Indiana Press.

_____. 1992b. "War in the Balkans." *Foreign Affairs* 71: 79–98.

Rao, Chandrasekhar R. V. R. 1985. "Regional Cooperation in South Asia." *Round Table.* January: 1–293.

Rao, Venkateshwar P. 1988. "Ethnic Conflict in Sri Lanka: India's Role and Perception." *Asian Survey* 28, 4: 419–36.

Redd, Steven. 2002. "The Influence of Advisers on Foreign Policy Decision Making." *Journal of Conflict Resolution* 46: 335–64.

Regan, Patrick. 1998. "Choosing to Intervene: Outside Interventions in Internal Conflicts." *Journal of Politics* 60, 3: 754–779.

_____. 2000. *Civil Wars and Foreign Powers: Interventions and Intrastate Conflict.* Ann Arbor: University of Michigan Press.

Republic of Cyprus. 1960. *The Constitution of the Republic of Cyprus.* Nicosia: Government Printing Office.

Riga, Lilliana. 1992. "The Yugoslav Crisis and the Unified Model." Unpublished manuscript. McGill University.

Riggs, Fred. 1964. *Administration in Developing Countries: The Theory of Prismatic Society.* Boston: Houghton Mifflin.

Rizvi, Hasan Askari. 1991. "The Military and Politics in Pakistan." *Journal of Asian and African Studies* 26, 1–2: 27–42.

Rogel, Carole. 1998. *The Breakup of Yugoslavia and the War in Bosnia.* Westport, Conn.: Greenwood.

Rosenau, James N., ed. 1969. *Linkage Politics: Essays on the Convergence of National and International Systems.* New York: The Free Press.

_____. 1990. *Turbulence in World Politics.* Princeton: Princeton University Press.

Rothchild, Donald, and Naomi Chazan, eds. 1988. *The Precarious Balance: State and Society in Africa.* Boulder, Colo.: Westview Press.

Rothschild, Joseph. 1981. *Ethnopolitics: A Conceptual Framework.* New York: Columbia University Press.

Rourke, John T., Ralph G. Carter, and Mark A. Boyer. 1996. *Making American Foreign Policy.* Guilford, Conn.: Dushkin/McGraw-Hill.

Rumley, Dennis, and Julian V. Minghi, eds. 1991. *The Geography of Border Landscapes.* New York: Routledge.

Rummel, Rudolph J. 1963. "Dimensions of Conflict Behavior within and between Nations." *General Systems Yearbook* 8: 1–50.

Rupesinghe, Kumar. 1989. "Sri Lanka: Peacekeeping and Peace Building." *Bulletin of Peace Proposals* 20, 3: n. pag.

Russett, Bruce. 1990. *Controlling the Sword: The Democratic Governance of National Security.* Cambridge, Mass.: Harvard University Press.

———. 1993. *Grasping the Democratic Peace.* Princeton: Princeton University Press.

Russinow, Dennison I. 1981. "The Cyprus Deadlock: Forever or Another Day." *American Universities Field Staff (DR-1-81).* Hannover, N.H.

Ryan, Stephen. 1988. "Explaining Ethnic Conflict: The Neglected International Dimension." *Review of International Studies* 14: 161–77.

———. 1998. "Preventive Diplomacy, Conflict Prevention, and Ethnic Conflict." In David Carment and Patrick James, eds., *Peace in the Midst of Wars: Preventing and Managing International Ethnic Conflicts,* 63–92. Columbia: University of South Carolina Press.

Saideman, Stephen M. 1997. "Explaining the International Relations of Secessionist Conflicts: Vulnerability versus Ethnic Ties." *International Organization* 51:4: 721–53.

———. 1998a. "Is Pandora's Box Half Open or Half Full? The Limited Virulence of Secessionism and the Domestic Sources of Disintegration." In David A. Lake and D. Rothchild, eds., *The International Spread of Ethnic Conflict: Fear, Diffusion, and Escalation,* 127–50. Princeton: Princeton University Press.

———. 1998b. "Inconsistent Irredentism: Political Competition, Ethnic Ties, and the Foreign Policies of Somalia and Serbia." *Security Studies* 7, 3: 50–94.

———. 2001. *The Ties That Divide: Ethnic Politics, Foreign Policy, and International Conflict.* New York: Columbia University Press.

Salih, Halil Ibrahim. 1978. *Cyprus: The Impact of Diverse Nationalism on a State.* Tuscaloosa: University of Alabama Press.

Samarasinghe, S. W. R. de A., and Kamala Liyanage. 1993. "Friends and Foes of the Indo-Sri Lanka Accord." In K. M. de Silva and S. W. R. de A. Samarasinghe, eds., *Peace Accords and Ethnic Conflict,* 156–72. New York: Pinter.

Sambanis, Nicholas. 1994. "Ancient Affections: Standing in the Way of Resolution in Cyprus." *SAIS Review* 14: 125–40.

Sandler, Todd. 1992. *Collective Action.* Ann Arbor: University of Michigan Press.

Sauldie, Madan M. 1987. *Superpowers in the Horn of Africa.* New Delhi: Sterling Press.

Sciolino, Elaine. 1993. "Bosnia Rivals Set New Talks as U.S. Weighs Action Plans." *New York Times.* 30 April: A1, A7.

Selassie, Bereket H. 1980. *Conflict and Intervention in the Horn of Africa.* New York: Monthly Review Press.

———.1984. "The American Dilemma on the Horn." *Journal of Modern African Studies* 22, 3: 249–72.

Shastri, Amita. 1997. "Government Policy and the Ethnic Crisis in Sri Lanka." In Michael E. Brown and Sumit Ganguly, eds., *Government Policies and Ethnic Relations in Asia and the Pacific,* 129–63. Cambridge: MIT Press.

———. 2002. "Sri Lanka in 2001."*Asian Survey* 42: 177–82.

Sisk, Timothy. 1996. *Power Sharing and International Mediation in Ethnic Conflicts.* Washington, D.C.: U.S. Institute for Peace.

Sivarajah, Ambalavanar. 1990. "Indo-Sri Lanka Relations and Sri Lanka's Ethnic

Crisis: The Tamil Nadu Factor." In Shelton U. Kodikara, ed., *South Asian Strategic Issues: Sri Lankan Perspectives*, 135–59. New Delhi: Sage.

Siverson, Randy, and Harvey Starr. 1990. "Opportunity, Willingness, and the Diffusion of War." *American Political Science Review* 84: 47–67.

———. 1991. *Diffusion of War: A Study of Opportunity and Willingness*. Ann Arbor: University of Michigan Press.

Sklar, Richard. 1979. "The Nature of Class Domination in Africa." *Journal of Modern African Studies* 17: 531–52.

———. 1980. *Nigerian Political Parties: Power in an Emergent African Nation*. New York: NOK Publishers.

Skocpol, Theda. 1979. *States and Social Revolution: A Comparative Analysis of France, Russia, and China*. Cambridge: Cambridge University Press.

Slengesol, Ibvar-Andre. 2000. "The United States and the 1974 Cyprus Crisis." *Mediterranean Quarterly* 11: 96–129.

Smith, Anthony D. 1986. "Conflict and Collective Identity: Class, *Ethnie*, and Nation." In Edward Azar and John Burton, eds., *International Conflict Resolution*, 63–84. Boulder, Colo.: Lynne Rienner.

———. 1993a. "A Europe of Nations—or the Nation of Europe." *Journal of Peace Research* 30, 2: 129–35.

———. 1993b. "The Ethnic Sources of Nationalism." *Survival* 35, 1: 48–64.

Snyder, Jack. 1993. "Nationalism and the Crisis of the Post–Soviet State." *Survival* 35, 1: 1–26.

Snyder, Richard C., H. W. Bruck, and Burton Sapin, eds. 1962. *Foreign Policy Decision Making: An Approach to the Study of International Politics*. New York: Free Press of Glencoe.

Sözen, Ahmet. 1999. "Cyprus Conflict: Continuing Challenge and Prospects for Resolution in the Post–Cold War Era." Ph.D. dissertation, University of Missouri, Columbia.

———. 2004. "A Model of Power-Sharing in Cyprus: From the 1959 London-Zurich Agreements to the Annan Plan." *Turkish Studies* 5, 1: 61–77.

———, and Birol Yesilada. 2002. "Negotiating a Resolution to the Cyprus Problem: Is Potential EU Membership a Blessing or a Curse?" *Journal of International Negotiation* 7, 2: 261–85.

Stack, John. 1997. "The Ethnic Challenge to International Relations." In David Carment and Patrick James, eds., *Wars in the Midst of Peace: The International Politics of Ethnic Conflict*, 11–25, Pittsburgh: University of Pittsburgh Press.

Stanovcic, Vojislav. 1992. "Problems and Options in Institutionalizing Ethnic Relations." *International Political Science Review* 13, 4: 359–79.

Starr, Harvey. 1978. "Opportunity and Willingness as Ordering Concepts in the Study of War." *International Interactions* 4: 363–87.

———. 1990. "Modelling the Internal-External Linkage: Rethinking the Relationship between Revolution, War, and Change." Paper presented at American Political Science Association annual meeting, San Francisco.

Stavenhagen, Rodolfo. 1987. "Ethnocide or Ethnodevelopment: The New Challenge." *Development: Seeds of Change* 1: 74–81.

Stavrou, Nikolas A. 1976. "Ethnicity in Yugoslavia: Roots and Impact." In Abdul Said and Luiz R. Simmons, eds., *Ethnicity in an International Context*, 134–49. New Brunswick, N.J.: Transaction Books.

Stein, Janice G., and Raymond Tanter. 1980. *Rational Decision Making: Israel's Security Choices*. Columbus: Ohio State University Press.

Stivachtis, Yannis A. 2000. "The Enlargement of the European Union: The Case of Cyprus." Working Paper, International Studies Association.

Stohl, Michael. 1980. "The Nexus of Civil and International Conflict." In Ted R. Gurr, ed. *Handbook of Political Conflict*, 297–330. New York: Free Press.

Suberu, Rotimi V. 1994. "The Travails of Federalism in Nigeria." In Larry J. Diamond and Marc F. Plattner, eds. *Nationalism, Ethnic Conflict, and Democracy*, 56–70. London: Johns Hopkins University Press.

Suhrke, Astri. 1977. "Loyalists and Separatists: Muslims in Southern Thailand." *Asian Survey* 17, 3: 237–50.

_____. 1981. "Southeast Asia: The Muslims in Southern Thailand." In Robert G. Wirsing, ed., *Protection of Ethnic Minorities: Comparative Perspectives*, 313–43. New York: Pergamon Press.

_____. 1989. "The Muslims of Southern Thailand." In Andrew D. W. Forbes, ed., *Politics of the Malay-Speaking South*, 2: 1–18. Bihar: Centre for South East Asian Studies.

Suhrke, Astri, and Lela Garner Noble, eds. 1977. *Ethnic Conflict and International Relations*. New York: Praeger Publishers.

Sullivan, Michael J. 1996. *Comparing State Polities*. New York: Greenwood.

Tamkoç, Metin. 1998. *The Turkish Cypriot State: The Embodiment of the Right of Self Determination*. London: K. Rustem and Brother.

Tanter, Raymond. 1966. "Dimensions of Conflict Behaviors within and between Nations, 1958–1960." *Journal of Conflict Resolution* 10, 1: 41–64.

Taras, Ray. 1997. *Nationalism, Ethnic Conflict, and World Politics*. New York: Addison-Wessley.

Taras, Ray, and Rajat Ganguly. 1988; 2nd ed. 2002. *Understanding Ethnic Conflict: The International Dimension*. New York: Longman.

Taylor, Charles L., and Michael C. Hudson. 1972. *World Handbook of Political and Social Indicators*. New Haven, Conn.: Yale University Press.

Taylor, Charles L., Michael C. Hudson, and David A. Jodice. 1983. *World Handbook of Political and Social Indicators*. 3rd ed. New Haven, Conn.: Yale University Press.

Theophanous, Andreas. 2000a. "Prospects for Solving the Cyprus Problem and the Role of the EU." *Publius: The Journal of Federalism* 30, 1–2: 217–41.

_____. 2000b. "Cyprus, the EU, and the Search for a New Constitution." *Journal of Southern Europe and the Balkans* 2: 213–33.

_____. 2003. "The Cyprus Problem: Accession to the EU: Broader Implications." *Mediterranean Quarterly* 14: 42–66.

Thomas, M. Ladd. 1977. "The Malayan Communist Insurgents and Thai-Malaysian Relations." *Asian Affairs: An American Review* 4, 6: 371–84.

_____. 1989. "Thai Muslim Separatism in South Thailand." In Andrew D. W. Forbes, ed., *Politics of the Malay-Speaking South*, 2. Bihar: Centre for South East Asian Studies.

Trigeorgis, Maria H., and Lenos Trigeorgis. 1993. "Cyprus: An Evolutionary Approach to Conflict Resolution." *Journal of Conflict Resolution* 37: 340–60.

Tsebelis, George. 1990. *Nested Games: Rational Choice in Comparative Politics.* Berkeley and Los Angeles: University of California Press.

Van Evera, Stephen. 1994. "Hypotheses on Nationalism and War." *International Security* 18: 5–39.

Vassilou, George. 2002. "EU Enlargement: Implications for Europe, Cyprus, and the Eastern Mediterranean." *Mediterranean Quarterly* 13: 12–20.

Vasquez, John A. 1992. "Factors Related to the Contagion and Diffusion of International Violence." In Manus I. Midlarsky, ed., *The Internationalization of Communal Strife,* 149–72. London: Routledge.

Väyrynen, Raimo. 1994. "Towards a Theory of Ethnic Conflicts and their Resolution." Inaugural Lecture of the Joan B. Kroc Institute for International Peace Studies, University of Notre Dame.

———. 1997. "International Stability and Risky States: The Enforcement of Norms." In Gerald Schneider and Patricia A. Weitsman, eds., *Enforcing Cooperation: Risky States and Intergovernmental Management of Conflict,* 149–72. London: Macmillan.

———, ed. 1991. *New Directions in Conflict Theory: Conflict Resolution and Conflict Transformation.* Newbury Park, Calif.: Sage.

Volkan, Vamik D. 1979. *Cyprus—War and Adaptation.* Charlottesville: University Press of Virginia.

Wallensteen, Peter, and Margareta Sollenberg. 1996. "The End of International War? Armed Conflict, 1989–1995." *Journal of Peace Research* 33: 353–70.

Waller, David V. 1992. "Ethnic Mobilization and Geopolitics in the Soviet Union: Towards a Theoretical Understanding." *Journal of Political and Military Sociology* 28: 37–62.

Weiner, Myron. 1971. "The Macedonian Syndrome: An Historical Model of International Relations and Political Development." *World Politics* 23, 4: 665–83.

———. 1986. "The State, Religion, and Ethnic Politics: Afghanistan, Iran, and Pakistan." Syracuse, N.Y.: Syracuse University Press.

———. 1987. *Understanding Political Development.* Boston: Little Brown, and Co.

———. 1992. "Peoples and States in a New Ethnic Order?" *Third World Quarterly* 13, 2: 317–33.

West, Rebecca. 1941. *Black Lamb and Grey Falcon: A Journey through Yugoslavia.* New York: Viking Press.

Wilkenfeld, Jonathan. 1968. "Domestic and Foreign Conflict Behaviour of Nations." *Journal of Peace Research* 5, 1: 56–69.

———. 1972. "Models for the Analysis of Foreign Conflict Behavior." In Bruce Russett, ed., *Peace, War, and Numbers,* 275–98. Beverly Hills, Calif.: Sage.

———, ed. 1973. *Conflict Behavior and Linkage Politics.* New York: David McKay.

Wilkenfeld, Jonathan, Gerald W. Hopple, Paul J. Rossa, and Stephen J. Andriole. 1980. *Foreign Policy Behavior: The Interstate Behavior Analysis Model.* Beverly Hills, Calif.: Sage.

Wilmer, Franke. 1993. *The Indigenous Voice in World Politics: Since Time Immemorial.* Newbury Park, Calif.: Sage.

Wright, Quincy. 1942. *A Study of War.* Chicago: University of Chicago Press.

Xydis, Stephen G. 1967. *Cyprus, Conflict, and Conciliation, 1954–1958*. Columbus: Ohio State University Press.

Yegar, Moshe. 2002. *Between Integration and Secession: The Muslim Communities of the Southern Philippines, Southern Thailand, and Western Burma/Myanmar.* Lanham, Md.: Lexington Books.

Yesilada, Birol A., and Joseph J. Hewitt. 1998. "Conflict, Negotiation, and Third Party Intervention in Cyprus: A Game Theoretic Analysis." Unpublished manuscript.

Young, Robert. 1997. "How Do Peaceful Secessions Happen?" In David Carment and Patrick James, eds., *Wars in the Midst of Peace: The International Politics of Ethnic Conflict*, 45–60. Pittsburgh: University of Pittsburgh Press.

Zartman, I. William. 1992. "Internationalization of Communal Strife: Temptations and Opportunities of Triangulation." In Manus I. Midlarsky, ed., *The Internationalization of Communal Strife*, 27–42. London: Routledge.

———. 1998. "Putting Humpty-Dumpty Together Again." In David A. Lake and Donald Rothchild, eds., *The International Spread of Ethnic Conflict: Fear, Diffusion, and Escalation*, 317–36. Princeton: Princeton University Press.

INDEX